# China's Pension System

# China's Pension System
*A Vision*

Mark C. Dorfman, Robert Holzmann, Philip O'Keefe,
Dewen Wang, Yvonne Sin, and Richard Hinz

**THE WORLD BANK**
**Washington, D.C.**

# Contents

**Boxes**

**Figures**

## Tables

# Preface and Acknowledgements

This volume was prepared to develop a medium-term vision for strengthening old-age income protection in China. The manuscript originated as a World Bank report initiated in discussions beginning early in 2009. A key objective of the report was to develop a vision consistent with principles articulated by the Chinese authorities to bring together fragmented policy designs into a common framework, strengthen coverage of the elderly, and ensure flexibility to adapt to rapidly changing needs in the Chinese economy and society.

Preparation of this report has been punctuated by important policy announcements. In mid-2009, the authorities announced a national pilot program for rural pensions. After a draft of this report was completed, the National Urban Residents Pension pilot program was announced in 2011. As a result of these announcements, this volume reconciles the policy designs suggested with these programs.

This report was very much a team effort. The core team members and authors were Mark C. Dorfman, Robert Holzmann, Philip O'Keefe, Dewen Wang, Yvonne Sin, and Richard Hinz. Though not an author, Xiaoqing Yu was a key member of the core team providing essential guidance throughout the process. The volume was prepared under the direction of Xiaoqing Yu (sector director, Human Development Department, East Asia and Pacific Region), Emmanuel Jimenez (former sector director,

Human Development Department, East Asia and Pacific Region) and Klaus Rohland (China country director). Sergiy Biletskyy, Yu-Wei Hu, and Wei Zhang contributed to the volume by providing analytical inputs. Yuning Wu provided inputs for the evolution of rural pension system. We are grateful for the useful comments provided by peer reviewers of earlier versions of the volume: Robert Palacios, David Robalino, Lawrence Thompson, and Cai Fang. Useful comments were also provided by Ardo Hannson, Louis Kuijs, and John Giles. Logistics and production staff included Lansong Zhang, Limei Sun and Sabrina Terry. Paola Scalabin and Mark Ingebretsen of the World Bank's Office of the Publisher managed the publication of the volume.

We would also like to thank the Chinese Ministry of Finance, Ministry of Human Resources and Social Security, National Development and Reform Commission, Development Research Center of the State Council, and National Social Security Fund for providing very useful inputs and feedback in researching the volume.

# About the Authors

**Mark C. Dorfman** is a senior economist with the World Bank's Social Protection Team, where he works on pensions, social security, and contractual savings reform. Earlier he worked in the Bank's Debt Department where he assessed debt sustainability and debt relief under the Heavily Indebted Poor Countries (HIPC) Initiative. Since 1999 he has prepared multiple reports and projects on the Chinese pension system. During his 24 years with the World Bank, he has worked on different areas of pensions and financial market reform in three of the Bank's regions: Latin America and the Caribbean, Sub-Saharan Africa, and East Asia and the Pacific. Mr. Dorfman holds an MBA in finance from the Wharton School.

**Robert Holzmann** is professor of economics and the director of the RH Institute for Economic Policy Analysis, Vienna, and holds the Old Age Financial Protection Chair at the University of Malaya, Kuala Lumpur, Malaysia. From mid-1997 to early 2011, he was director of the World Bank's Social Protection Team and Labor Department and research director of the Marseille Center for Mediterranean Integration. Before joining the World Bank he was professor of economics at the Universities of Saarland (Germany) and Vienna (Austria) and a senior economist at the International Monetary Fund (IMF) and the Organisation for

Economic Co-operation and Development (OECD). He has published over 30 books and over 150 articles on social, fiscal, and financial policy issues.

**Philip O'Keefe** is lead economist for the Human Development Sector for East Asia and Pacific, and was previously Human Development Sector coordinator for China and Mongolia, at the World Bank. He coordinates the Bank's work on social protection issues, including social security, social assistance and welfare services, and labor markets. Prior to his China role, he was based in India as the social protection coordinator, following a decade of work on social security, labor market, and social services issues in Eastern Europe and the former Soviet Union. Prior to joining the World Bank in 1993, he was a university lecturer at the University of Warwick (Coventry, U.K.). He holds undergraduate degrees from the University of Sydney, Australia, and postgraduate degrees from the London School of Economics and Oxford University in economics and law.

**Dewen Wang** is a social protection economist in the World Bank's China Country office. He was professor and division chief of the Institute of Population and Labor Economics, Chinese Academy of Social Sciences (Beijing, China), before he joined the Word Bank's Social Protection Team in the East Asia and Pacific region. He served as deputy division director of China's Ministry of Agriculture and was a research fellow at the Ministry's Research Center for Rural Economy. His work focuses on China's pension and social protection programs, population aging, labor market dynamics, and economic reform and growth.

**Yvonne Sin** is the general manager of Risk and Financial Services at Towers Watson, a global professional consultancy firm. Ms. Sin worked at the World Bank from 1993 to 2007 and was head of the Pensions Thematic Group of the Social Protection Team from 2005 to 2007. She is a research fellow of the China Centre for Insurance and Social Security Research at Peking University, a member of the Advisory Board of the Risk and Insurance Research Centre at National Chengchi University (Taiwan, China), and a board member of the Asia Pacific Risk and Insurance Association. She is also a member of the Society of Actuaries, the Canadian Institute of Actuaries, the American Academy of Actuaries, the Actuarial Society of Hong Kong, and the International Actuarial Association.

**Richard Hinz** is a pension policy adviser to the Social Protection Team of the Human Development Network at the World Bank. Since joining the World Bank in 2003, his work has been focused on the reform of social security systems and the development, regulation, and supervision of funded pension arrangements—subjects on which he has authored and edited a number of articles and publications. Prior to this, he was the director of the Office of Policy and Research at what is now the Employee Benefits Security Administration (EBSA) of the U.S. Department of Labor, where he managed economic research and legislative analysis for the agency responsible for the regulation and supervision of private employer-sponsored health insurance and pension programs in the United States.

# Abbreviations

| | |
|---|---|
| CE | coverage expansion |
| CHNS | China Health and Nutrition Survey |
| CIRC | China Insurance Regulatory Commission |
| CPI | consumer price index |
| CSP | Citizens' Social Pension |
| CSRC | China Securities Regulatory Commission |
| CURES | China Urban and Rural Elderly Survey |
| EA | Enterprise Annuity (scheme) |
| EET | exempt-exempt-taxable (tax treatment) |
| FA | financial asset |
| FDC | Funded Defined Contribution (Scheme) |
| GA | pay-as-you-go asset |
| GDP | gross domestic product |
| IA | individual account |
| IBRD | International Bank for Reconstruction and Development |
| ILO | International Labour Organization |
| IPD | implicit pension debt |
| MDC | matching defined contribution (scheme) |
| MHRSS | Ministry of Human Resources and Social Security |
| MOCA | Ministry of Civil Affairs |

| | |
|---|---|
| MOLSS | Ministry of Labor and Social Security (later constituted under the MHRSS) |
| MORIS | Mandatory Occupational Retirement Insurance Scheme (proposed) |
| NBS | National Bureau of Statistics |
| NCMS | new cooperative medical scheme |
| NDC | notional or nonfinancial defined contribution (scheme) |
| NDRC | National Development Reform Commission |
| NRPP | New Rural Pension Pilot Program |
| NRPS | New Rural Pension Scheme |
| NSSF | National Social Security (Trust) Fund |
| OA | Occupational Annuity (scheme, proposed) |
| OECD | Organization for Economic Cooperation and Development |
| PA | pension asset |
| PAYG | pay-as-you-go |
| PROST | Pension Reform Options Simulation Toolkit |
| PSU | public service (or sector) unit |
| RAW | regional average wage |
| RMB | renminbi (yuan) |
| RPPP | Rural Pension Pilot Program |
| SC | solidarity contribution |
| SOE | state-owned enterprise |
| TBL | target benefit level |
| TEE | taxable-exempt-exempt (tax treatment) |
| TTE | taxable-taxable-exempt (tax treatment) |
| URPS | Urban Residents Pension Scheme |
| VAT | value added tax |
| VIRIS | Voluntary Individual Retirement Insurance Scheme (proposed) |

# Overview

## Introduction

China is at a critical juncture in its economic transition. Comprehensive reform of its pension and social security systems is an essential element of a strategy aimed toward achieving a harmonious society and sustainable development. A widely held view among policy makers is that the current approach to pension provision is insufficient to enable China's economy and population to realize its development objectives in the years ahead. The government has articulated principles for what it would like to achieve in a reformed pension system: an urban system that "has *broad coverage, protects at the basic level*, is *multilayered* and *sustainable*," while for the rural system[2] "has *broad coverage, protects at the basic level*, is *flexible* and *sustainable*." This volume aims to articulate such an integrated holistic vision for strengthening old-age income protection in China consistent with the principles outlined.

Over the last few years, the government has considered various options and initiated several significant measures. A major reform of the urban old-age insurance system was undertaken in 1997 and subsequently has had refinements. In 2009 the authorities established a national framework for rural pensions, the new Rural Pension Pilot Program (NRPP), which became the New Rural Pension Scheme (NRPS), and in mid-2011 announced a national pilot Urban Residents Pension Scheme (URPS), completing a national framework aimed at universal pension coverage.

Although substantial reforms have been initiated, some policy makers have suggested that additional reforms are needed to meet the needs of China's rapidly changing economy and society. Issues such as legacy costs, system fragmentation, and limited coverage have not been fully addressed. At the same time, many new challenges have emerged, such as rapid urbanization, income inequality, urban-rural disparities, informalization of the labor force, changes in family structure, and the effects of increased globalization. A reform vision needs to address policy issues that the current design does not sufficiently provide for, consider reform needs that have also emerged, and anticipate the future needs of China's rapidly changing society.

This volume is organized as follows: The main text outlines the vision. It focuses on summarizing the key features of a proposed medium-term pension system, and the appendixes provide the deeper analysis and context that underpins the recommendations of the main text. The main text first examines key trends motivating the need for reform then outlines the proposed three-pillar design and the rationale behind the design choices and moves on to examine financing options. The main text continues by introducing institutional reform issues, and the final section concludes. The appendixes provide additional analytical detail supporting the findings in the main text. Appendix A evaluates the pension needs of nonsalaried rural and urban citizens and outlines the rationale for the proposed instruments. Appendix B evaluates a notional or nonfinancial defined-contribution design applied to China's urban old-age insurance system. Appendix C evaluates pension legacy costs and financing options for addressing them. Appendix D evaluates issues of aging, retirement, and labor markets in China in the context of old-age insurance provisions. Appendix E examines voluntary pension savings arrangements.

## Motivations for Pension Reform

China is in the midst of a major demographic and economic transition, including the following changes:

- China is facing a dramatic aging process and demographic transition as a result of declines in fertility combined with significant increases in longevity. Old-age dependency ratios are therefore projected to almost triple over three decades.

- The country's rapid growth and economic transformation have increased the demand for a mobile and dynamic labor force that can effectively adjust to the pace of change. At the same time, demographic change will constrain the size of the working-age population. Fragmented pension provisions and limited portability of accrued benefits are just two of the barriers to labor mobility. Moreover, low urban retirement ages contribute to rigidities in the face of growing labor demand.

- Although the authorities have placed a growing premium on more balanced growth between households, rural and urban areas, and different regions, to date the pension system has in some ways contributed to divergence.

- As the authorities seek to rebalance the growth model toward greater reliance on domestic consumption, the lack of coverage and uncertainty with regard to financial protection secured with current pensions encourage overly high precautionary savings.

The pension system design can play an important role in supporting or constraining such economic and demographic transitions: (1) fragmentation and lack of portability of rights hinder labor market efficiency and contribute to coverage gaps; (2) multiple schemes for salaried workers, PSU employees, civil servants, and, in some areas, migrants similarly impact labor markets; (3) legacy costs that are largely financed through current pension contributions weaken incentives for compliance and accurate wage reporting; (4) very limited risk pooling and interurban resource transfers limit the insurance function of the urban pension system and create spatial disparities in old-age income protection; (5) low retirement ages affect incentives and benefits and undermine fiscal sustainability; and (6) relatively low returns on individual accounts result in replacement rates significantly less than anticipated while at the macro level, are likely to inhibit wider efforts to stimulate higher domestic consumption.

Although the government has undertaken important reforms, a holistic long-term vision is needed to guide future policies. The urban old-age insurance system has several positive design features but needs to better respond to the needs of China's increasingly complex and mobile labor force. Although the authorities have introduced significant programs to cover rural and urban citizens, a long-term vision would recognize the integration of rural and urban economies. Second, a framework is needed to serve workers inside and outside the formal sector who have until recently not been served, including nonsalaried, informal, self-employed, rural, and migrant workers. Finally, the scope of the Enterprise Annuity (EA) provides supplementary pension arrangements, but has focused on formal sector enterprises. The regulatory and supervisory framework needs substantial reform, as does the incentive framework, including tax treatment, in order to be broadened to provide supplementary pension arrangements for small companies and the self-employed and for other individual pension arrangements.

The rationale behind the multipillar approach proposed in this volume is fully aligned with the government's philosophy: (1) the pension system can redistribute income between individuals, income groups and cohorts to protect the elderly from poverty; (2) the pension system should provide an efficient form of retirement savings and risk pooling for different types of workers and income groups; and (3) regulated supplementary pension savings arrangements are needed to justify investments in human capital and preferences for additional retirement savings.

## Pension System Design Proposal and Options

This volume proposes a three-pillar design consisting of the following components (see table O.1):

(a) A *basic benefit pillar* providing minimum elderly poverty protection through urban and rural noncontributory *Citizens' Social Pension* (CSP) benefits
(b) A *contributory pillar* with a mandatory notional defined-contribution (NDC) scheme for salaried workers with labor contracts (modifying the current urban old-age insurance system) and a voluntary defined-contribution pension savings scheme for the urban and rural populations with nonwage incomes such as temporary workers, the self-employed, and farmers, and
(c) A *supplementary savings pillar* for urban and rural residents providing voluntary occupational and individual pensions, which may supplement other pension benefits.

This volume suggests a vision of a national pension system that no longer distinguishes along urban and rural locational or *hukou* lines yet takes account of the diverse nature of employment relations and capacity

**Table O.1    Summary of Proposed Pension Design (Architecture and Financing)**

| | *Pensions for Wage-Based Work* | *Pensions for Non-Wage Work* |
|---|---|---|
| Basic benefit pillar | *Citizens' Social Pensions (CSP)*<br>• Benefit level linked to regional average wages (urban)/regional per capital incomes (rural)<br>• Benefits adjusted when recipients receive alternative pension income<br>• Noncontributory—financed from general revenues<br>• Provincial and national subsidies to reduce regional benefit disparities | |
| Contributory pillar | *Mandatory Occupational Retirement Insurance Scheme (MORIS)*<br>• Mandatory contributions linked to individual wages<br>• Notional defined-contribution design<br>• Applied to all workers with labor contracts, including migrants, public service units, and civil servants<br>• Portable accumulations<br>• Individual notional accumulation determines an annuitized benefit<br>• Liquidity and buffer fund management at a provincial or national level<br>• Legacy costs financed outside the pension system | *Voluntary Individual Retirement Insurance Scheme (VIRIS)*<br>• Voluntary, tiered contributions by nonwage residents<br>• Funded defined-contribution design<br>• Applied to all nonwage residents not covered by other schemes<br>• Contributions matched with government subsidies<br>• Portable accumulations<br>• Individual accumulation determines an annuitized benefit<br>• Reserve management at a provincial or national level |
| Supplementary savings pillar | *Voluntary Occupational and Individual Annuities*<br>• Provide a common regulated, secure, and tax-neutral instrument for employer-based (occupational) and individual-based (personal) supplementary retirement savings<br>• Defined contribution in design with annuitization options<br>• Fully funded<br>• Decentralized account and investment management under a unified framework<br>• Strong regulatory framework and supervisory institutions | |

of individuals to make contributions. The proposed separation of mandatory salary-based and voluntary non-salary-based contributory schemes is intended as an interim measure until the overall tax collection and compliance framework can be extended to nonsalaried workers including the informal sector, the self-employed, and farmers. Over the very long term, it is anticipated that the urban old-age insurance system will extend to all citizens, while the distinction between salary-based and non-salary-based incomes would likely remain.

### The Basic Benefit Pillar

A Citizens' Social Pension (CSP) is proposed to ensure a basic level of income support for the rural and urban elderly who are unable to meet basic subsistence needs from contributory pension sources. Such a benefit would be designed according to a national framework with structured regional variation. The benefit level would be based on a proportion of the regional average wage (in urban areas) or regional average per capita income (in rural areas) and would provide minimum income support higher than the per capita *dibao* or social assistance threshold. Individuals aged 65 and above would be entitled to a minimum CSP benefit with a *pensions test* applied that would reduce the benefit amount by a proportion of other pension benefits received for those aged 65–74. The extent of the reduction would be a policy choice guided by the relative emphasis on retirement savings incentives and fiscal costs. The benefit would be indexed on the same basis as are other proposed contributory benefits, that is, based on a mix of one-third wages (in urban areas) or per capita income (in rural areas) and two-thirds prices. Although financing the scheme would fall upon different levels of government, provincial and municipal authorities would be accountable for observance of the national framework.

### The Contributory Pillar, Part 1: The Mandatory Occupational Retirement Insurance Scheme

The contributory pillar would consist of two instruments, the first of which would be a Mandatory Occupational Retirement Insurance Scheme (MORIS). The design of the MORIS would build upon the existing policy design and institutional structure for the urban old-age insurance system. The proposed scheme would be defined contribution in design, follow a notional financing approach, and provide an integrative framework across different types of employers. The scheme's rights and responsibilities would therefore extend to all salaried employees regardless of sector, ownership structure, or location. In this way, in the medium term the MORIS would include civil servants and Public Sector Unit (PSU) workers. Although this volume does not advocate a particular target replacement rate, a replacement rate of about 45 percent of lifetime pre-retirement income could be provided by a contribution rate of about 16 percent of wages on a sustainable basis. This range would be applicable under three conditions: (1) the retirement age would be increased to age 65 over time, (2) the benefit would be indexed one-third to wage increases and two-thirds to price increases, and (3) legacy costs would be separately financed from outside the urban old-age insurance system. Figure O.1 compares current urban old-age insurance and proposed MORIS designs.

Inclusion of civil servants and PSU workers in the proposed MORIS would undoubtedly create special financial and institutional challenges but could promote a less rigid labor market and a more integrated pension system. By combining benefits from the proposed MORIS NDC account and a supplemental benefit from a revised Occupational Annuity scheme, current levels of income replacement could be supported while also freeing workers to move in and out of positions in accordance with the demand for their skills. Transition challenges may justify postponing integration of civil servants and PSU workers into the MORIS while the necessary accounting, financial control, and remittance systems are developed.

Key advantages of the proposed MORIS design include the following:

- *Strong labor market incentives*: An NDC approach establishing a sound link between contributions and benefits.
- *Supporting labor mobility and competitiveness* through a simple accounting framework.

**Figure O.1    Current and Proposed Urban Old-Age Insurance Design**

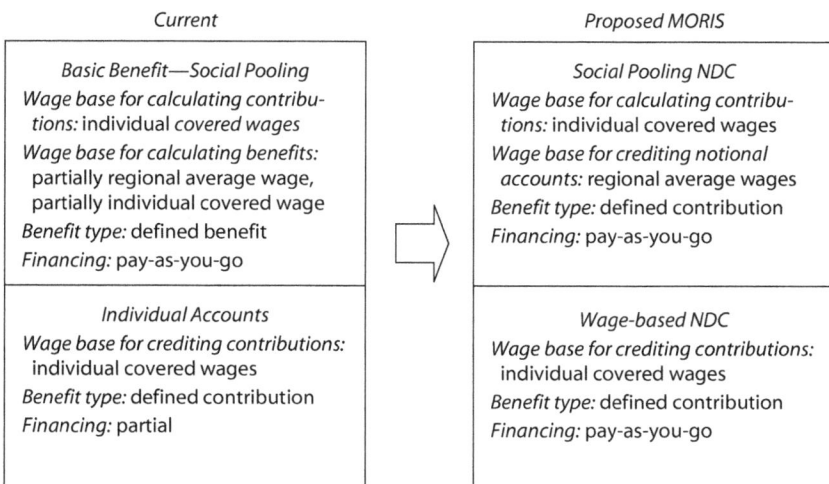

|     | *Current* |     | *Proposed MORIS* |
| --- | --- | --- | --- |
|     | *Basic Benefit—Social Pooling* | | *Social Pooling NDC* |
|     | *Wage base for calculating contributions:* individual *covered wages* | | *Wage base for calculating contributions:* individual covered wages |
|     | *Wage base for calculating benefits:* partially regional average wage, partially individual covered wage | | *Wage base for crediting notional accounts:* regional average wages |
|     | *Benefit type:* defined benefit | | *Benefit type:* defined contribution |
|     | *Financing:* pay-as-you-go | | *Financing:* pay-as-you-go |
|     | *Individual Accounts* | | *Wage-based NDC* |
|     | *Wage base for crediting contributions:* individual covered wages | | *Wage base for crediting contributions:* individual covered wages |
|     | *Benefit type:* defined contribution | | *Benefit type:* defined contribution |
|     | *Financing:* partial | | *Financing:* pay-as-you-go |

- *Substantial reduction in contribution rates* when compared with the current scheme.
- *Very limited transition costs* as the NDC framework is financed on a pay-as-you-go basis.
- *Stronger old-age income protection* for workers who do not meet current vesting requirements.

### The Contributory Pillar, Part 2: The Voluntary Individual Retirement Insurance Scheme

The second instrument of the contributory pillar would be the Voluntary Individual Retirement Insurance Scheme (VIRIS). The VIRIS would establish a framework supportive of voluntary savings for retirement for nonwage residents of urban and rural areas. The VIRIS design has several similarities to the NRPS and URPS.[4] The scheme would be voluntary, with individual contributions matched with a governmental subsidy reflected in individual account statements. The matching subsidy would be based on a national framework providing for a minimum match, which could be supplemented from provincial and local finances. The scheme would be fully funded, with a rate of return guaranteed by the central authorities to reduce the risk to contributors from empty accounts. The proposed scheme would provide an annuitized benefit at retirement based on a worker's lifetime contributions, matching contributions provided by the local and central governments, and a rate of return applied to the individual's retirement savings account.

The approach to the VIRIS design has numerous advantages, most of which are shared by the NRPS and URPS:

- The matching subsidy creates a strong incentive for worker participation and savings.[5]
- The minimum contribution design provides simplicity.
- The defined-contribution design facilitates the consolidation of balances across both wage- and non-wage-based schemes.
- The interest formula and investment management arrangements minimize the investment risks borne by contributors.
- The funded design can mitigate worker uncertainty over potential risks to benefits.

### The Supplementary Savings Pillar

Supplemental occupational and individual annuity schemes provide an essential part of the overall design for a multitiered pension system architecture. The proposed Occupational and Personal Annuity scheme design could build upon the current Enterprise Annuity but would require substantial reform of the regulatory, supervisory, and incentive framework. Reformed tax treatment should provide incentives to save for retirement while limiting tax shields. The regulatory framework should address actual and perceived potential conflicts of interest. A framework for personal pension savings arrangements is needed to support the long-term individual savings needs of the self-employed, the unemployed, farmers, or other individuals without wages or institutional affiliations while in addition supporting supplemental savings options for those who participate in state-sponsored pension schemes but seek additional retirement income.

## Design Considerations

The proposed design is motivated by key design principles to provide an integrated framework for all Chinese workers and retirees while allowing for diverse economic and demographic circumstances:[6]

- A reform vision should *address current and long-term future needs* under the assumption that reform should be infrequent.
- *Policies should have uniform national standards* yet sufficient flexibility to accommodate China's diverse regional needs and economic characteristics.
- Reforms should reflect the *decentralized nature of current policies and administration* while at the same time seeking to achieve risk pooling at least at the provincial level and ultimately at the national level in the long term.
- Pensions savings and insurance require *sharing financing and risk management burdens at multiple levels*, including the central government; provincial, municipal, county, and prefecture governments as well as between employers, workers, retirees, and families.

The rationale behind the design choices includes the following:

- *Overall*: The rationale for proposing a unified framework for all citizens while providing flexibility for local circumstances is to accommodate the diversity of economic circumstances and decentralized administrative structure, reduce the fragmentation and coverage gaps, provide portable instruments for labor mobility and ensure that elderly poverty protection as a policy objective is satisfied for all citizens.

- *MORIS:* An NDC design has been suggested for the mandatory contributory scheme: (a) This directly links contributions and benefits, thereby eliminating the need for periodic benefit adjustments in the face of aging and a demographic transition. (b) Benefits based on notional account accumulations can reduce labor market distortions and incentives for wage underreporting and noncompliance. (c) The NDC design provides a uniform basis for adding up pension entitlements for workers from different locations, sectors and types of employers. (d) A pay-as-you-go financing approach largely eliminates costly transition costs while minimizing the performance risk of reserve management.

- *VIRIS*: (a) The design would apply to all nonsalaried workers addressing a coverage gap. (b) The matching subsidy provides a strong incentive to motivate those in the nonwage sector to save in long-term retirement accounts. (c) The proposed design provides a matching subsidy for nonwage workers to save for their own retirement. (d) A voluntary scheme was proposed in view of the difficulties suggested by international experience in achieving meaningful coverage of nonwage workers through mandatory contributory schemes. (e) The central and local financing of the VIRIS could ensure a more uniform set of contribution incentives nationwide by insulating the matching contributions from local fiscal conditions.

- *The Occupational and Individual Annuities Scheme*: Broadening occupational and individual pension savings arrangements can provide a secure retirement savings vehicle for employers and workers seeking to supplement those benefits provided under the contributory pillar. The rationale for proposing a funded defined-contribution (FDC) design is: (a) to build upon the legal and institutional infrastructure for the EA scheme, (b) individual accounts under an FDC design can be transparent and portable and entitlements easily aggregated across places of employment, (c) fully funding benefit obligations and separating the management of assets eliminates the risk to the participant of sponsor bankruptcy or otherwise defaulting on obligations, and (d) placing additional savings in a separately managed fund diversifies the risk borne by participants.

## Implementation Issues and Options

The authorities face several institutional, financing, and implementation challenges, regardless of the nature and extent of further reforms. Key decisions include (1) target replacement rates across the pension system, (2) the degree of income redistribution that is desired in the system, (3) the approach to indexation, (4) the mechanisms for financing both legacy costs and future pension rights as the demographic transition matures, and (5) the promotion of a more robust institutional architecture and capacity to regulate the system. In taking these decisions, several key issues are the following:

***Improving the analytical base for ongoing pension reform:*** A more sustainable pension system will require policy development based on robust projections of system liabilities, monitoring and reporting of current performance, and more rigorous evaluation of current experience and emerging reforms.

***Financing current and future pension costs:*** Establishing the policy framework for financing past, present, and future pension rights is a core component of the proposed reform. The following elements need to be considered in the policy framework for pension financing: (1) the framework for financing of past and new legacy costs, (2) the financing plan for future benefit accruals for civil servants and PSU employees, (3) the subsidy framework for compensating those provinces that have demographic and economic conditions requiring additional fiscal subsidies, (4) the subsidy framework supporting the proposed VIRIS and CSP, and (5) the financing plan and anticipated prefunding of future pension liabilities via the National Social Security Fund or other reserve funds that may be established.

Defining, estimating, planning for, and ultimately financing legacy costs are a key part of the proposed reform program even in the absence of further reforms. Legacy costs include: (1) those costs that exist in the unreformed system and reflect accrued rights in excess of those supported by a sustainable contribution rate and (2) those costs that are created by the reform if the sustainable contribution rate is lowered. Separating these costs for the different schemes that may be integrated in the proposed urban system is the first step toward fully understanding what has already been committed and must be delivered. Ongoing actuarial exercises are required to evaluate and adjust financing decisions for the best outcomes.

Estimates of gross legacy costs depend, among other factors, upon the estimated existing implicit pension debt (IPD) and the expected steady-state contribution rate for the reformed scheme. So for example, initial estimates of legacy costs under a low IPD assumption range from 44 percent assuming a contribution rate of 25 percent to 89 percent assuming a contribution rate of 15 percent. Similarly, legacy cost estimates under a high IPD assumption range from 56 percent assuming a contribution rate of 25 percent to 113 percent assuming a contribution rate of 15 percent (see main text and appendix C for a more detailed discussion). Such gross legacy costs would not fully translate into additional fiscal costs, even if they were made explicit. The existing old-age insurance system, as well as schemes for civil servants and PSUs, already receives government subsidies, which are included in these estimates. Up to three-quarters of legacy costs for the civil service and PSU schemes are, in any case, already financed by government revenues.

Although individual acquired rights under preexisting schemes could, in principle, be translated into notional account balances any time before individual retirement, the sooner such rights can be quantified under a common accounting framework, the sooner public credibility could be strengthened and the challenges of portability addressed.

*Portable pension rights:* Achieving national portability will require careful consideration of design and administrative policy options. Guidance from the State Council on the issue provides an important step forward in this regard. Key choices will include the framework for (1) record keeping and information flows across space, including when, where, and how data are consolidated for worker entitlements from several venues, urban and rural, intra- and inter-provincial, (2) pooling of contributions and reserves, (3) benefit calculation that accommodates China's diverse conditions, and (4) reconciling differences in financial flows between cities and between provinces.

*Transition policies and institutional arrangements* will be needed for multiple groups of workers, including:

- Policy and administrative changes in the urban old-age insurance system to ensure its attractiveness for urban migrants; additional changes to effectively cover civil servants and PSU employees, and over the long term to extend coverage to include nonwage workers.
- Transition arrangements applied to older cohorts in the urban old-age insurance system. The phasing and transition period for parametric changes is needed, such as changes in the minimum retirement age.
- Transition arrangements supporting the integration of PSU employees and civil servants into the proposed MORIS scheme, with supplementary benefits provided to protect replacement rates as needed.

*Investment management:* Regulations, guidelines and strengthened supervision are needed for liquidity and reserve management for investment accumulations under the MORIS at the county, municipal, and provincial levels.

*Regulation and supervision of voluntary pension arrangements:* A multiyear strategy will be needed to develop policies for such arrangements and establish the institutional capacity for supervising such policies. This will include regulations and guidelines for investment management, custodianship, trustee relationships and record keeping. It will also require substantial strengthening of supervision of voluntary pension arrangements, including financial market intermediaries and instruments.

Developing and implementing the proposed vision will require additional study and consideration, including (1) quantifying individual rights for conversion to NDC account balances, (2) quantifying legacy costs, (3) establishing a detailed financing framework, (4) establishing and strengthening the framework for investment management, (5) establishing the legal and institutional framework for regulation and supervision, and (6) in the future refining pension policy provisions through systematic monitoring and evaluation.

## Conclusion

This volume outlines a medium-term vision for strengthening old-age income protection. The proposed design provides a common framework for a minimum Citizens' Social Pension (CSP) for all citizens and strengthening of the old-age insurance system, including the integration of all salaried workers, such as civil servants, PSU employees, and migrants. Furthermore, it proposes—in line with the NRPS and URPS—a Voluntary Individual Retirement Insurance Scheme (VIRIS)—that would provide state subsidies as incentives for individuals to save for retirement over and above those currently in place. Finally, it proposes a common framework for voluntary occupational and individual savings arrangements.

The proposal builds on existing policies and institutional arrangements yet strengthens them to address key reform needs identified:

(1) Contributory instruments are defined-contribution in design to adjust benefits in line with anticipated aging.

(2) Sustainability is achieved by aligning contributions and benefits, eliminating transition costs with the NDC design, and establishing a modest target benefit level and a factor reduction in the CSP benefit to constrain fiscal costs.

(3) Coverage gaps are reduced through matching contribution incentives and a social pension for all elderly.

(4) The design is aligned with China's dynamic and changing labor markets supporting transparent and portable pension rights and providing a secure and uniform foundation for nationwide old-age income security.

## Notes

1. 广覆盖、保基本、多层次、可持续.
2. 保基本、廣覆蓋、有彈性、可持續.
3. In addition, secondary objectives of the social security system would be to support labor market efficiency, business competitiveness, and financial market development.
4. 新型农村社会养老保险.
5. The VIRIS suggests a substantially higher matching subsidy of perhaps 1:1 compared with the minimum local matching subsidy of the NRPS of 0.3:1.
6. Additional common principles were suggested above, including broad coverage, protects at the basic level, is multilayered, flexible, and sustainable.

# China: A Vision for Pension Policy Reform

## Introduction

China is at a critical juncture in its economic transition. A comprehensive reform of its pension and social security systems is an essential element of a strategy aimed toward achieving a harmonious society and sustainable development. Among policy makers, a widely held view is that the approach to pension provision and reform efforts piloted over the last 10–15 years is insufficient to enable China's economy and population to realize its development objectives in the years ahead. Over the last few years, the government has initiated several significant measures, considered various reform options, and articulated principles for what it would like to achieve in a reformed pension system. The principles (indicated by 12 Chinese characters)[1] call for an urban system that "has broad coverage, protects at the basic level, is multilayered and sustainable," while the principles articulated for the rural system[2] are "broad coverage, protects at the basic level, is flexible, and sustainable." Recognition is widespread among policy makers that an integrated approach toward pension provision and a medium-term vision consistent with such principles are necessary to realize China's core objectives.

This volume has been prepared to develop a long-term vision of a holistic framework for strengthening old-age income protection in China, consistent with the principles outlined, that could be realized by 2040, and to propose design options toward achieving it.

A well-functioning social security system is essential for sustained growth and for people-centered development in the context of China's rapidly aging society. Investing in a well-functioning social security system is one of several measures supportive of the macroeconomic objectives of increasing domestic consumption and reducing precautionary household savings. It can also support labor markets conducive to growth while providing minimum old-age income protection and a framework for retirement savings. A national framework would remove barriers to labor mobility between both locations and professions and afford equal treatment as workers save toward retirement. A social security system that is affordable to businesses, workers, and the budget can strengthen incentives for business development and job creation and create a more equalized financial burden throughout China. Finally, a sustainable social security system can ensure sufficient resources to honor current and future pension commitments.

Although substantial reforms have been undertaken over the last two decades, many policy makers believe that additional reforms are needed to meet the needs of China's rapidly changing economy and society. Several reform issues previously raised by the authorities have not been fully addressed, such as legacy costs, fragmentation, and limited coverage. Simultaneously, many new challenges have emerged, such as rapid urbanization, income inequality, urban-rural disparities, informalization of the labor force, changes in the family structure and residence arrangements, and the increasing effects of globalization.

The government is actively pursuing measures to further develop and improve the social security system for all of its citizens. It undertook a major reform of the urban enterprise pension system in 1997 and has refined the system since that time. Moreover, it has piloted pension reforms for Public Sector Units (PSUs) and for migrants and farmers. In 2009 the authorities established a national framework for rural pensions, the New Rural Pension Scheme (NRPS) and in mid-2011 announced an Urban Residents Pension Scheme (URPS) completing a national framework for expanding pension coverage and for eventual integration of rural and urban resident schemes. The plan enjoys political support, motivation of relevant agencies and local governments, and strong overall fiscal capacity. The country also has more than two decades of experience piloting different approaches to social security reform for different sectors of the Chinese population. Yet in spite of such strong motivation and experience, the government has found it difficult to identify a holistic vision to achieve a coherent and integrated pension system. As seen in the pronouncements of the 17th Congress of the Communist Party, it is recognized that an integrated reform effort is essential to avoid the long-term economic and social consequences of a fragmented and inefficient system. This volume aims to articulate such an integrated holistic vision.

This volume suggests a national pension system that no longer distinguishes along urban and rural locational or *hukou* lines yet takes account of the diverse nature of employment relations and capacity of individuals to make contributions. The proposed separation of mandatory wage-based and voluntary nonwage-based contributory schemes is intended as an interim measure until the overall tax collection and compliance framework could be extended to the nonwage sector. Over the long term, it is anticipated that the urban old-age insurance system will extend to all citizens while the distinction between wage-based and nonwage-based incomes will remain.

This volume is organized as follows: The main text outlines this vision, focusing on summarizing the key features of a proposed long-term pension system. It first examines key trends motivating the need for reform then outlines the proposed three-pillar design and the rationale behind the design choices. It then moves on to examine financing options. The text continues by discussing institutional reform issues, and the final section concludes. The six appendixes provide additional analytical detail supporting the findings in the main text. Appendix A evaluates the pensions needs of nonwage rural and urban citizens and outlines the rationale for the instruments proposed. Appendix B evaluates a notional or nonfinancial defined-contribution design as applied to China's urban old-age insurance system. Appendix C evaluates pension legacy costs and financing options for addressing them. Appendix D evaluates issues of aging, retirement, and labor markets in China in the context of old-age pension provisions. Appendix E examines voluntary pensions savings arrangements.

## Current and Future Trends Motivating Reform

### Addressing the Demographic and Economic Transition
China is in the midst of a major demographic and economic transition, including aging, changes in the family structure, urbanization, labor mobility, informalization of the labor force, and high income inequality. China's dramatic aging process and demographic transition have resulted

in part from the one-child family policy introduced in the late 1970s, combined with significant increases in longevity. Old-age dependency ratios are projected to rise from 13.5 percent and 9.0 percent in 2008 in rural and urban areas, respectively, to 34.4 percent and 21.1 percent by 2030 (figure 1). In the urban old-age insurance system, the system dependency rate, which was 34 percent in 2001, is projected to increase to 100 percent (one worker for each retiree) within 30 years.[3] China will undergo this transition in approximately half the time of other countries while starting the transition with a per capita gross domestic product (GDP) roughly one-fifth that of the developed world. Just as old-age dependency ratios are increasing, the so-called 1-2-4 family pattern (1 child–2 parents–4 grandparents) has contributed to declining family

**Figure 1    China Population Projections: Growth in the Aged and Dependency Ratios**

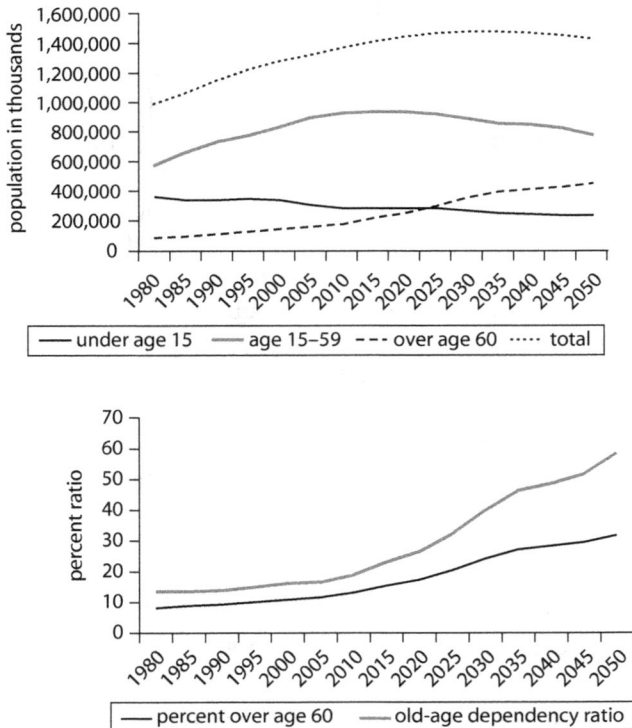

*Source:* Population Division of the Department of Economic and Social Affairs of the United Nations Secretariat, *World Population Prospects: The 2008 Revision.* http://esa.un.org/unpp.

resources to support the elderly. Moreover, changes in the family structure (including an increasing divorce rate) are creating new demands on the traditional old-age support arrangements.

Aging and the demographic transition have been key factors in the projected financing gap for the urban old-age insurance system.[4] Long-term actuarial projections suggested a financing gap (present value of projected yearly financial shortfalls) from 2002 to 2075 of 95 percent of China's GDP for 2001. The same projections suggested marginal system-wide cash surpluses between 2009 and 2018 and then deficits thereafter, in spite of the maturation of "new men" with lower replacement rates.[5] Faster coverage expansion would delay the turning point but make the negative cash flow larger thereafter.

The country's rapid growth and economic transformation have increased the demand for a dynamic labor force that can effectively adjust to the pace of change. Fragmented pension provisions create a barrier to labor mobility. Moreover, low urban retirement ages discourage participation of older workers in the labor force, thereby creating rigidities in the face of growing labor demand (see box 1 and appendix D). China's urban retirement ages (60 for men and 50 or 55 for women) have remained unchanged since the 1950s, during which time the proportion

**Box 1**

## The Effect of the Minimum Retirement Age on Employment and Labor Markets

*Demographic trends and labor force shortage.* Changes in China's demographic structure have important implications for the labor supply, pension schemes, old-age income support, fiscal sustainability, and long-term growth (see appendix D). The size of China's working-age population will peak in about 2015, and so continued growth will require both higher labor force expansion and skill development. Since 2003 the issue of labor shortages has emerged, with such shortages not limited to the coastal areas. Indeed, the transfer of labor-intensive industries into inland areas has also replicated similar shortages in those areas. Accelerated growth coupled with demographic conditions has led to growth of migration and in some cases labor scarcity. Increasing the minimum retirement age could be one of several options to simultaneously address the labor shortages and population aging.

*(continued next page)*

**Box 1**    *(continued)*

The *lump of labor fallacy* assumes that the level of labor demand is fixed in the economy and that a substitution effect exists between older and younger workers, so that gradually raising the minimum retirement age will reduce the number of jobs for young workers entering the labor force. Such a view originated from the high and sustained unemployment in Europe in the 1980s and 1990s. It has been a widespread perception in China. Empirical evidence from 21 OECD countries, however, suggests that changes in employment of older workers aged 55–64 have small but *positive* effects on the employment of younger workers aged 16–24 and on prime-working-age people aged 25–54 because job-specific knowledge and differences in noncognitive skills that develop with age render such individuals useful complements to younger new workers, who often enter with different skill sets. In China, the modest and gradual increase of older workers' participation suggested by an increase in the retirement age very likely will not worsen the situation of youth employment.

*Effects of employment and labor markets.* Encouraging the elderly to stay longer in the labor market, and retool their skills will have a certain and (in most cases) gradual effect on the labor supply. Simulations illustrate that an increase in retirement age for women from 51 to 60 years old would increase the proportion of the population group between age 15 and retirement age by 0.5 percent in 2010, but this proportion is projected to keep increasing over time to about 10.0 percent after 2029. If the retirement age is further increased from 61 to 65 for both men and women, the proportion of the increased labor force will rise from 10.9 percent in 2029 to 18.4 percent in 2039, whereafter it is projected to remain constant. In practice, other factors that affect labor supply and labor demand should be considered, such as wages, wealth, preferences, skills, job opportunities, discrimination, and informalization. Therefore, the effect of an increase in retirement age could be marginally less than one-third of the supply of older workers aged 51–65.

*Effects of the minimum retirement age on the urban old-age insurance system.* Increasing the minimum retirement age is one of several options to address the financial consequences of aging. The existing old-age insurance system will be financially unsustainable because of various factors, including legacy costs and aging. An increase in retirement age could materially affect the financial sustainability of the existing social pooling component, increase the benefit level from Individual Accounts and slow the growth of the system old-age dependency

*(continued next page)*

**Box 1**    *(continued)*

ratio, leaving more financial resources available to support the aging society. Increasing the retirement age has different effects on pension revenues and expenditures. Encouraging older workers to work longer means more pension contributors who otherwise would be retired, which increases pension revenues. In the meantime, social pooling expenditures are reduced because the number of years of benefits is reduced even though the annual benefit received at retirement would increase because of additional years of accrual.

of the population represented by the elderly, as well as life expectancy at the time of retirement, have both increased. Demands on the labor force will increase as the working-age population is projected to be stagnant and then decline in the coming years (figure 2).

A national pension framework including the portability of pension rights is essential to remove barriers to China's increasingly mobile labor force. Workers in China have become increasingly mobile in recent years, and such a trend will undoubtedly continue with projected urbanization (figure 2).[6] Establishing a framework for the portability of urban and rural pension rights will strengthen old-age income security for a growing population with work histories that span locations in urban and rural areas. With fully portable pension rights, individuals can make labor market decisions without the distorting effects of losing accumulated rights because of changes in profession or location.

High contribution rates to the urban old-age insurance scheme impact labor costs and competitiveness, thereby discouraging participation. China's urban old-age insurance system contribution rates of 28 percent of covered wages are relatively high when compared with those of Organisation for Economic Co-operation and Development (OECD) countries.[7] Such rates do not include other social security contributions, which together with pension contributions can total about 41 percent depending upon local regulations. Such high rates create strong incentives for evasion, distorting labor markets. Moreover, regional differences in contribution rates impact labor and business competitiveness.

The authorities have placed a growing premium on more balanced growth between households, rural and urban areas, and different regions of the country. To date, the pension system has in some ways contributed to increased divergence. The divergence in urban old-age insurance contribution rates only narrowed over the last decade.

**Figure 2    Projected Size and Composition of the Working-Age Population**

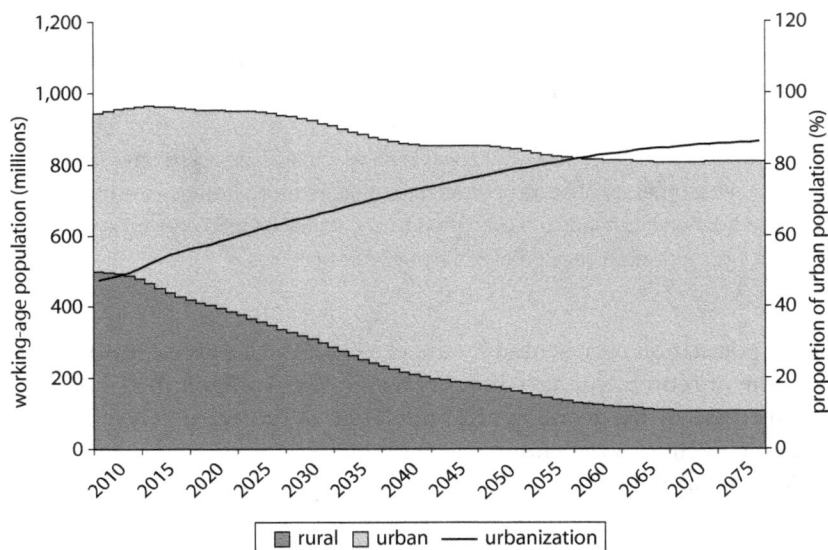

Source: World Bank estimates.

There is a weak framework for voluntary pension savings, including occupational schemes. Enterprise Annuity (EA) schemes at year-end 2008 covered less than 5 percent of contributors to the urban old-age insurance system, and the EA framework has not been adapted to the special needs of PSUs or small enterprises. Structured instruments for voluntary pension savings are also increasingly important due to decreases in replacement rates from the urban old-age insurance system. A strengthened framework for occupational and personal pensions affords the opportunity for workers to improve the returns on funds saved as well as diversify the sources of old-age income protection.

As the authorities seek to rebalance the growth model toward greater reliance on domestic consumption, limited coverage and uncertainty over income protection from current pensions discourage consumption and encourage precautionary savings. Strengthening the design and transparency of the old-age insurance system can reduce uncertainty, improving public confidence. Strengthening old-age income protection is one of several measures to improve social protection (such as also improving health and unemployment insurance and social assistance— dibao), which together can reduce vulnerability and thus support current consumption.

## Proposed Design

### *Summary Description and Principles behind Design Choices*

This volume proposes a three-pillar design consisting of the following components (see figure 3):

(a) A *basic benefit pillar* providing minimum elderly poverty protection through noncontributory *Citizens' Social Pension* (CSP) benefits

(b) A *contributory pillar* with a mandatory notional defined contribution (NDC) scheme for workers with labor contracts (modifying the current urban old-age insurance system) and a voluntary defined-contribution pension savings scheme for the urban and rural populations with nonwage incomes (for example temporary workers, migrants, the self-employed, and farmers)

(c) A *supplementary savings pillar* for urban and rural residents providing voluntary occupational and personal pension savings options that may supplement other pension benefits.

Maintaining separate wage and nonwage-based contributory schemes is intended as an interim measure for perhaps 30 years or more, after which provisions under the Mandatory Occupational Retirement Insurance Scheme (MORIS) potentially could absorb workers without labor contracts—the informal sector, self-employed, migrants, and farmers. The rationale behind this approach is that (1) the experience in developed countries suggests that extending coverage of mandatory contributory schemes to the rural and informal sectors generally is a prolonged process even with rapid and sustained high rates of growth and (2) the projected rural working population in 2040 will still be about 200 million (figure 3). Because the authorities have committed to providing old-age income protection for the largely uncovered rural and urban populations, an interim (30+ year) arrangement is necessary under

**Figure 3    Proposed Overall Design**

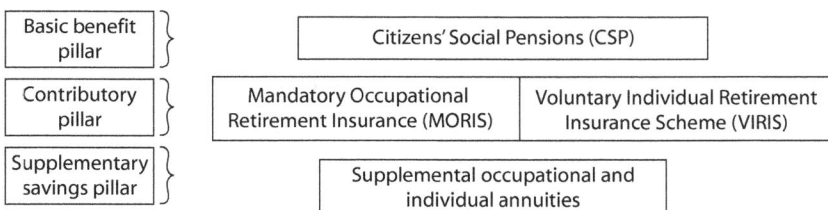

the assumption that over time urbanization will make it easier to integrate the MORIS and the Voluntary Individual Retirement Insurance Scheme (VIRIS).

The proposed design is motivated by principles of providing an integrated framework for all Chinese workers and retirees while allowing for diverse economic and demographic circumstances:

(1) Reforms should *address current and long-term future needs* under the assumption that reform should be infrequent.
(2) Policies should have *uniform national standards yet sufficient flexibility* to accommodate China's diverse regional needs and economic characteristics.
(3) Reforms should *reflect the decentralized nature of current policies and administration* while at the same time seeking to achieve risk pooling at least at the provincial level and ultimately at the national level in the long term.
(4) Pension savings and insurance functions are collective responsibilities that require *sharing the financing and risk management burden at multiple levels,* including the central government; provincial, municipal, county, and prefecture governments; and among employers, workers, and families.

The proposed design has been chosen to satisfy the principles articulated by the authorities. The proposed design should accomplish the following:

(1) Provide *broad coverage* providing minimal elderly poverty protection. The CSP aims to cover all of the elderly with little or no pension income. The VIRIS provides strong incentives for coverage expansion to nonwage workers.
(2) Target benefits *at a basic level* for all retirees and a retirement savings and insurance option for the vast majority of workers.[8] The CSP benefit level is suggested to be a proportion of the individual consumption requirements for minimum subsistence as currently is the rationale behind the *dibao.* Although the authorities have not specified the targeted level of income replacement in old age, if mandatory contributions target only a modest proportion of income replacement then well-regulated occupational and personal pensions savings arrangements can supplement the mandatory scheme.

(3) Be *multilayered* to diversify the risks and sources of income for China's elderly. The three-pillar design has separate financing sources and risk characteristics for each instrument, which together diversify contributors' and retirees' sources of risk.

(4) Be *sustainable* for contributors, the government, and the broader economy. The proposed NDC design and separate financing of legacy costs for the contributory pillar aims in part to satisfy the *sustainability* objective. The CSP would be fiscally sustainable in spite of demographic change provided that the benefit is established and maintained at a very modest level. The supplementary pillar has been proposed as a defined-contribution design in part to satisfy this sustainability criterion.

(5) Be *flexible* not only for rural schemes but for all schemes. The design has been formulated according to national standards while allowing for adaptation to local circumstances. Further, the design and institutional configuration aim to ensure the portability of pension rights.

An additional objective supported by this volume though not explicitly indicated by the authorities is *affordability*. Affordability refers to the cost to employers and employees of saving for a targeted income replacement in retirement. Moreover, fiscal *affordability* refers to the fiscal burden for providing a social pension, financing legacy costs, financing pension promises for government or PSU workers attributable to fiscal resources, and backstopping potential fiscal costs for the MORIS and VIRIS.

### Basic Benefit Pillar—Citizens' Social Pension (CSP)

*Need and rationale for the CSP*. The elderly are vulnerable to shocks and are likely to grow more vulnerable in the years ahead. Information on elderly poverty and sources of income suggests that the urban elderly are not uniformly at risk as a group; many of them rely on sources of support that are vulnerable to shocks or are dependent on family members who may be unable to provide adequate levels of support and may themselves be subject to shocks that reduce the level of support they can provide (see appendix D). The pressures on family support are likely to become more acute in coming decades as old-age dependency ratios rise. The old-age insurance system will also continue to have major gaps in coverage of the urban elderly for some time to come, and family support will continue to be an important although not uniform source of support to fill the gap for the uncovered urban elderly, especially women.

Although the elderly are growing more vulnerable, substantial weaknesses are seen in existing provision of poverty protection for the elderly poor:

- *Dibao* assistance presently reaches less than half of the urban elderly poor.
- Means-testing criteria for *dibao* programs have not been uniform.
- A common framework for the *dibao* benefit level does not exist, and the benefit level and access criteria have been dependent upon local fiscal capacity.
- Without some form of universality, an increasing number of elderly have been left vulnerable, though the NRPS and URPS should substantially increase the coverage of the elderly.

Although the NRPS and URPS are important steps forward towards universal elderly coverage, some elderly may likely not satisfy the criteria to receive benefits under these programs. The poorest often have the least capacity to save for retirement and thus meet the savings or family binding criterion for the minimum basic benefit. Communities with weak fiscal capacity may also likely have insufficient matching resources to motivate savings for retirement by rural and informal sector workers, resulting in some of the elderly population left uncovered.

In line with an assessment of vulnerability and weaknesses in existing policies, analysis of elderly poverty and vulnerability supports a solid rationale for greater public intervention in support for the rural elderly:[9] (1) Historically, rural elderly have been consistently poorer, have been more vulnerable, and have suffered a higher incidence of chronic poverty than have both working-age households and the urban elderly in China. Households headed by older people are consistently the poorest in rural areas, even though rural poverty head counts have fallen sharply. (2) The demographic transition is accelerating with aging, and the increase in old-age dependency is far more pronounced in rural than in urban areas. (3) Rural elderly depend more on labor income and informal sources of support, which will come under increased pressure over time, particularly for the rural poor (figure 4). (4) Although savings rates are high across the income distribution in China and remain positive even in old age, they are strongly correlated with household income, and the rural poor are not saving on average.[10] Concerns have also been expressed that people are saving too much as a precaution against old age, health costs, and other shocks, contributing to macroeconomic imbalances between saving and consumption.

***Proposed design.*** The objective of the proposed CSP is to ensure basic living subsistence for the elderly not covered by existing pension provisions or otherwise unable to generate an adequate retirement income from contributions during their working age.[11] This could be for a variety of reasons, including sickness or disability or time out of the workforce for various reasons such as child rearing or acquiring an education (figure 4).

The proposed benefit would have uniform design parameters nationwide, although the benefit level would reflect local characteristics (see table 1). Provincial authorities would be held accountable for observance of the national framework and its implementation at the city and county levels. The benefit level proposed for urban beneficiaries would be a proportion of the regional average wage, whereas that for rural beneficiaries would be a proportion of the regional average rural per capita income.[12] Both benefits would aim to be higher than the per capita benefit under the existing *dibao* scheme. A "pensions test" would reduce the benefit by a proportion of benefits received under other pension arrangements. The factor reduction applied to the

**Figure 4    Primary Source of Support for Rural Elderly by Age**
*percentage of total individual incomes*

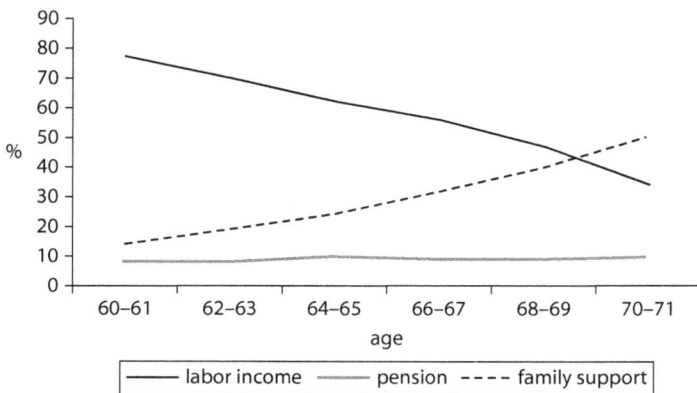

*Source:* Cai and others 2012.

**Table 1    Citizens' Social Pensions (CSP)—Proposed Parameters**

| Issue | Provision/parameters |
| --- | --- |
| Applicability | • All urban and rural residents age 65 and over |
| Eligible beneficiaries | • Urban or rural elderly that apply and have other pension income lower than an applicable threshold for those aged 65–74 and any retiree aged 75 and above. |
| Benefit level (before pension test reduction) | • Percent of regional average wage (urban) or regional per capita income (rural)<br>• Minimum benefit above *dibao* standard<br>• Benefit partially offset by other pension income, factor reduction may be 40–60 percent depending upon desired incentives and fiscal constraints |
| Financing | • Noncontributory<br>• Financed from general revenues<br>• Shared responsibility between central and subnational governments, with minimum benefit guarantee from the central government |
| Interaction with *dibao* | • Benefit included in family income for purposes of determining eligibility for *dibao* |

CSP benefit needs to be designed to provide meaningful incentives for contributions to other pension schemes while at the same time targeting the benefit to those with the least source of income from other pensions benefits. Figures 5 and 10 illustrate the effect on a benefit of applying a pensions test in a stylized example. Given the intention to increase the MORIS retirement age to 65 over time for men and women, age 65 has been proposed for the minimum age necessary to qualify for the CSP. This would be important from a labor supply incentive viewpoint and to maintain the coherence of urban pensions policy. Such a benefit would be noncontributory and financed by national, provincial, municipal, and local resources.

An important design parameter of the CSP would be the benefit's relativity to the rural *dibao* threshold in counties. In this respect, the practice of most rural pension pilot schemes seems appropriate, that is, to set the benefit at a level above the rural *dibao* per capita threshold. It would be important for incentive reasons to be sufficiently above the *dibao* threshold, but for fiscal reasons not to be too far above it. If the CSP benefit is set too high, the incentives to contribute to the MORIS or VIRIS would be weak, while if it is set too low, the objective of mitigating old-age poverty through the pension system may be undermined. Under the NRPS, the central government has initiated a minimum flat benefit level at 55 renminbi (RMB) monthly, with additional funds that can be

**Figure 5    Stylized Example of Rural CSP Benefit Levels and Composition**

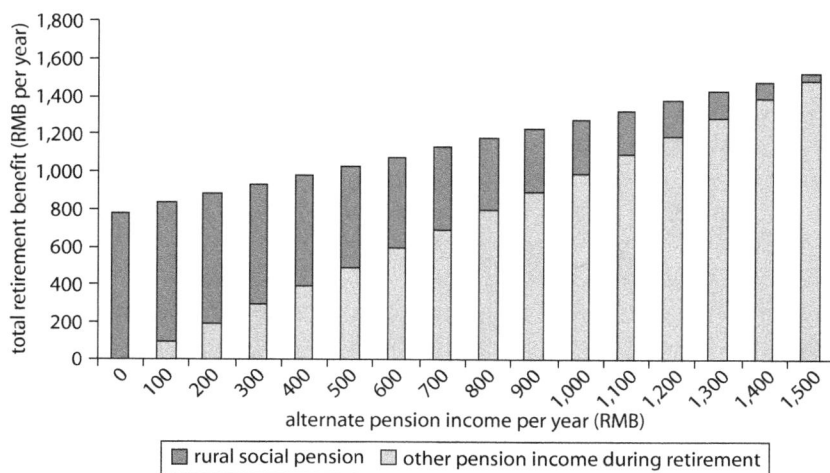

*Source:* World Bank simulations.

*Note:* Assumes a CSP benefit of 788 RMB/year, which is the 2003 Ravallion-Chen rural consumption poverty level increased by the CPI from 2003 to 2009. In this example, the CSP benefit is reduced by 50 percent of the alternative pension income.

provided from subnational sources. This compares to an average annual rural *dibao* threshold of 988 RMB nationally in 2008, with a range from 26 to 267 RMB (about 6.6–67.3 percent of the national average net rural per capita income). The *dibao* threshold rates suggest that closer attention will be needed to the relative level of the CSP benefit "floor" to align protections and incentives appropriately. Finally, pensions from under the NRPS, URPS, and the proposed CSP would have no effect on the receipt of the supportive allowance for following the family planning policy, although some Chinese researchers have proposed integrating the programs through using the family planning subsidy as an additional subsidy toward individual pension contributions.[13]

Key open policy design decisions that need to be made include (1) a more detailed framework for the minimum benefit level, (2) the benefit reduction factor applied to other pension income, (3) qualifying conditions including age and residency, (4) central, provincial, and local financing arrangements (see discussion below), (5) linkages to the *dibao*, and (6) administrative arrangements.

***Projected costs.*** Indicative cost estimates suggest that a CSP benefit for both rural and urban elderly poor would cost about 0.24 percent of GDP in 2010, rising to about 0.43 percent of GDP in 2040 (figure 6).[14] A benefit at about the urban income poverty line would cost about 0.11 percent of 2010 GDP, rising to 0.31 percent of GDP in 2040 with the benefit level at about 4 percent of the urban average wage. Similar cost estimates suggest that a CSP for the rural elderly poor with a benefit at about the rural individual poverty consumption line would be about 0.13 percent of 2010 GDP, declining to about 0.12 percent of GDP in 2040 (figure 6). These estimates would vary substantially based on the benefit level, growth in the benefit level, level of urbanization, and observed benefit reductions arising from the "pensions test." The cost increases reflect population aging and urbanization. By comparison, by adopting a benefit level of about 28 percent of the urban average wage (the OECD country average), the urban CSP cost would be 0.75 percent of GDP in 2010, rising to 2.1 percent of GDP by 2040.[15]

***Comparison of proposed design with current arrangements and justification for policy changes.*** What are the differences in incentives

**Figure 6    Indicative Cost Projections for Urban and Rural Citizens' Social Pensions**

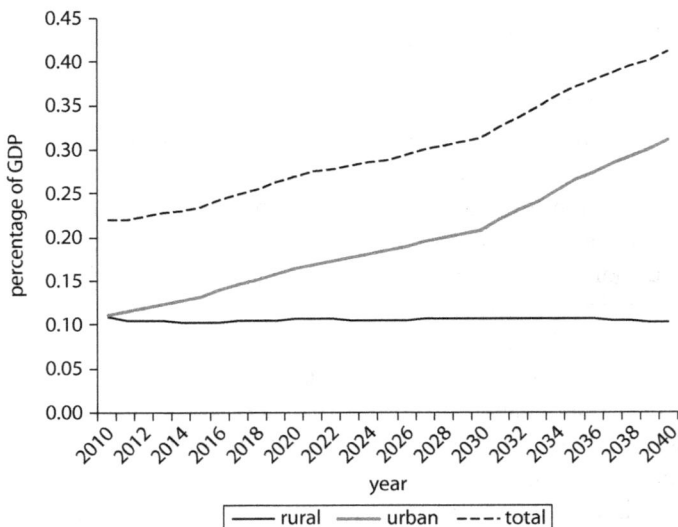

*Source:* World Bank estimates.
*Note:* This assumes median variant urbanization 2010–2040, total fertility rate 1.8, and age distribution for the beneficiary population over age 60 is the same as for the total population. Assumed rural factor reductions attributed
to a pensions test as follows: 5 percent in 2011, rising by 3 percent each year up to a maximum of 50 percent.
Assumed urban factor reductions attributed to a pensions test are as follows: 40 percent in 2010 rising by 1 percent
each year up to a maximum of 60 percent. The benefit level is assumed to grow at the same rate as GDP.

created by the proposed CSP qualifying conditions and benefits compared with those of the NRPS and URPS?

- *Benefit level—Minimum national standards with scope for regional variation.* The CSP has a similar design to the NRPS and URPS in that both establish a national basis for the benefit formula with the opportunity for localities to increase the benefit provided. Although the NRPS and URPS provide a minimum benefit of 55 RMB, the CSP has proposed a benefit that would uniformly be linked to a local rural per capita income or urban wage index with no minimum national benefit level.

- *Financing.* The financing plans for the CSP, NRPS, and URPS are similar. The CSP suggests that the central government will guarantee a minimum benefit (linked to a local index), and the NRPS and URPS provide for central government financing of a minimum benefit in all but the eastern coastal provinces.

- *Qualifying conditions and incentives.* The CSP establishes Chinese residency, age (65), and pension income (under a threshold to be determined) as the only qualifying conditions, whereas the NRPS and URPS have qualifying conditions of age (60), residency, and 15 years of contributions (or buyback or family binding provisions). Although the NRPS and URPS vesting or family binding provisions create strong incentives for participation by those approaching retirement age and their children, these incentives may also lead to elderly coverage gaps for those poor elderly not able to satisfy such conditions. The CSP proposal therefore does not include contribution or family binding conditions although it does reduce CSP benefits resulting from alternative pension income. In respect to the age requirement, a retirement age of 65 can not only align with the other contributory pension retirement age proposals but also create stronger incentives for individuals to work longer.

- *Work and savings incentives.* This volume shares the authorities' concern that a CSP may discourage incentives to work, save, and contribute to a pensions saving or old-age insurance scheme. The NRPS and URPS, on the other hand, have contribution or family binding requirements established as a savings incentive. Although the CSP benefit may discourage incentives for some to work and save for retirement, the primacy of the objective of ensuring full beneficiary coverage accepts this tradeoff.

- *Targeting.* The pensions test applied to the CSP would target benefits to those elderly with the limited alternative pension benefits while at the same time limiting program costs. The NRPS and URPS are also designed for those elderly without pension benefits but do not provide a supplement for those with very low pension benefit levels.

- *Needs of urban nonwage workers.* Recognizing the changing nature of urban and rural residency distinctions in China and the vulnerability of the nonwage sector, this volume proposes the CSP to apply equally to urban and rural dwellers and therefore cover the informal sector, self-employed, and migrants that may not realize sufficient retirement income to prevent poverty in old age.

*If the differences between the CSP, on the one hand, and the NRPS and URPS, on the other, are only marginal, is the suggested policy change justified by the anticipated results?*

Overall, the basic benefit of the NRPS and URPS is similar to the CSP provisions proposed here. Table 2 provides stylized examples comparing the NRPS and CSP benefits. The differences in policy parameters (retirement age, pensions test, elimination of contribution requirements) would marginally improve the design of the NRPS and URPS. Of greater importance, however, is the suggestion to extend the CSP framework to include both rural and urban nonwage workers, and, in this way, the benefit would be much better aligned with China's increasingly mobile workforce and the government's desire to reduce the distinction between urban and rural residents. This would also create an alignment between the CSP and urban old-age insurance system. Reducing the risk of old-age poverty in China can therefore be much more effectively achieved by a CSP that is provided to all of the aged regardless of their rural or urban residency.

### Contributory Pension Provisions
*Motivations for reform of current urban old-age insurance.* Urban old-age insurance provisions face various weaknesses that constrain China's objectives of realizing sustained growth and a harmonious society:[16]

(a) *Fragmentation and limited portability obstruct labor mobility.* Maintaining separate schemes for civil servants, employees of PSUs, and other urban workers creates a barrier to labor mobility that impacts labor markets and the career choices of affected workers. The lack of portability of rights between schemes and between cities also inhibits labor mobility. Pension administration is also decentralized in most places,

**Table 2  Stylized Examples Comparing NRPS and CSP Benefits**

| Example | Retiree characteristics | NRPS benefits | CSP benefits | Comparison |
|---|---|---|---|---|
| 1. Rural retiree with no pension | Rural resident, 65 years old in 2011, has not contributed to the NRPS or any other pension plan and receives no other pension income. | Retiree receives the minimum benefit of 55 RMB per month, and in this case there is no increase in the benefit level by the local government. Contributions of 100 RMB/year are made by his or her relatives through the family binding requirement. | Retiree receives the minimum benefit (percent of regional average per capita income to be determined). In this case there is no increase in the benefit provided by the local government. No contributions are required by family members. | • Benefits under the CSP may be lower or higher than under the NRPS.<br>• Under the CSP, no contributions are required by family members. |
| 2. Rural retiree with no pension and no children | Rural resident, 65 years old in 2011, has no other sources of pension income and has made no contributions to the NRPS. Retiree has no surviving children or any other pension income. | Retiree cannot qualify for benefits because he/she cannot meet the family binding requirement. | Retiree receives the minimum benefit. | CSP removes a potential coverage gap by eliminating family binding or historical contribution requirements characteristic of the NRPS. |

*(continued next page)*

**Table 2** (continued)

| Example | Retiree characteristics | NRPS benefits | CSP benefits | Comparison |
|---|---|---|---|---|
| 3. Rural retiree with small urban pension | Rural resident, 65 years old in 2011, and receives a small pension of 50 RMB per month from years of work in an SOE. | Retiree receives minimum benefit of at least 55 RMB/month in addition to the 50 RMB/month from the SOE for a total of 105 RMB/month. Contributions of 100 RMB/year are made by his/her children through the family binding requirement. | Retiree entitled to the minimum benefit (assumed 55 RMB/month) reduced by 40 percent of the SOE benefit (0.4 × 50 = 20). The CSP benefit is 35 RMB (in addition to the 50 RMB/month from the SOE) for a total of 85 RMB/month. | Benefit adjustment applied to the CSP reduces fiscal costs while providing an incentive for workers to find additional means of savings or mobilizing other retirement income. |
| 4. Urban retiree with no pension income | Urban resident, 65 years old in 2011, has worked in the informal sector and has no other sources of pension income. | As an urban resident, retiree cannot qualify for NRPS benefits though he/she may qualify for a URPS benefit. | Retiree receives the minimum CSP benefit plus additional benefits as may be provided by the municipality. | Both URPS and CSP ensures that a minimum benefit is provided for urban nonwage retirees. |
| 5. Rural retiree age 60 | Rural resident, 60 years old in 2011 and has no other sources of pension income. Retiree has not contributed to the NRPS or any other pension plan and receives no other pension income. | Retiree receives the minimum benefit of at least 55 RMB/month subject to family binding requirements. | Retiree does not meet the age requirement and does not qualify for a benefit. | CSP does not cover population aged 60–64 under the rationale that such individuals can work and find nonpension income sources. |

*Note:* CSP = Citizens' Social Pension; NRPS = New Rural Pension Scheme; SOE = state-owned enterprise; URPS = Urban Residents Pension Scheme.

with collections, record keeping, account management, compliance monitoring, benefit calculation, and disbursement carried out at a county, prefecture, municipal, or city level.

(b) *Very limited risk pooling.* The experience of the urban old-age insurance system in pooling of contributions, benefit disbursements, and reserves has been very limited since being established in the late 1990s.[17] Such limited pooling creates fiscal stress for those cities and counties with the oldest covered populations and a risk that some beneficiaries receive eroded benefits.

(c) *Poor returns.* The old-age insurance system's individual accounts have yielded rates of return inferior to covered wage growth, resulting in replacement rates for new retirees well below what had been anticipated at the time of the reform in 1996–1997 (figure 7). Expectations that individual accounts could achieve market returns in excess of wage growth have not materialized.

(d) *A growing threat to sustainability.* Although reforms to the urban old-age insurance system have improved projected sustainability in the long term, several factors, including population aging, have continued to pose important challenges. Although urban schemes as a whole have run cash-flow surpluses, many provinces and cities have been paying out more in benefits than they receive in contributions and are therefore running current deficits requiring increasing subsidies (see figure 8). Such future deficits are expected to substantially increase over the coming years as system dependency ratios increase before moderating over the long term.[18]

(e) *Barriers to competitiveness and coverage.* Combined employer-employee contribution rates of 28 percent present a burden on formal labor and enterprise competitiveness in those areas of China generally with the largest pension liabilities. Such contribution rates create incentives for weak labor force coverage, wage underreporting, and early exit from the labor force just as China's labor markets become increasingly competitive (see appendix B and box 1). Weak compliance enforcement and high minimum contributions for low-income workers also contribute to poor coverage. Migrant and informal sector employees have generally not participated in the urban old-age insurance system, although pilot provisions for migrants have provided lower contribution rates.

**Figure 7    Comparison of Rates of Inflation, Wage Growth, and One-Year Term Deposits Interest Rates**

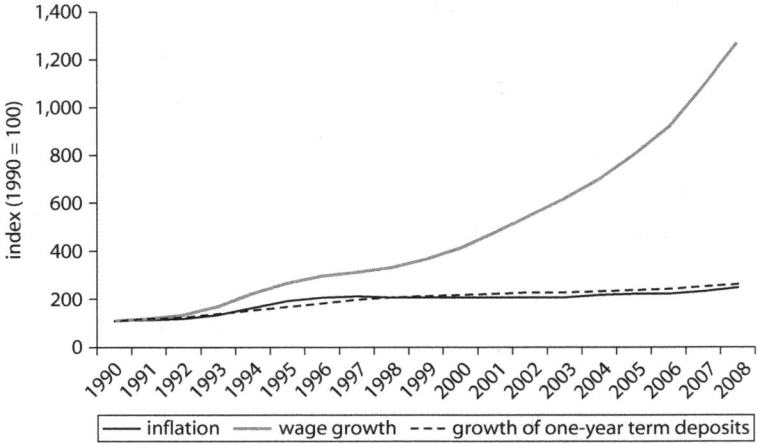

*Sources:* Sin 2008 and World Bank estimates.

**Figure 8    Chinese Government Subsidies to Pensions, 2003–2007**

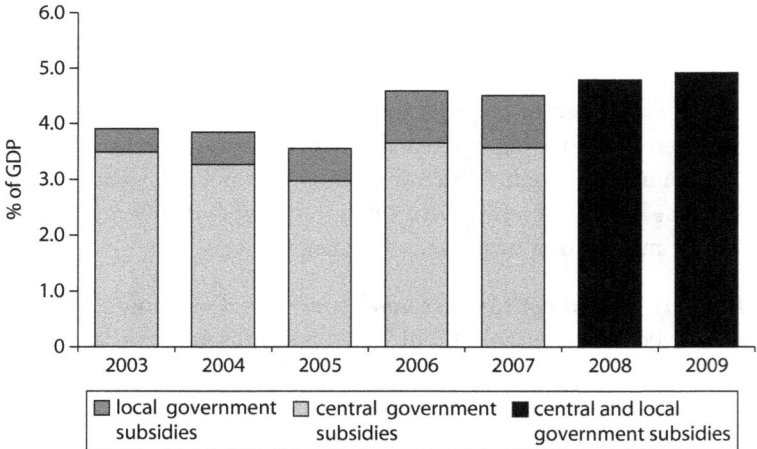

*Source:* World Bank estimates.

## Mandatory Occupational Retirement Insurance Scheme (MORIS)

*MORIS Description.* An NDC design is proposed as a reform measure applied to the old-age insurance system—a Mandatory Occupational Retirement Insurance Scheme (MORIS) (see appendix B; see also figure 9 and box 3). The proposed MORIS design would build on the existing old-age insurance design and institutional structure. The proposed scheme would be defined-contribution in design, follow a notional pay-as-you-go financing approach, and establish an integrated framework across different types of employers. The scheme's rights and responsibilities would extend to all wage-based urban employers and workers—regardless of sector, ownership structure, or location—including civil servants and PSU workers in the medium term. The parameters of such a scheme— that is, the qualifying conditions, the contribution rate, the benefit formula, and the indexation and annuitization framework—should be uniform nationwide, although grounded in local indices.

A key design issue is the *target replacement rate* and, therefore, the optimal contribution rate for the MORIS scheme. Target replacement rates generally reflect social policy choices of desired income replacement, elderly poverty protection, and redistribution. There is a trade-off between the adequacy of income replacement, the affordability of the contribution rate, and the retirement age. A modest target replacement rate would result in equally modest contributions for enterprises and individuals across China, limiting the contribution burden and leaving space for supplementary retirement savings or contributions to other forms of social insurance.

**Figure 9    Current Urban Old-Age Insurance and Proposed MORIS Design**

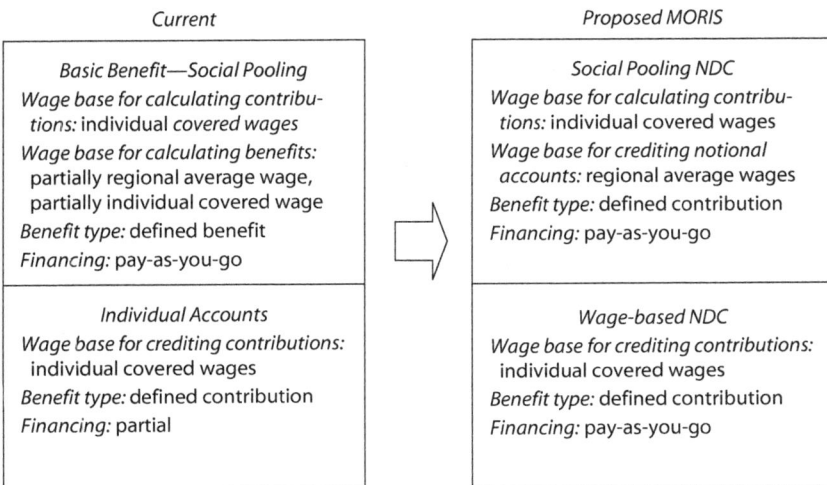

|  *Current*  |  *Proposed MORIS*  |
| --- | --- |
| *Basic Benefit—Social Pooling*<br>*Wage base for calculating contributions:* individual *covered wages*<br>*Wage base for calculating benefits:* partially regional average wage, partially individual covered wage<br>*Benefit type:* defined benefit<br>*Financing:* pay-as-you-go | *Social Pooling NDC*<br>*Wage base for calculating contributions:* individual covered wages<br>*Wage base for crediting notional accounts:* regional average wages<br>*Benefit type:* defined contribution<br>*Financing:* pay-as-you-go |
| *Individual Accounts*<br>*Wage base for crediting contributions:* individual covered wages<br>*Benefit type:* defined contribution<br>*Financing:* partial | *Wage-based NDC*<br>*Wage base for crediting contributions:* individual covered wages<br>*Benefit type:* defined contribution<br>*Financing:* pay-as-you-go |

The proposed design of the MORIS scheme is indicated in figure 9, and table 3 provides a more in-depth comparison of key features of the old-age insurance system and the proposed MORIS.

- *Contribution rate.* The contribution rate depends primarily on the target replacement rate, retirement age, indexation provisions, and income redistribution through the benefit formula. Contributions are determined by multiplying the contribution rate by the individual's wage. By financing legacy costs outside the pension system and increasing the retirement age to 65, the total contribution rate could be reduced from the current 28 percent to between 14 percent and 22 percent for a 40–60 percent average target replacement rate.[19]

- *Notional account accumulation.* Wage-based NDC contributions would credit amounts to an individual's notional account based on the contribution rate multiplied by his or her individual wage. To replicate some of the redistributive properties of the existing social pooling benefit formula, under the *Social Pooling NDC*, the contribution would be levied based on an individual's wage, but the amount credited to the notional account would be calculated based on the contribution rate multiplied by the regional average wage. In this way, some of the income redistribution provided under the social pooling formula of the old-age insurance system would be achieved under the MORIS. The notional account balance would increase at the *notional interest rate*, which would include the *national GDP growth* plus a *balancing mechanism* (see appendix B).

- *Benefit formula.* As suggested in box 2, benefits would be calculated at retirement based on the notional balance accumulated and the annuity factor, which includes the life expectancy at retirement and the prevailing notional interest rate (see box 2), similar to the benefit formulation under current individual accounts.

- *Retirement age.* The urban old-age insurance system should gradually phase in a minimum retirement age of 65 for both men and women.[20] Not only is increasing the retirement age essential to reducing contribution rates and improving benefits, it is also one of a series of measures needed to remove disincentives for workers to work longer (see box 1).

- *Indexation.* In any pension system, the higher the indexation factor, the lower the initial pension. Although price indexation protects a retiree

**Table 3  Comparison of Key Features of the Old-Age Insurance System and the Proposed MORIS**

| | Current old-age insurance system | Proposed MORIS |
|---|---|---|
| 1. Coverage | Regular employees of registered enterprises | All urban and rural wage-based workers (enterprises, PSUs, civil servants, urban migrants with labor contracts) |
| 2. Qualifying conditions | Retirement age: 60 for men; 55 for managerial women; 50 for women workers; earlier ages for hazardous professions 15-year vesting | Retirement age: 65 (men and women, gradually phased in) 30-day vesting |
| 3. Target replacement rate | 58 percent (est. 1997), although currently replacement rates for new retirees estimated at 45–55 percent | According to objectives to be determined, possibly 40–60 percent. |
| 4. Benefit | Social pooling—1 percent/year of service after 15 years Indexation: Individual Account—in accordance with accumulations and returns realized Annuity factor based on life expectancy at retirement and projected changes in life expectancy | Social pooling—A proportion of the contribution rate credited to the notional account based on the regional average wage Notional account formula = notional account, accumulation/projected life expectancy at retirement Indexation = minimum of CPI, mix of 2/3 CPI and 1/3 covered wage growth Notional interest rate = national GDP growth + balancing mechanism Annuity factor based on life expectancy at retirement and projected changes in life expectancy |
| 5. Contribution rates | 20 percent employer 8 percent employee | Total contribution rate depends upon target replacement rate (possibly 14–22 percent) redistribution, assuming legacy costs financed outside the pension system |
| 6. Contribution base | Minimum: 60 percent of regional average wage Maximum: 300 percent of regional average wage | Base for calculating contributions: individual-covered wage Maximum: 300 percent of regional average wage; no minimum |
| 7. Portability | Very limited | Notional accumulations can be transferred across localities and public and private sectors |
| 8. Management | Accounts managed by local social security bureaus Investment management managed by local finance bureaus according to national guidelines | Target to achieve accounts and fund management at least at the provincial level, recognizing that city and county management may exist according to a unified provincial management framework |

*Note:* CPI = consumer price index; GDP = gross domestic product; PSU = public sector unit.

**Box 2**

## Benefit Calculation and Illustrative Examples for the Proposed MORIS

*Design and financing.* Under an NDC scheme, employers and employees make contributions to "notional" accounts, which are unique to each individual employee participant in the scheme. Accounting entries record such contributions, and "notional interest" is accrued and recorded on an ongoing basis. The cash contributions are used to pay the social insurance benefits of other retirees so that the account balance is "notional" or a pension promise based on an accounting entry. The notional interest rate is specified by law and is tied to an index and accrued on notional balances. In one sense, notional accounts are "empty" accounts by design and have an interest rate formula to ensure that the retiree is paid what he or she is promised, which also can be reviewed and accounted for. There often is also a "balancing mechanism," an adjustment to the notional interest rate that aims to adjust for unanticipated long-term differences in the contributions made and benefits paid. In addition, a "buffer fund" is generally established to make sure that all retirees are paid even in the event of an unanticipated short-term shortfall in contributions.

*Benefit calculation.* At retirement, benefits are calculated much in the same way that Individual Account benefits are calculated under the old-age insurance system. All of the retiree's notional balances (and imputed notional interest) are added together from each of the places of work to create a total notional account balance. The individual receives an annuity computed on the basis of (1) projected cohort life expectancy at the individual's age of retirement, (2) notional interest rates and (3) an applicable discount rate. If a retiree waits to retire, the benefit is proportionally greater because he or she has a shorter life expectancy than at the minimum retirement age. Each month a worker participates in the scheme, contributions by the employer and employee are made at a contribution rate to be determined. Such a contribution amount would be calculated as the contribution rate *multiplied by the individual's wage.* The amount credited to his or her notional account would be divided into two parts as follows:

1. One part would be credited to the notional account an amount equal to a contribution rate (for example, 12 percent) *multiplied by the individual's wage;* and
2. One part would be credited to the notional account an amount equal to a rate (for example, 3 percent) *multiplied by the regional average wage.*

*(continued next page)*

**Box 2**   *(continued)*

*Illustrative examples.* This can be illustrated as follows: Suppose that the NDC contribution rate is 12 percent, and the Social Pooling NDC contribution rate is 3 percent, and the individual's monthly salary is 1,750 RMB or one-half of an average monthly salary of 3,500 RMB:

Monthly contribution = (0.12 × 1,750) + (0.03 × 1,750) = 263.

Monthly increase in notional account balance = (0.12 × 1,750) + (0.03 × 3,500) = 298.

The final replacement rate at age 65 for a worker earning one-half of the average wage (assuming 30 years of work and contributions, real growth in wages of 4.5 percent, notional interest rate of 4.5 percent, and life expectancy at retirement age 65 of 17.8 years–men) would be 56 percent.

Two more illustrations indicate the redistributive character of the benefit:

Final replacement rate at age 65 for an *average wage worker* (men—same assumptions) = 46 percent.

Final replacement rate at age 65 for *worker earning two times the average wage* (7,000 RMB—same assumptions) = 42 percent.

*Redistribution.* The contribution to a Social Pooling NDC account would achieve redistribution through the pension system much in the same way as the Social Pooling basic benefit of the old-age insurance system.

against price inflation, because wages generally rise faster than prices, price indexation will result in a decrease in pension benefits after retirement relative to prevailing wages. This volume proposes that the indexation factor applied to notional account benefits be determined based on one-third from the growth in covered wages and two-thirds based on the growth in prices with the indexation not to be less than price growth.[21]

- *Vesting and minimum benefits.* A 30-day vesting period and no minimum benefit provision are proposed to justify the administrative costs of employee registration.[22]

*Rationale behind MORIS design choice.* What is the rationale behind the proposed NDC design in place of the existing Social Pooling and Individual Accounts of the current old-age insurance system?

- *Aging and financial sustainability.* The NDC design when compared to the defined-benefit Social Pooling benefit design has an automatic balancing mechanism to address the demographic effect of aging. In contrast, the Social Pooling defined-benefit design would require periodic adjustments to the contribution rate, accrual rate, and/or retirement age to maintain a balance between contributions and benefits in China's aging society.

- *Coverage incentives.* Benefit determination based on defined-contribution account accumulations establishes a sound link between contributions and benefits, eliminating many of the labor market distortions and incentives for wage underreporting and noncompliance under the current Social Pooling benefit formula. A notional interest rate of GDP growth also provides an attractive incentive to contribute when compared with the returns on Individual Accounts, which have been less than wage growth for more than a decade, and often less than price growth.

- *Accounting framework supportive of labor mobility.* An NDC framework provides a uniform basis for adding up pension entitlements for work from different counties, cities, and provinces and in different sectors and types of employers such as PSUs and enterprises. In this way the NDC framework can remove a substantial barrier to labor mobility. Although in principle it is possible to add up entitlements under the Social Pooling and Individual Account benefit frameworks, an NDC framework offers a far more simple process. Individual Account balances under the current system can, in principle, be added together between employers.

- *Simplicity for fiscal accounting and transfers.* An NDC framework provides a simple basis for transferring acquired rights at retirement although it does require that existing Social Pooling rights are translated into notional account balances. Interregional or interprovincial transfers can be calculated based on such notional account balances. Under the current Social Pooling arrangement, transferring acquired rights between locations requires proper actuarial valuation of these rights.

- *Transition costs and consistency with macroeconomic objectives.* Consistent with China's objective of consumption-driven growth, the NDC approach requires setting aside far less savings for future pension commitments when compared with the transition cost financing requirements for funding existing Individual Accounts. In this way, more resources can be made available for current consumption.

- *Enabling conditions and performance risks for current Individual Accounts.* The governance and financial market requirements for the management of reserves in current Individual Accounts will grow over the coming years. Although many observers have suggested that over time China can develop the regulatory framework and governance capacity to ensure the proper management of such reserves, many have also pointed out the substantial risks posed by such a large concentration of resources that have been mandatorily contributed by employers and employees throughout China. The NDC design eliminates the need for workers to bear these performance risks by setting a formula for notional account returns. Moreover, reserves needed under the NDC design are limited to liquid resources to finance short-term disbursements and a buffer fund to cover potential cash flow imbalances from economic shocks (see appendix B).

What are common design characteristics between the MORIS and the current Social Pooling and Individual Accounts in the old-age insurance system?

- *Target income replacement.* The MORIS can be designed to target the same replacement rate for workers at different income levels as the old-age insurance system.

- *Redistribution.* The existing Social Pooling benefit provides income redistribution by calculating the benefits based on a combination of one-half individual wages and one-half regional average wages. The same effect can be achieved by the Social Pooling NDC calculation, which credits some of the individual contribution to the notional account based on regional average wages instead of individual wages.

- *Annuity calculation and risks.* The proposed benefit calculation under the MORIS is very similar to that of the existing Individual Account benefits.

Can the advantages of the MORIS design be achieved without a major policy change?

- It is possible to enact parametric adjustments to the current Social Pooling benefit to emulate an NDC scheme: (1) the wage base for benefit determination would need to be extended from a final wage basis to lifetime wages and the reference wages indexed or "valorized" to take account of wage or GDP growth during an individual's working life; (2) the accrual rate would need to be changed from the current 1 percent to reflect a projected long-term equilibrium between contributions and benefits; (3) the retirement age would need to be increased to 65 for men and women; and (4) an automatic stabilizer would need to be established to either increase the contribution rate, decrease the accrual rate, and/or increase the retirement age as the system dependency ratios increase in the future.

- It is also possible to prescribe a fixed rate of return to current Individual Accounts, although a financing vehicle would need to cover the deficiency between the rate of return on reserves and such a prescribed interest rate.

- Moving from a fully funded objective of the current Individual Accounts to an NDC framework would require a policy change as well as financial management and institutional arrangements to make such accounts "notional." Those localities that have accumulated significant reserves could place such reserves in regional or national social security funds to achieve diversification and some level of uniformity in investment management.

- Legacy costs could be calculated and separately financed from current revenues while retaining the current old-age insurance system policy design as has been suggested.

*Unifying pension provisions for wage-based workers.* How does the MORIS design create a unifying framework for the diversity of wage-based workers in China?

- *Civil servants and PSU workers.* The proposed MORIS design can readily accommodate PSU and civil servant employees (box 3), thereby facilitating labor mobility to and from the public sector. Past entitlements can be reflected in the notional balances transferred to participants' notional accounts. Future benefit entitlements that exceed the anticipated replacement rate under the MORIS could be supported by additional benefits structured under the proposed Occupational Annuity (OA) scheme. Legacy costs associated with past entitlements would need to be explicitly financed in the MORIS.

**Box 3**

# Proposed Pensions for Civil Servants and Employees of Public Service Units

*Obstacles to inclusion in the old-age insurance system.* An obstacle to the inclusion of civil servant and PSU employees in the old-age insurance system has been the large disparity between the target replacement rates of PSUs (88–94 percent of the standard wage) compared with the old-age insurance system target of 40–60 percent of total wages. Financing arrangements in the existing old-age insurance system have also been in place since 1997 or before, while most PSUs and civil servants have not adopted contributory financing arrangements until more recently, if at all. Moving PSUs from being largely noncontributory to 28 percent combined contribution rates (or less, as proposed) has substantial implications for PSU workers' financial position as well as net wages after employee contributions. Moreover, such contributions have fiscal implications because funds are supposed to be set aside on behalf of future pension liabilities in addition to paying current beneficiaries. Finally, provisions have yet to be finalized under the EA scheme so that PSU employees can have in place a means of covering all or part of the difference between their current target replacement rates and the income replacement provided under the old-age insurance system.

*Proposed approach.* Both civil servant and PSU employers and workers alike would substantially benefit from modernizing the modalities by which such employees accrue pension benefits. This could happen by maintaining target replacement rates yet changing the modality from either the current noncontributory defined-benefit schemes or pilot PSU provisions, to a combination of (1) benefits from the proposed MORIS and (2) a supplemental benefit from a revised OA scheme. Together these arrangements could ensure promised income replacement while also freeing workers to move in and out of positions in the civil service and at PSUs in accordance with the demand for their skills while not sacrificing pension entitlements.

*Examples of treatment under the MORIS and OA arrangements.* Under the proposed design, income replacement for PSU workers and civil servants could be structured between the MORIS and the OA scheme. For example, the government may decide that it wants to maintain a target replacement rate for all existing PSU workers in a given PSU sector or type. If one supposes the target replacement rate for such workers is 88 percent and if the MORIS would deliver

*(continued next page)*

**Box 3**   *(continued)*

a 55 percent replacement rate, then the worker at retirement could receive the MORIS benefit as well as an OA benefit with a target replacement rate of 33 percent.

*Legacy costs and transitional arrangements.* As discussed in appendix C and below, substantial legacy costs are associated with the past service liabilities of PSU workers and civil servants. Financing such costs will be required whether or not a reform program is undertaken and whether or not PSU workers and civil servants are integrated into the old-age insurance system under the proposed MORIS. Under the MORIS design, fully delivering on past pension promises of PSU workers and civil servants requires the recognition of past service liabilities by translating such benefit accruals into a notional balance, which would be recorded in such workers' notional accounts (see appendix C). This recognition of past service would work in a way similar to that of other workers who entered the labor force before the establishment of the MORIS. The government would need to explicitly finance the legacy costs associated with past service for these workers.

*Institutional issues.* Inclusion of civil servants and PSU workers into a reformed old-age insurance scheme poses institutional challenges. These include developing the collections, accounting, financial control, information, and remittance systems in government units and PSUs that are compatible with the proposed institutional requirement of the MORIS policy design. China may therefore seek to delay the incorporation of PSU employees and civil servants into the old-age insurance system until such time as the administrative policy and institutional conditions are in place to effectively support such measures.

- It is widely accepted that inclusion of civil servants and PSU workers in the MORIS or an otherwise reformed urban old-age insurance system poses substantial financial and institutional challenges. A key challenge would be to finance the legacy costs associated with past entitlements of these workers. Moreover, future entitlements which may exceed those provided under the MORIS or old-age insurance system would need to be prefinanced through a supplementary OA scheme. Finally, collections, accounting, financial control, and information and remittance systems would need to be established in government units and PSUs that are compatible with the institutional requirements of the MORIS policy design.

- *Migrants*. Although efforts have been made to incorporate migrants into the current old-age insurance system, several deterrents to participation remain, namely, a relatively high contribution rate[23] and the application of a minimum contribution requirement (see box 4).[24] Moreover, the absence of portability results in practice (despite regulations which provide a framework for transfer of entitlements in the urban workers' scheme) in migrants facing obstacles to fulfilling the 15-year vesting requirements making it difficult for them to collect benefits. Without urban residency, migrants also face uncertainty over whether they will be entitled to receive benefits toward which they may contribute. Most important, many employers and employees alike prefer to avoid the costs of social insurance contributions in an effort to have competitive wages.

Together the MORIS and VIRIS would materially improve the participation incentives for migrants. The MORIS would eliminate an effective minimum contribution requirement (28 percent × 60 percent × the regional average wage), decrease vesting to 30 days, and materially reduce

---

**Box 4**

## Rural-Urban Migrants and Informal Sector Workers

*Migrants are a growing proportion of China's labor force.* This increases the importance of ensuring their old-age income security (see figure 3). The proposed policy design distinguishes between migrants with labor contracts who would be covered under the MORIS and those without such contracts who could contribute to the VIRIS and supplementary personal pension arrangements.

*Proposed urban old-age insurance reforms.* Three policy design proposals should make it more attractive for employers to cover migrants with labor contracts under the MORIS when compared with the existing old-age insurance system: (1) financing legacy costs outside the pension system should materially reduce the current contribution rate for workers with employment contracts, including migrants, (2) the minimum wage subject to mandatory contributions should be materially reduced or eliminated (depending upon the size of the Social Pooling NDC), and (3) reduction in the vesting period would remove the disincentive for reporting for short-term workers close to retirement age.

*(continued next page)*

**Box 4**    *(continued)*

*Incentive issues.* The 2008 labor law requires migrant workers to be included in urban social insurance programs. However, migrant workers apparently in many cases have preferred higher wages in lieu of social insurance contributions. Avoidance of such contributions is one source of labor competitiveness whereby migrants can compete based on lower all-in labor costs. Concerns about portability of pension entitlements also act as a disincentive for mobile workers. The effect can be seen in findings from the 2010 China Urban Labor Survey (CULS) in six provinces which found only around 20 percent participation in the urban workers' pension scheme by migrants, against an average of around 80 percent for local *hukou* workers.

*Proposed VIRIS.* Establishment of the proposed VIRIS should create a strong incentive for migrants without employment contracts to contribute toward retirement. Contributions under the VIRIS could be added to those accrued under the MORIS at retirement. It will be particularly important for migrants for the account accumulations from work in different locations to be portable and added together to determine a pension benefit.

*Institutional reforms* are needed regardless of the policy design adopted. These include (1) establishment of a unified data management system that can consolidate benefit entitlements across localities and (2) continued measures to increase the efficiency of record keeping and contribution remittance to limit employer transaction costs.

contribution rates if legacy costs are financed outside the pension system. For migrants without labor contracts, the VIRIS would offer a substantial matching subsidy to encourage pension savings.

### *Voluntary Individual Retirement Insurance Scheme (VIRIS)*

*Motivations for the establishment of specialized retirement savings instruments for nonwage workers.* A growing need is seen for pension savings instruments for nonwage urban and rural populations because of the increasing importance of the nonwage work in the Chinese economy. Rural-urban migration will change the demographic profile of rural areas and leave the elderly increasingly vulnerable (see appendix C). Relatively high rural household savings rates among all but the poorest rural households are held in short-term savings instruments, and a dearth of options are encountered for managing longevity risks. Although the NRPS and URPS include a savings component with a matching subsidy, additional specialized retirement savings instruments can improve long-term voluntary savings.

*VIRIS objectives and proposed design.* The objectives of a Voluntary Individual Retirement Insurance Scheme (VIRIS) would be (1) to provide a uniform framework for pension savings for nonwage urban and rural residents, including temporary workers, the informal sector, the self-employed, the unemployed, and farmers; (2) to subsidize a minimal savings level as a means of creating incentives for individuals to save for future retirement benefits; and (3) to support the labor mobility and efficiency through a uniform framework. More detailed design parameters are summarized in table 4, and a more detailed discussion of the rationale and proposed design is provided in appendix D.

The VIRIS design is very much along the lines of the contribution provisions in the NRPS and URPS building upon the experience of earlier pilots.[25] The scheme would be voluntary, with individual contributions "matched" with a governmental subsidy reflected in employees' Individual Account statement.[26] The matching subsidy would be based on a national framework allowing for a minimum match subsidized by the central government, which could be supplemented from local finances. The scheme would be fully funded, with a rate of return of national GDP growth guaranteed by the central authorities to reduce the risk to contributors from empty accounts. This would align the rate of return on such individual accounts with the notional interest rate applied to the proposed MORIS and facilitate account consolidation at retirement.

The target benefit should be at least as great as the regional poverty line and the *dibao* threshold for individuals and preferably well above both. The purpose of such a minimum target benefit is to mobilize sufficient individual savings matched with government contributions to have a savings fund that protects against old-age poverty. This objective is also reinforced through the CSP which provides noncontributory payments during retirement. The minimum and matching contributions can then be determined based on the minimum targeted benefit level. It may also be useful to consider the target benefit as a proportion of regional per capita income, keeping in mind the trade-off between affordability of the contributions and adequacy of the benefits.[27]

The proposed scheme would provide an annuitized benefit at retirement based on a worker's account accumulation. Payout options would

**Table 4  Voluntary Individual Retirement Insurance Scheme (VIRIS)—Key Parameters**

| | |
|---|---|
| 1. Participation and coverage | • Participation *voluntary* for all nonwage workers not contributing to other pension schemes<br>• Actual participation and coverage will depend upon the matching subsidy and other incentives in the design |
| 2. Qualifying conditions | • Retirement age: 65 (men and women)<br>• Immediate vesting |
| 3. Annuitized benefit | • Benefit formula = benefit level and amortization schedule determined by Individual Account accumulation, projected life expectancy at retirement, and projected indexation<br>• Form of payment = annuitized at retirement<br>• Benefit indexation = the higher of (1) 1/3 national GDP growth and 2/3 national growth of the CPI of the previous year or (2) CPI growth of the previous year |
| 4. Contributions and subsidies | • Minimum individual contribution level established by central authorities<br>• Tiered contribution amounts (such as 100, 200, …, 500 RMB per year)<br>• Multiple options for the frequency of contributions (monthly, quarterly, annually)<br>• Matching contribution subsidies from central authorities and subnational authorities<br>• Amount of marginal matching contribution reduced the greater the individual contribution |
| 5. Portability | • Account balances can be transferred across localities<br>• Account balances can be transferred to the reformed urban old-age insurance system |
| 6. Financing, subsidies, and interest rates | • Minimum matching contribution subsidies from central government to be established by the central authorities<br>• Additional subnational matching contribution subsidies in accordance with local fiscal conditions<br>• Accounts fully funded with interest rate of national GDP growth, guaranteed by the central authorities |
| 7. Management, administration, and oversight | • Accounts and fund management responsibility at the provincial level<br>• Central government (MHRSS) would establish an oversight framework to ensure that the scheme operates according to national guidelines |

*Note:* CPI = consumer price index; GDP = gross domestic product; MHRSS = Minister of Human Resources and Social Security.

depend on the size of the accumulation. Annuities would be computed according to national guidelines that specify the basis for computation of life expectancy at retirement, the projected benefit indexation, and the discount rate applied.

An important transition design consideration would be how to handle those workers already at or approaching retirement who will have insufficient time as contributors to generate an adequate Individual Account balance. Figure 10 indicates a stylized annuitized benefit supported by annual contributions of 360 RMB (half presumably from workers and half from the government) for between 1 and 40 years. For older residents with insufficient remaining work years to accumulate an adequate VIRIS account balance, one option would be to provide additional matching contributions, although such subsidies may have adverse incentive effects. In any event, the proposed CSP could provide a safety net for the poorest elderly until such time as the VIRIS matures.

*Rationale for VIRIS design choices.* The proposed matching contribution subsidy is based on Chinese and international experience that suggests that such a subsidy can mobilize long-term savings. Such a subsidy is already part of the NRPS and URPS and has been part of various pension

**Figure 10    Stylized Example of Annuitized Monthly VIRIS Benefits Based on Different Contribution Histories**

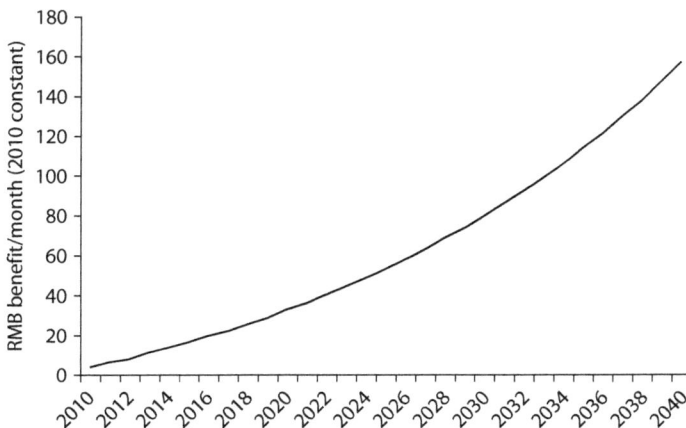

Source: World Bank estimates.
Note: Assumes contributions of 30 RMB/month beginning in 2010, retirement age of 65, male life expectancy in 2008 remaining constant through the projection period, real interest rate on account balances 5.0 percent. Projections are in constant real terms.

pilots. The policy direction is also consistent with experience in some OECD countries and a new generation of rural pension and coverage expansion programs in middle-income countries.

The VIRIS design aims to create strong incentives for retirement savings for nonwage workers. The design therefore aims to create incentives to reduce the coverage gap for urban nonwage, self-employed, or unemployed workers left out of the urban old-age insurance system, migrant workers with weak incentives to contribute to such a system, and rural dwellers who will not be covered under the NRPS. The combined central and local financing of the VIRIS can ensure a more uniform set of incentives nationwide because part of the matching contributions would not be subject to local fiscal conditions. The simplicity in the contribution and benefit design is intended to support the portability of pension savings.

The employment of matching contributions (as under the NRPS and URPS) is motivated by several factors:[28] (1) The nature of work among farmers, the self-employed, and the informal sector and the variability of employment relationships makes it difficult to mandate participation for these types of workers and suggests that an incentive to set aside their savings in a pension scheme during their working lives is likely to be necessary. (2) An individual account accumulation provides the possibility of crafting rules for selective borrowing of some of the accumulation during people's working lives in the face of specified shocks.[29] Finally, (3) keeping the design simple supports strong implementation, understanding among participants, fiscal planning, and allocation.

Determining the appropriate rate of subsidized matching contributions (and hence the fiscal costs) should be based on the anticipated effect such matching contributions will have in mobilizing long-term savings. This will depend on several factors, including available fiscal resources, the elasticity of take-up against different rates of matching, and the interaction of the contributory scheme with other public transfers for the elderly. Almost no robust evidence is available to correlate rates of contribution matching with participation under varying scenarios. For simplicity, a 1:1 match on individual contributions is not uncommon and is proposed as a starting point here. A monitoring and evaluation process can then discern the basis for different levels of savings mobilization that will inevitably result.

Table 5 summarizes commonalities and differences between the VIRIS and the NRPS/URPS. The combination of the VIRIS and CSP share many commonalities with the NRPS/URPS, including a shared view that workers are primarily responsible for assuring their old-age income security.

Although the two proposals share many commonalities, some differences can be identified:

(1) The matching subsidy proposed under the VIRIS (perhaps 100 percent of the minimum contribution amount) is higher than the minimum matching subsidy provided for under the NRPS/URPS (30 percent of the first 100 RMB/month). Although the VIRIS proposes a *higher* matching subsidy during an individual's work life (compared to the NRPS/URPS), the CSP after retirement is subject to a pension test, thereby *reducing* the fiscal expenditures when compared to the NRPS/URPS. Such additional matching subsidies provide greater incentives to save when compared to the NRPS/URPS. Moreover, although the NRPS/URPS minimum 15-year vesting period provides savings incentives (to receive the basic benefit), the VIRIS has much stronger savings incentives beyond the 15-year period.

(2) Providing an interest rate on VIRIS savings linked to a national index (of national GDP growth) and guaranteeing this rate by the central authorities mitigates the risks for savers and therefore contributes to long-term savings incentives. By contrast, the NRPS/URPS does not have such an interest rate guarantee or financing features.

(3) Under the VIRIS, NRPS, and URPS, a key assumption is that a guaranteed minimum level of subsidized matching contribution is needed to establish a credible floor as an incentive for participation. The VIRIS design makes it the responsibility of the central authorities for assuring the minimum matching subsidy, whereas the NRPS and URPS establish the minimum subsidy but leave the financing to the local level.

(4) The VIRIS design starts with a prevailing assumption that the nonwage sector should have the same pension savings incentives whether urban or rural. Applying a unified policy framework to everybody with only wage and nonwage distinctions is consistent with the objective of removing artificial differences between target groups (urban/rural). The NRPS/URPS, however, retains the rural and urban residency distinctions.

## Occupational and Personal Savings Arrangements

Occupational and personal savings arrangements are an essential part of old-age income protection in China (see appendix E).[30] The rationale behind these instruments includes the following: (1) the dramatic aging of the population and increases in old-age system dependency rates suggest that the urban old-age insurance system will be able to provide

Table 5 Commonalities and Differences between the Proposed VIRIS Design and the NRPS and URPS

| | NRPS/URPS | Proposed VIRIS design | Rationale for differences |
|---|---|---|---|
| Fundamental principles | Basic insurance, wide coverage, flexibility, and sustainability | Same principles as NRPS/URPS and affordability and portability | |
| Individual contributions | Five levels for the NRPS, 100–500 RMB, and local governments can add additional levels. The URPS has additional levels up to 1000 RMB. | Level of minimum contribution should be calculated as either a proportion of per capita income (rural) or average wages (urban) | The diversity of economic circumstances in China will make the 100 RMB contribution very low in some places |
| Collective subsidy and support by local people's governments | Village collectives can subsidize individual contributions. For disadvantaged groups in urban areas that have difficulty in paying contributions, local people's governments should pay a part of their pension contributions or all of their minimum pension contributions. | Same | |
| Central government subsidy: basic pension | Central government pays full basic pension (central and western areas) and a 50 percent subsidy to eastern areas | A minimum CSP benefit is assured by the central government | |
| Central government subsidy: matching contributions | None | The central government subsidy for matching contributions should be sufficient to finance an annuity for full-career contributors with a benefit in excess of that provided by the CSP | Central government subsidies are believed to be essential as incentives for contributions by low-income individuals in areas with low fiscal capacity |
| Local government subsidy: matching contributions | Subsidy no less than 30 RMB per person per year | Local government subsidy is not mandated by the central authorities | |
| Local government subsidy: basic pension | Local governments encouraged to increase the level according to the local situation | Same | |

54

| | | | |
|---|---|---|---|
| Individual Account records | Individual pension accounts to be set up for each new rural pension enrollee | Same + record system should be on a common platform with urban old-age insurance. A centralized data management system should manage benefit processing and disbursements. | Coordination of locally managed Individual Account record keeping has proven difficult in old-age insurance and will likely continue to be difficult in the future using that approach |
| *Benefits* | | | |
| Individual Account benefit calculation | Applying an annuity factor of 139 | Annuity factor should be periodically revised according to cohort-specific life expectancy rates | |
| Inheritance rights | Individual Account balance can be inherited | Joint annuity providing spousal inheritance | |
| Indexation | "According to economic development and changing prices" | Proposed indexation formula: The maximum of: 2/3 changes in prices and 1/3 changes in per capita income; or price changes. | Formula aims both to ensure retirees against price increases while keeping benefits roughly consistent with prevailing per capita income |
| Retirement age | 60 | 65 | To align with proposed MORIS and to support benefit adequacy |
| Transition arrangements: individuals near retirement age | Family binding and buyback arrangements | Possibly additional matching contribution subsidies | |
| Fund management | Managed by counties with transfer to higher levels in places with required conditions. | Funds should aim to be managed at provincial level, with financial reporting to central government unified data management system | |

*Note:* CSP = Citizens' Social Pension; MORIS = Mandatory Occupational Retirement Insurance Scheme; NRPS = New Rural Pension Scheme; URPS = Urban Residents Pension Scheme.

only about 40–60 percent of pre-retirement income in the long term; (2) changes in the traditional family structure result in an increasing number of people that need alternative savings opportunities for old-age income protection; (3) voluntary occupational schemes can provide a framework to compensate for the uneven level of benefits between different types of enterprises, PSUs, and civil servants; (4) occupational schemes can enhance the economic efficiency of enterprises and government employers because the structure of the benefits can be tailored to increase the willingness of employers to invest in training and skills development; (5) occupational schemes can create an incentive for labor force participation by older workers as China's working-age population begins to decline from 2015; and (6) privately managed pension funds can support the development and stability of financial markets, which in turn can be supportive of overall economic development.

Although the EA scheme is a notable initiative aimed at motivating voluntary enterprise-sponsored contractual savings, a broader framework is needed to serve the large number of workers inside and outside the formal sector that so far have not been served.[31] The 2004 legislation and subsequent amendments provide a basic framework for the operation of enterprise-based occupational schemes but fall short of providing the scope of instruments needed for several reasons: (1) Employer participation and worker coverage remain low because of uncertainty about the design and security of the system and because the tax treatment of savings is uneven. (2) Additional populations that need voluntary savings arrangements include workers in small enterprises and informal, self-employed, rural, and migrant workers. (3) The legal framework for the system is not fully developed and cannot, in its current form, provide an adequate foundation to ensure that the system can be effectively regulated to provide the degree of security for an occupational pension system to flourish. (4) The supervision of the system is not developed, lacks an adequate institutional basis, and lacks sufficient resources. The regulatory and supervisory framework needs substantial strengthening as does the incentive framework to include the issue of tax treatment.

The proposed design features for occupational and personal savings arrangements are summarized in table 6 and appendix D. Some of these features are the following:

- The schemes should be *defined contribution* and *fully funded* to provide a framework for portability of benefits, as well as a transparent means of verifying pension entitlements through account accumulations.
- Account accumulations should be fully portable.

**Table 6   Occupational and Personal Pension Arrangements**

| Issue | Provision/parameters |
|---|---|
| Architecture | • Defined contribution |
| Funding | • Fully funded |
| Tax treatment | • Consistent tax treatment (such as EET or TEE see note 32)<br>• Tax deductibility up to a cap (percent of income and absolute amount cap) |
| Financing | • Through individual, employer, and/or employee contributions |
| Withdrawal and annuitization provisions | • Withdrawal provisions (lump-sum, phased-withdrawal, and annuities) to be developed<br>• Withdrawal should be permitted at a retirement age close to that of social insurance<br>• Age of withdrawal linked to individual tax treatment |
| Regulation | • Strengthened regulatory framework for investment management, custodianship, and account management<br>• Revision of role, responsibilities, and accountabilities of a trustee; provision of governing standards<br>• Regulatory framework and institutional infrastructure supporting a private annuity market to be developed |
| Supervision | • Strengthened supervisory capacity |

• Account and investment management should be market based to maximize risk-adjusted returns and support essential risk management.
• Taxation provisions should be consistent across time (for example, exempt-exempt-taxable (EET) or taxable-taxable-exempt (TEE)).[32]
• Account balances above a level to be determined should in principle be provided in an annuitized form so that individuals can have a means of managing longevity risks.
• Occupational schemes should be positioned to support firms and organizations of all types, including PSUs and civil servants.
• A strengthened regulatory framework and supervisory capacity is essential to ensure employer compliance with minimum standards and adequate consumer protection.

The current EA provides some of the building blocks for a proposed OA, but substantial strengthening of the regulatory, supervisory, and incentive framework would be needed for the OA to realize its true potential in the reformed pension system. The following principles could be considered for the OA to realize such potential:

• Permissible levels of income that can be contributed under the scheme need to be sufficient to provide for a meaningful savings for retirement.

- Tax incentives need to be clear and consistent across time and limited to mitigate potential regressive effects.
- The benefit needs to be perceived as secure and fair by workers and employers, through a complete and coherent set of rules and regulations and effective and reliable supervision.
- The design needs to be sufficiently flexible to adapt to varying needs of different enterprises and workers, such as providing more conservative investment portfolios for older workers and providing a framework for savings options for both large and small employers.
- The OAs must operate with sufficiently low administrative costs and provide long-term investment returns consistent with alternative savings instruments.

Realizing these principles will require various steps to develop both the policies and institutional oversight to support the development of this important instrument.

Establishment of an OA framework can play a pivotal role in facilitating the integration of PSU and civil servant workers into a unified urban pension system. One means of such integration is to retain a target income replacement, through the MORIS and an OA. Together these instruments could offer a target income replacement similar to that currently provided. Moreover, although the MORIS would provide a framework for basic income replacement for wage-based workers, targeted income replacement could be adjusted to the compensation arrangements of specific industries and groups of workers. For example, the OA arrangement in the mining sector might target a relatively high replacement rate at a relatively early retirement age.

## Overall Design Conclusions

The combination of proposed instruments would strengthen old-age income protection by improving incentives and addressing coverage gaps:

(1) The CSP would apply to all qualifying citizens, urban or rural, removing an important level of insecurity and precautionary retirement savings for retirement for many workers.
(2) Nonwage workers, farmers, the informal sector, and the self-employed would all have a much stronger incentive to set aside savings until retirement age (through VIRIS).
(3) Workers with employment contracts would have a common platform for old-age pensions so that they could navigate between employers across space and time with minimal losses in benefits.

(4) The instruments are grounded in a common defined-contribution architecture that provides a basis for compiling benefit entitlements across different pension instruments (MORIS, VIRIS, OA). This can provide a much clearer and more transparent idea to workers of their anticipated pension benefit so they can make more rational labor market decisions.

## Financing Options

### Fiscal Costs and Financing Arrangements

Fiscal costs are associated with the current pension schemes as well as with the proposed reforms (see table 7, figure 8, and appendix C). The position of this volume is that the pension system and the broader economy will benefit from making such costs explicit and developing a viable and orderly financing strategy to cover them. Some costs, such as the proposed CSP, are additional for benefits not currently provided. So-called legacy costs (see below) will be incurred regardless of whether or not a reform is undertaken. These costs could be financed from within or outside the contributions to the pension system. Benefit promises for many PSU workers and civil servants are implicit, although not explicitly recognized and financed.

Various sources can be identified for financing current or future pension costs. The options for financing different components of the proposed pension system are discussed in turn below. They include (1) contributions, returns on pension reserves, or drawing down reserve stocks; (2) other general revenue sources, such as asset sales, corporate, or individual income taxes (financed from general revenues); (3) dedicated revenue sources, such as a portion of the proceeds from share flotations, as is currently the practice for dedicated financing for the National Social Security Fund (NSSF); (4) prefinancing through alternative fiscal savings vehicles, such as the NSSF;[34] or (5) partial financing by beneficiaries through the tax treatment of benefits.

### Citizens' Social Pension (CSP)

The central government could guarantee a minimum CSP benefit and subnational authorities provide additional financing to guarantee any additional benefits as is currently the case for the NRPS and URPS (see appendix A).[35] Although the central government would guarantee a minimum benefit, it may finance only part of such a minimum for some provinces. The cost of CSP would depend on the benefit level and the application of a "pensions test" or benefit reduction from alternative

**Table 7  Description of Pension Costs and Possible Financing**

| | Cost description | Evolution of costs over 30+ years | Costs incurred only with reform? | Proposed financing source(s) |
|---|---|---|---|---|
| 1. Citizens' Social Pension | Fiscal costs of CSP (net of benefit reductions from applying a "Pensions Test") | Depends upon benefit level and income threshold applied. Elderly population will grow over time because of demographics, although the elderly poverty prevalence may decrease. | Yes, though the NRPS and URPS have a basic benefit cost already incurred by the central government. | Central government to finance a guaranteed minimum with local and provincial authorities bearing the costs for benefits provided above the minimum |
| 2. Urban old-age insurance system—MORIS—legacy costs | See text | Depends upon proportion of age cohorts required to enter into a reformed system | • Costs incurred regardless of reform<br>• Proposed alternative source of financing | Current (nonwage) tax revenues—national and provincial |
| 3. PSU and civil servant legacy costs | Costs of accrued rights for PSU workers above the long-term benefit promises under the reformed urban system | Same | • Costs incurred regardless of reform | For PSUs categorized as dependent upon government financing, the same financing source from which the PSU receives fiscal support; for civil servants, financing from general revenues |

| | | | Benefits are prefinanced through contributions resulting from the reform | |
|---|---|---|---|---|
| 4. PSU contributions | For qualifying PSUs, future contributions to reform | In accordance with the worker profile | | See note 33 |
| 5. Civil servant contributions | • Contributions to reformed MORIS on behalf of civil servants<br>• Contributions to an occupational annuity | Costs move from long term to spread over time from short term, brought forward through MORIS and OA contributions. | As for cost evolution | Financed according to a similar formula as for civil servant wages |
| 6. Matching contributions—VIRIS | Costs of matching contributions for participants | Costs will rise during an implementation period to gradually cover participants. Costs will level off and decline as the working-age population declines over time. | Yes, but subsidies to finance matching contributions also reduce the later subsidy requirements for the CSP | Central government finances a guaranteed minimum with local and provincial authorities bearing the costs for benefits provided above the minimum. |
| 7. Occupational scheme contributions | • Contributions on behalf of civil servants and PSU workers<br>• Forgone tax revenue from tax exemption provided | In accordance with the worker profile | Yes, although cost share between budget and enterprises for PSU workers uncertain | For civil servants and PSUs, by the level of government and sectoral authority responsible |

**Note:** CSP = Citizens' Social Pension; MORIS = Mandatory Occupational Retirement Insurance Scheme; NRPS = New Rural Pension Scheme; PSU = public sector unit; URPS = Urban Residents Pension Scheme; VIRIS = Voluntary Individual Retirement Insurance Scheme.

income sources. As suggested above, indicative costs estimates in 2010 for a benefit level that provides just enough resources to cover the urban and rural elderly at age 65 in poverty were about 0.11 percent and 0.12 percent of GDP for urban and rural areas, respectively. By comparison, by adopting a benefit level of about 28 percent of the urban average wage (the OECD country average); the urban cost would be 0.75 percent of GDP in 2010, rising to 2.1 percent of GDP by 2040.

## MORIS—Financing Legacy Costs

The MORIS design utilizes a pay-as-you-go financing approach, although it will require a fully funded buffer fund to accommodate unanticipated shocks. This compares with the pay-as-you-go financing approach of the social pooling basic benefit of the urban old-age insurance system while Individual Accounts have been partially funded. This volume proposes separately addressing legacy costs.

Addressing legacy costs—defining, estimating and planning for their financing—is both an essential part of the proposed reform and worthy of consideration even if the broader reform program is not adopted (see appendix C). In any pension system, the accrued-to-date liabilities must at least be matched by corresponding assets to be financially sustainable. Such legacy costs can be broadly defined as the actuarial deficit of the reformed system and have two main sources: (1) the legacy cost of the unreformed system that would have to be financed in any case, resulting from prior reforms and the move from higher (for older and middle-aged men) to lower benefits for new entrants (new men) and (2) the legacy costs introduced by a new reform as the result of reducing contribution rates and benefit levels for future beneficiaries. To properly assess the scope of the legacy costs to design a viable long-term financing plan, one must be able to (a) estimate the accrued-to-date liabilities,[36] (b) estimate the pay-as-you-go assets[37] and measure the overall legacy costs that need to be financed against total liabilities, and (c) translate the overall legacy costs into annual financial transfers and establish a financing plan.

This volume proposes that legacy costs be financed from general revenues rather than from pension contributions. The rationale behind such a recommendation is the following:

- Separately financing legacy costs from general revenues is a means of transferring the financial burden from current contributors to broader sources of fiscal revenues, and because a considerable proportion of legacy costs are associated with benefit promises made before the 1997 reforms, having current contributors pay for these costs amounts to a substantial intergenerational transfer, which can be moderated and phased through a well-considered financing plan over a period of about 30 years (see below).

- Financing legacy costs from outside the pension system would materially reduce contribution rates, thereby substantially improving the affordability of the MORIS or old-age insurance system.

- A manageable and fiscally sound plan for financing legacy costs from general revenues can be developed that gradually pays for such costs over a period roughly consistent with the period in which the costs will be borne through disbursement.

- Legacy costs associated with earlier entitlements of PSU and civil servant workers would be a fiscal responsibility of the government authorities in any event, so justifiably the legacy costs should also be shouldered from general revenues.

If it is assumed that legacy costs are about 80 percent of GDP,[38] the initial annual costs would be 4 percent of GDP, declining to zero after about 40 years (see table C.1 in appendix C). The wide range of legacy costs estimates results from the equally wide range of assumed steady-state contribution rates for the new NDC scheme based on a similar range of target replacement rates. The lower the target replacement rate, the higher the legacy costs. Estimates of gross legacy costs depend upon, among other factors, the estimated existing implicit pension debt (IPD) and the expected steady-state contribution rate for the reformed scheme. So, for example, initial estimates of legacy costs under a low IPD assumption range from 44 percent assuming a contribution rate of 25 percent to 89 percent assuming a contribution rate of 15 percent. Similarly, legacy cost estimates under a high IPD assumption range from 56 percent assuming a contribution rate of 25 percent to 113 percent assuming a contribution rate of 15 percent (see appendix C). Such gross legacy costs do not fully translate into additional fiscal costs, even if they are made explicit. The current urban old-age insurance system, civil servants, and PSU schemes already receive government subsidies that are included in these estimates. These implicit and explicit subsidies are of particular importance for the public sector schemes that levied no contributions (state organs, that is, civil servants) or imposed low-contribution rates on participants (PSUs) to finance pension expenditures. As much as 75 percent of the legacy costs for the civil service and PSU schemes are already financed by government revenues.

The phasing of the legacy costs (how much the costs will be during which periods in the future) is determined by the transition from the old to the new scheme. If the transition is immediate (that is, all active workers are immediately transferred to the NDC scheme), then the legacy costs are front-loaded with the highest value in the first year gradually reduced to zero over approximately 40 years. If the NDC scheme is applied only to new entrants, then the legacy costs are back-loaded, rising initially from small amounts and peaking after about 40 years before gradually being reduced in another 40 years. Moving the entrance cohorts to the new scheme somewhere in the middle—for example, all below the age of 40—advances the peak to 20 years after the reform.

The legacy costs can be financed by the government at different levels and could also be shared with workers and retirees. The central government could establish a framework by which it finances a minimum level of acquired rights, and the remainder could be financed by provinces and municipalities. Moreover, the indexation provisions adopted for future benefits will impact the size of the legacy cost and, implicitly, whether and how much current and future retirees bear the burden of financing.

Another realistic possibility is an increase in urban old-age insurance coverage resulting from economic growth and better incentives. Such coverage growth can serve as a means of generating the contribution revenue to finance some of the legacy costs. From 1998 to 2008 coverage (measured as the proportion of the urban labor force contributing to the scheme) increased from 39.2 percent to 54.9 percent—that is, 15.4 percentage points. This helped increase the reserves of the urban old-age insurance system from 0.7 percent to 3.3 percent of GDP, or 2.6 percentage points. A rough calculation suggest that over the next 40 years of coverage expansion, additional cash reserves of about 40 percent of GDP or more could be achieved.

Legacy costs may therefore be reduced by roughly one-half through anticipated coverage expansion and reform measures that reduce acquired rights. A net legacy cost of about 40–60 percent of GDP over a period of 40 years could be financed in various ways, with the annual fiscal impact posing what would appear to be a manageable fiscal burden.

### Matching Contributions for the VIRIS
The cost of financing matching contributions under the proposed VIRIS depends on parameters established and participation in the scheme. Key parameters affecting financing include the match formula and cost sharing with provincial, municipal, and local governments. Furthermore, guaranteeing a rate of return of GDP growth when market instruments cannot yield

such returns would require another subsidy. Finally, the volume of resources raised under the scheme will profoundly affect the costs of the scheme.

It is proposed that the central government would finance a guaranteed minimum with subnational authorities financing the costs for matching contributions provided above the minimum. This approach would establish compatible incentives between the financing strategies of the VIRIS and CSP. The ratio between the minimum matching contribution and the worker contribution and the financing source for such matching contributions should be uniform nationwide (as under the NRPS). Above a minimum matching contribution, the provincial and municipal authorities could have a common framework for providing additional resources, fiscal resources permitting.

Above a minimum guaranteed level, it would be up to the provincial and municipal authorities to determine the level of matched contributions. The higher the contribution, the lower the level of matched contribution that should be provided by the government. The matching contributions could be, for example, 100 RMB for the first 100 RMB individual contribution, 60 RMB match for the second 100 RMB individual contribution, and 30 RMB for the third 100 RMB individual contribution.

### Occupational Schemes for PSUs and Civil Servants

Four sets of costs are found for PSUs and civil servants: (1) contributions to the MORIS, (2) contributions to supplemental OA schemes, (3) legacy costs associated with current workers, and (4) continuing pension disbursements. As suggested above, legacy costs are now implicit but would become explicit. Contributions to the MORIS scheme would likely be used to pay existing retirees, so those contributions would not have a direct fiscal impact. Finally, contributions to OA schemes would prefund future benefits. Tax receipts could also be affected under the OA schemes, depending on the tax treatment of OA contributions, accumulations, and benefits.

## A Reform Process: Cross-Cutting Analysis and Institutional Reform Issues

Translating a broad vision into a policy reform program will require numerous decisions guided by further analysis. These include the following:

- The *target replacement rate* from the mandatory old-age insurance system
- The *level of income redistribution* that the authorities seek to achieve through pensions, including reduction in the geographical income dispersion

- The desired level of adequacy and affordability of *elderly poverty and vulnerability protection* in urban and rural areas, respectively
- The *approach to benefit indexation*
- A *financing strategy*, including the approach to legacy costs (see earlier discussion)
- The *desirability and feasibility of integrating all wage earners into a unified pension scheme* and
- The *institutional framework* for achieving the desired policy objectives.

Improvements will be needed in the analytical base for ongoing pension reforms. A pension system that meets the criteria established by the authorities will require policy development based on a combination of robust projections of system liabilities, monitoring and reporting of current performance, and rigorous evaluation of current experience and emerging reforms. This could be facilitated through multiple processes, including the following:

(1) The development of a more systematic process for monitoring and evaluating pension pilot programs (including, in particular, the NRPS and URPS) and emerging reforms in areas such as portability. A key step to piloting a new policy design or institutional setup is to establish the monitoring framework and evaluation criteria that will determine how successful the design is as well as lead to useful outputs to determine how to adjust or fine-tune the design in accordance with unfolding experience.
(2) Strengthening the capacity for actuarial projections to measure long-term financial impacts of pension provisions and evaluate potential refinements to pension parameters.
(3) Strengthening the process for data collection and measurement, including data on mortality essential for life expectancy and benefit calculation.
(4) Integrating analysis of the impact of pension provisions on labor and financial markets. Such analysis should draw on related recent and ongoing research in China.

Achieving national portability will require careful consideration of design and institutional policy options and phasing of the reform process. The 2009 circular from the State Council on the issue provides an important step in this regard. A key choice will be the framework for record keeping and information flows across space, including when, where, and how data are consolidated for worker entitlements from several venues: urban and rural, intra- and interprovincial. Facilitation of the policies and institutional requirements for portability include reconciling rights accumulations across space and communicating such entitlements to members. A framework is needed for benefits processing and disbursement at retirement to facilitate portability regardless of whether a central or parallel processing approach is adopted.[39] One option that should be considered is the establishment of a central clearinghouse responsible for compiling member contribution and account balance data, thereby aggregating entitlements across space and time. Such a national clearinghouse could act as the channel for data exchange across provinces, provided that a common data model can be implemented nationally and data exchange protocols enforced. It may also be possible in the longer term to centralize benefit processing and disbursements. As an intermediate step, such a consolidated data management system following common national data standards is a pressing need at the provincial level.

A framework for pooling contributions and reserves is needed. Pooling contributions and reserves establishes a means of smoothing inevitable disparities in demographic and economic conditions across communities as well as diversifying the risks to members. Provincial pooling is an essential part of the medium-term reform process, as recognized in the 1990s with the establishment of the urban old-age insurance system. Although the NDC design places less urgency on pooling than the current defined-benefit urban pension design, such pooling is nonetheless an important objective to be realized over time. Realizing the insurance benefits of a pooled buffer fund will necessitate guidelines that ensure a fair distribution according to transparent parameters that provide strong incentives for widespread participation.

Several conditions must be satisfied to support the integration of PSU workers and civil servants into a reformed old-age insurance system. These include (1) the categorization of PSUs establishing their level of fiscal autonomy,[40] (2) establishment of the legal framework for a more robust occupational annuity savings scheme as a means of topping up PSU and civil servant workers' benefits, (3) creation of a financing framework for past and future benefit entitlements of PSU workers and civil servants, and (4) satisfaction of institutional and operational requirements for integrating with the old-age urban system.[41]

These financial and institutional challenges may justify postponing the integration of PSU workers and civil servants until conditions are ripe. To promote a smooth transition of PSU workers and civil servants into an integrated urban workers' pension scheme, three options could be considered: (1) phased harmonization of the benefit structure with that of the old-age insurance system before integration, (2) piloting of specific classes of civil servants or other public sector workers for harmonization and/or integration, and (3) only integrating new entrants or younger cohorts or new employees into the integrated urban old-age insurance system.

Three areas require improvements in the policy and institutional arrangements for investment management and regulation: (1) short-term liquidity, buffer fund, and medium-term reserve management guidelines and processes at the county, municipal, and provincial levels; (2) investment management, custodianship, trustee relationships, and record-keeping requirements for management of supplemental occupational annuity and personal savings arrangements; and (3) strengthening the clarity of the mandate of the NSSF to enhance the financing of medium-term urban pension requirements to enable the NSSF to better structure its investments to match the profile of its anticipated obligations.

Establishment of a CSP could proceed relatively expeditiously, provided that financing responsibilities are agreed among the national and subnational authorities. At the same time, reform would need to consider existing and future policies, including (1) the basic benefit provisions of the NRPS and/or the URPS where they are operating, (2) the impact of the minimum target benefit on the VIRIS design, and (3) minimum vesting provisions and redistributive characteristics of the social pooling benefit in the urban old-age insurance system.

As the importance of voluntary savings arrangements for old-age income protection increases, so too should the robustness of the regulatory framework and institutional infrastructure for them. This will require a multiyear strategy aimed at development of policies for such arrangements while simultaneously establishing the institutional capacity for supervising such policies. Because voluntary pensions savings arrangements are and will be undertaken by financial intermediaries under other supervisory authorities, the Ministry of Human Resources and Social Security (MHRSS) will need to interface with these authorities.

Over the long term, coordinating and potentially integrating income tax and social security contribution collections systems are supportive of achieving the universality of coverage desired. Although many provincial and municipal authorities have already integrated collections, reconciliation of individual income tax and social insurance contributions could also improve compliance over time as more people come into the income tax net. A first step toward this will be ensuring a completely smooth interface between the management information systems of the tax and social security authorities. The shift to budgetary management of public pension funds from 2010 is a positive step in this direction.

## Conclusion

This volume has assessed the key objectives articulated by the authorities and suggested a design for a medium-term vision of a mandatory and voluntary pension program that seems appropriate to China's needs and enabling conditions. In developing such a vision, it has paid particular attention to both the principles articulated by the authorities (broad coverage, at a basic level, multileveled, sustainable, and flexible) as well as additional criteria suggested of affordability, predictability, and equity. As China's economy becomes increasingly developed and integrated, its pension system will play an increasingly important role in providing strong labor market incentives, including the portability of rights.

The proposed design is a multipillar approach that essentially provides a basic benefit to ensure against poverty in old age, a mandatory contributory scheme for those with wage incomes, a voluntary retirement savings vehicle for the nonwage sector that provides subsidized matching contributions, and a strengthened framework for voluntary occupational and individual pension savings arrangements to supplement retirement benefits from state-sponsored sources. This is summarized in table 8.

The proposed design addresses key reform needs that have been identified:

(1) Contributory instruments proposed have automatic mechanisms that adjust benefits in line with anticipated aging, thereby explicitly confronting China's aging challenge;

(2) Sustainability is achieved by (a) proposed reforms that align contributions and benefits, (b) eliminating transition costs with the NDC design, and (c) moderating the target benefit and establishing a pensions test in the CSP to constrain fiscal costs;

(3) Coverage gaps resulting in elderly poverty and vulnerability are eliminated through both contribution incentives in the VIRIS and a CSP for all elderly; and

(4) The design is aligned with China's dynamic and changing labor markets by facilitating transparent and portable pension rights and providing a secure and uniform foundation for old-age income security nationwide.

**Table 8  Summary of Proposed Design Parameters**

| | Citizens' Social Pension (CSP) | Mandatory Occupational Retirement Insurance Scheme (MORIS) | Voluntary Individual Retirement Insurance Scheme (VIRIS) | Occupational annuity/ Individual savings product |
|---|---|---|---|---|
| Target benefit | To be determined by the authorities<br>Suggest a minimum benefit of at least the regional poverty line<br>Benefit should be a proportion of the rural per capita income or urban regional average wage<br>Minimum benefit should be greater than the individual *dibao* benefit | To be determined by the authorities<br>Could be in the range of 40–60 percent | Target benefit should be a proportion of the rural per capita income or urban regional average wage | As determined by individual sectors, employers, and individual contributors |
| Rate of return on individual funded or notional accounts | Not applicable | Annual growth rate of national GDP | Annual growth rate of national GDP | In accordance with the portfolio return |
| Benefit calculation and form | Monthly benefit based on national framework; benefit reduced by an adjustment factor for other pension benefits received | Annuitized benefit depending upon individual notional account balance, life expectancy at retirement, notional interest rate; phased withdrawal or lump sums depending upon notional account balance | Annuitized benefit depending upon Individual Account balance, life expectancy at retirement, and notional interest rate; phased-withdrawal or lump sums depending upon account balance | Lump sum, phased withdrawal, or annuity according to retiree preferences and account balance at retirement |
| Pensions testing | Benefit reduced by an adjustment factor multiplied by the monthly pension benefit received from other sources for those aged 65–74 and no reduction for those aged 75 and above. | None | None | None |

| | | | | |
|---|---|---|---|---|
| Contributions | None | Based on the target replacement rate—assuming a retirement age 65, in the range 14–22 percent | • Flat minimum amount per year, matched by government contribution • Matching could be scaled to different contribution levels | No limit, but tax deductibility would be limited to an absolute cap and a percentage |
| Mandatory or voluntary | n.a. | Mandatory | Voluntary | Voluntary |
| Indexation | New and existing benefits would adjust in accordance with a percent of regional average wages (urban) or regional per capita incomes (rural) | Minimum (CPI, mix of 2/3 CPI and 1/3 covered wage growth) | The higher of (1) 1/3 national GDP growth and 2/3 national growth of the CPI of the previous year; or (2) CPI growth of the previous year | According to the specifications of the individual product |
| Retirement age | 65 for men and women | 65 for men and women, phased in over time | 65 for men and women | Eligibility age lower than for mandatory schemes |
| Vesting period | None | 1 month | None | According to sponsor guidelines |
| Funding | Noncontributory-budget transfers | Notional | Funded | Fully funded Individual Accounts |
| Tax treatment | Tax exempt | • To be determined by the authorities • Should be consistent (EET or TEE) | • To be determined by the authorities • Should be consistent (EET or TEE) | To be determined, should be on a consistent basis (EET or TEE) |
| Record keeping | By MHRSS bureaus at a county level | By MHRSS bureaus at a county, city, and provincial level | By MHRSS bureaus at a county level | By enterprises and account administrators |

*Note:* CPI = consumer price index; GDP = gross domestic product; MHRSS = Minister of Human Resources and Social Security; n.a. = not applicable; TBD = to be determined; see note 36 for an explanation of EET and TTE.

Although the proposed vision provides a design to work toward for a future pension system, multiple transition paths can be taken toward achieving it; developing and implementing the proposed vision proposed will require additional study and consideration. The following areas have been identified for additional study: (1) quantifying individual rights for NDC Individual Accounts; (2) quantifying legacy costs; (3) establishing a detailed financing framework; (4) establishing a framework and institutional agreement on the portability of rights, including the approach toward data management; (5) establishing transition provisions for specific classes of workers; (6) establishing and strengthening the framework for investment management; (7) establishing the legal and institutional framework for regulation and supervision; and (8) refining pension policy provisions through systematic monitoring and evaluation.

## Notes

1. 广覆盖、保基本、多层次、可持续 (Broad coverage, basic protection, mutiple-layer, and sustainable).
2. 保基本、廣覆蓋、有彈性、可持續 (Basic protection, broad coverage, flexible, and sustainable).
3. See Sin (2005, 36).
4. Ibid.
5. The Chinese nomenclature refers to those workers entering the labor force after the introduction of changes to the urban old-age insurance scheme in the late 1990s as "new men," those workers that have started work prior to the reform but will retire after it is implemented as "middle men," and those workers that have retired before the introduction of such reform as "old men."
6. The estimated number of migrants (including family migrants) by the National Bureau of Statistics Rural Household Surveys was over 150 million in 2011, almost doubling the number a decade earlier. See World Bank (2009, 93). Growth in the urban and migratory labor force requires pension policies that can provide old-age income security for China's increasingly mobile urban population.
7. Although the national guidelines are for combined employer and employee contribution rates not to exceed 28 percent, contribution rates in some municipalities have ranged up to 31 percent. Some municipalities and provinces, however, have lower contribution rates.
8. Provision of benefits *at a basic level* appears to be consistent with the principle of *adequacy* in the World Bank's conceptual framework.

9. See Cai and others (2012).

10. Ibid.

11. There is widespread international experience with noncontributory social pensions at all levels of country incomes, and the experience in reducing old-age poverty is generally found to be positive. Consistent with the coverage objectives in China, social pensions are an increasingly popular method for helping address the old-age coverage gap in pension systems. Schemes in countries such as Brazil, Bolivia, South Africa, Mauritius, Botswana, and Namibia have been shown to reduce old-age poverty significantly, while supplementary schemes have varied more widely in their targeting and poverty reduction outcomes. See Kakwani and Subbarao (2005) on African schemes; Barrientos (2009) on four developing countries, and Palacios and Sluchynsky (2006) for an international overview. See also Holzmann and others (2009).

12. These benefit levels would apply to both new and existing beneficiaries so that the benefit level would be implicitly indexed to the two respective indices.

13. See Yang, J. (2007), Mi (2007), and Yang, C. (2007).

14. These figures assume a benefit level of 1,200 RMB per year beginning in 2010, or about 4.1 percent of the projected urban average wage.

15. For the purposes of comparison, the reduction was left due to the application of the "pensions test" the same in the two scenarios. Realistically, the cost reduction to the application of the pensions test should be greater in this second scenario because the benefit before reduction is far higher.

16. This includes the urban old-age insurance system, pensions for PSUs, pensions for civil servants, and pilot programs for migrants to urban areas.

17. The 2011 decision by the Ministry of Finance is important in this regard.

18. The simulated results show that the projected pension liability of the baseline scheme is equivalent to 141 percent of 2001 GDP. The system dependency ratio is projected to increase from 16 percent to over 50 percent in about seven years and increase further to 100 percent over a 30-year time span under the pension policy framework adopted in 1997. See Sin (2005).

19. This assumes, however, that the retirement age is increased to age 65 over time for both men and women, and the benefit is indexed at one-third of the growth in regional average wages and two-thirds of the growth in regional average prices and provided that all "legacy costs" are separately financed from resources other than pension contributions.

20. An increase in the retirement age could be phased in at a rate of a six-month increase each year so that women who currently retire at age 50 would retire at age 65 in 30 years' time. This phased approach to increasing the retirement age eliminates an abrupt impact on specific cohorts.

21. By comparison, the State Council guidelines for indexation of current old-age insurance benefits are 40–60 percent of regional average wages.

22. A 30-day vesting period is necessary to reduce administrative/transaction costs by employers and by the social security departments. By comparison, although there is no minimum benefit under the current old-age insurance system, the minimum vesting period is 15 years, and the minimum covered wage is 60 percent of the regional average wage. This therefore effectively results in a minimum social pooling benefit of 15 (years) × 1 percent (the social pooling accrual rate) × 60 percent of the regional average wage, or about 9 percent of the regional average wage at retirement.

23. Twenty-eight percent not including other social insurance contributions. The 2008 labor law requires migrant workers to be included in urban social insurance programs.

24. This is generally the applicable minimum wage × the employer and employee contribution rates in a given locality.

25. 新型农村社会养老保险 (The New Rural Pension Scheme).

26. Voluntary participation is essential given the nature of the income volatility for rural workers targeted by VIRIS. This is also supported by international experience, which generally has been poor with respect to coverage of rural workers in contributory schemes in low- or middle-income countries. It would be advisable to have flexibility on the periodicity of contributions within a year to allow for the specificities of rural incomes and access. Such an incentive-based approach (rather than mandated participation) has resulted in high coverage in numerous rural pension pilots in China in recent years. See Palacios and Robalino (2009).

27. For example, if one assumes contributions of 15 RMB per person per month and a one-for-one matching by the government, 3 percent real return on assets, this is projected to yield an annuitized benefit of about 85 RMB per month at age 65 after 40 years of contributions (in present-value terms). Real GDP growth (which could be the basis for the rate of return) has been much higher than this in recent years, so the annuitized benefit could be greater if the notional accounts grow at the rate of GDP growth. A remuneration that is one percentage point higher over 40 years increases benefits by almost 20 percent.

28. See Palacios and Robalino (2009) for a discussion of matching defined-contribution schemes, demonstrating the model and design questions, empirical evidence, and theoretical framework.

29. Some areas of China in existing pilot schemes also allow use of the accumulation as collateral on loans for business activities. Although this is an interesting approach, it carries obvious risks if the share of accumulations pledged is not capped at a reasonable level and is not common practice internationally.

30. Such thinking dates back to 1991 when the first arrangements for voluntary occupational pension savings were put in place. See Hinz (2007).

31. At the year end 2006, an estimated 24,000 employers and 9.64 million workers (about 6.0 percent of participants in the old-age insurance system) were covered under the EA scheme. See Sin and Mao (2007). Also see Cui (2007) and Chen (2007).

32. "Exempt-exempt-taxable" (EET) means that contributions (up to a ceiling) are exempt from corporate and/or personal income taxation, account accumulations (interest, dividends, and capital gains) are exempt from tax, and distributions during retirement are taxable as personal income at the personal income tax rate applicable. "Taxable-exempt-exempt" (TEE) means that contributions are subject to tax while account accumulations are exempt, and distributions during retirement are exempt from personal income tax.

33. PSU financing is a broader issue of which PSU pension financing is only a part.

34. The mandate of the NSSF is to finance some of the pension liabilities for China's aging population.

35. This is the framework adopted for the Basic Benefit in the 2009 NRPS.

36. This is a complex task because the accrued rights not yet in disbursement reflect a variety of prior reforms as well as special ad hoc provisions.

37. The pay-as-you-go asset is defined as the present value of future contributions minus pension rights accruing to these contributions.

38. Net of ongoing existing government transfers already in the system.

39. In principle, a retiree could receive a benefit from each of the locations where he or she has worked. With central processing an individual receives a single benefit based on rights entitlements from various locations during his or her work life. Central processing would necessarily require a framework for data sharing, consolidation, and reconciliation.

40. It is useful to note that the five PSU pension reform pilot provinces had faced difficulties in such a categorization, thereby making integration very challenging to date.

41. Institutional needs include the accounting, financial control, and record-keeping systems associated with moving to become contributory schemes and the institutional foundations for data submission and reconciliation.

## References

Asher, M. 2009. "Social Pensions in Four Middle-Income Countries." In *Closing the Coverage Gap: The Role of Social Pensions and Other Retirement Income Transfers*, ed. R. Holzmann, D. Robalino, and N. Takayama, chap. 6. Washington, DC: World Bank.

Asian Development Bank. 2002. *Rural Pension Reform in China*. Manila: Asian Development Bank.

Barrientos, A. 2009. "Social Pensions in Low-Income Countries." In *Closing the Coverage Gap: The Role of Social Pensions and Other Retirement Income Transfers*, ed. R. Holzmann, D. Robalino, and N. Takayama, chap. 5. Washington, DC: World Bank.

Cai, F., J. Giles, P. O'Keefe, and D. Wang. 2012. *The Elderly and Old Age Support in Rural China: Challenges and Prospects*. Directions in Development Series. Washington, DC: World Bank.

Chen, L. 2007. "A Preliminary Analysis on Enterprise Pension and Multiple-Layer Pension System." www.cnpension.net,2007-06-24.

China Economic Research and Advisory Program. 2005. *Social Security Reform in China: Issues and Options*. Beijing. http://economics.mit.edu/files/691.

Cui, S. 2007. Keynote Speech at Asian Investor Summit. May, Hong Kong.

Dollar, D. 2007. *Poverty, Inequality and Social Disparities during China's Economic Reform*. Policy Research Working Paper 4253, World Bank, Washington, DC.

Dorfman, M., D. Wang, P. O'Keefe and J. Cheng. 2013. "China's Pension Schemes for Rural and Urban Residents." In *Matching Contributions for Pensions*, edited by R. Hinz, R. Holzmann, D. Tuesta and N. Takayama. chapter 11. Washington, DC: World Bank.

Drouin, A., and L. Thompson. 2006. "Perspectives on the Social Security System of China." ESS Extension of Social Security Paper No. 25, International Labour Organization, Geneva.

Dunaway, S., and V. Arora. 2007. "Pension Reform in China: The Need for a New Approach." IMF Working Paper, Asia and Pacific Department, International Monetary Fund, Washington, DC.

Frazier, M. 2004. "After Pension Reform: Navigating the 'Third Rail' in China." *Studies in Comparative International Development* 39 (2): 43–68.

Ge, Y., ed. 2002. *Research into the Reform of the Pension System in State Institutions and Public Service Units in China*. Beijing: Foreign Language Press.

Grosh, M., and P. Leite. 2009. "Defining Eligibility for Social Pensions: A View from a Social Assistance Perspective." In *Closing the Coverage Gap: The Role of Social Pensions and Other Retirement Income Transfers*, ed. R. Holzmann, D. Robalino, and N. Takayama, chap. 12. Washington, DC: World Bank.

He, J., and L. Kuijs. 2007. "Rebalancing China's Economy—Modeling a Policy Package." World Bank China Research Paper No. 7, World Bank, Washington, DC.

Hinz, R. 2007. "The New Enterprise Annuities: The Need to Strengthen a Key Element of the Chinese Pension System." Mimeo, World Bank, Washington, DC.

Hinz, R., R. Holzmann, D. Tuesta, and N. Takayama. 2013. *Matching Contributions for Pensions: A Review of International Experience.* Washington, DC: World Bank.

Holzmann, R., and R. Hinz. 2005. *Old Age Income Support in the 21st Century.* Washington, DC: World Bank.

Holzmann, R., and E. Palmer. 2006. *Pension Reform: Issues and Prospects for Nonfinancial Defined Contribution Schemes.* Washington, DC: World Bank.

Holzmann, R., E. Palmer, and D. Robalino, eds. 2012. *Nonfinancial Defined Contribution Pension Schemes in a Changing Pension World: Progress, Lessons, and Implementation* (vol. 1) and *Gender, Politics, and Financial Stability* (vol. 2). Washington, DC: World Bank.

Holzmann, R., D. Robalino, and N. Takayama, eds. 2009. *Closing the Coverage Gap: The Role of Social Pensions and Other Retirement Income Transfers.* Washington, DC: World Bank.

Hu, Y.-W., C. Pugh., F. Stewart, and J. Yermo. 2007. *Collective Pension Funds— International Evidence and Implications for China's Enterprise Annuities Reform.* OECD Working Papers on Insurance and Private Pensions No. 9. Paris: OECD.

Jackson, R., and N. Howe. 2004. *The Graying of the Middle Kingdom: The Demographics and Economics of Retirement Policy in China.* Washington, DC: Center for Strategic and International Studies.

Jackson, R., K. Nakashima, and N. Howe. 2009. *China's Long March to Retirement Reform: The Graying of the Middle Kingdom Revisited.* Washington, DC: Center for Strategic and International Studies.

Jiang, L. 2008. *Aging China, Who Pays?* Caijing Annual Edition.

Jiang, L., M. Dorfman, and W. Yan. 2007. *Notional Defined-Contribution Accounts: A Pension Reform Model Worth Considering.* Fiscal Reform in China.

Kakwani, N., and K. Subbarao. 2005. "Aging and Poverty in Africa and the Role of Social Pensions." Social Protection Discussion Paper No. 0521, World Bank, Washington, DC.

McKinsey Global Institute. 2009. "Preparing for China's Urban Billion." Executive Summary. McKinsey Global Institute, Shanghai, China.

Mi, H., and C. Yang. 2008. "Basic Theoretic Framework Research on Rural Pension System." [In Chinese.] Shanghai: Guang Ming Publishing House.

Organisation for Economic Co-operation and Development (OECD). 2009. *Pensions at a Glance. Retirement-Income Systems in OECD Countries.* Paris: OECD.

———. 2011. Pensions at a Glance. *Retirement-Income Systems in OECD Countries.* Paris: OECD.

Palacios, R., and D. Robalino. 2009. "Matching Defined Contributions: A Way to Increase Pension Coverage." In *Closing the Coverage Gap: The Role of Social*

*Pensions and Other Retirement Income Transfers*, ed. R. Holzmann, D. Robalino, and N. Takayama, chap. 13. Washington, DC: World Bank.

Palacios, R., and O. Sluchynsky. 2006. "Social Pensions Part I: Their Role in the Overall Pension System." Social Protection Discussion Paper No. 0601, World Bank, Washington, DC.

Reutersward, A. 2007. "Labour Protection in China: Challenges Facing Labour Offices and Social Insurance." OECD Social Employment and Migration Working Papers No. 30, OECD, Paris.

Salditt, F., P. Whiteford, and W. Adema. 2007. *Pension Reform in China: Progress and Prospects*. OECD Social Employment and Migration Working Papers No. 53, OECD, Paris.

Sin, Y. 2005. "China Pension Liabilities and Reform Options for Old Age Insurance." Working Paper 2005-1, World Bank, Washington, DC.

Sin, Y., and L. Mao. 2007. *China Pensions: Hidden Pot of Gold, CLSA Speaker Series*. n.p.: Watson Wyatt.

———. 2008. *Understanding China's Pension System—Yesterday, Today and Tomorrow*. n.p.: Watson Wyatt.

Song, L., and S. Appleton. 2008. "Social Protection and Migration in China: What Can Protect Migrants from Economic Uncertainty?" Institute for the Study of Labor (IZA) Discussion Paper No. 3594, IZA, Hamburg.

State Council of the People's Republic of China. 2008. "Circular of the State Council concerning the Printing and Distributing of the Pilot Reform Plan of the Pension System for Public Service Units Employees." *Guofa* No. 10.

———. 2009. "Guiding Suggestions of State Council on Developing New Rural Social Pension Scheme Pilot." *Guofa* No. 32, September 4.

———. 2011. "The Guiding Opinions of the State Council on Piloting Social Pension Insurance for Urban Residents." *Guofa* No. 18, June 7.

Trinh, T. 2006. *China's Pension System: Caught between Mounting Legacies and Unfavourable Demographics*. Frankfurt: Deutsche Bank Research.

United Nations Population Fund (UNFPA). 2006. *Population Aging in China: Facts and Figures*. New York: UNFPA.

United Nations. 2010. "Population Estimates and Projections." Population Division, Department of Economic and Social Affairs, United Nations, New York.

Wang, D. 2006. "China's Urban and Rural Old Age Security System: Challenges and Options." *China & World Economy* 14 (1): 102–16.

Whitehouse, E. 2007. *Pensions Panorama: Retirement-Income Systems in 53 Countries*. Washington, DC: World Bank.

World Bank. 1997. *Old Age Security: Pension System Reform in China*. Washington, DC: World Bank.

————. 2005. "Evaluation of the Liaoning Province Social Security Reform Pilot Analysis of Pension Liabilities and Fiscal Implications under Reform Scenarios," China and Mongolia Department, World Bank, Washington, DC.

————. 2007a. "Urban *Dibao* in China: Building upon Success," Human Development Unit, World Bank, Washington, DC.

————. 2007b. "China's Modernizing Labor Market: Trends and Emerging Challenges," Human Development Unit, World Bank, Washington, DC.

————. 2009. *From Poor Areas to Poor People: China's Evolving Poverty Reduction Agenda—An Assessment of Poverty and Inequality in China.* Washington, DC: World Bank.

Yang, C. 2007. "Studies on Rural Social Pension Insurance System in China: Practice, Theory, and Policy." [In Chinese.] Hangzhou: Zhejiang da xue chu ban she.

Yang, J. 2007. "Innovation and Selection of Financing Sources of Rural Social Security." *Developing Research* 2.

Yu, X., and Y. M. Sin. 2005. "Labor Market and Pension Reform Issues of PSU Reform." Study on Public Service Unit Reform Background Note No. 2, mimeo.

Yuebin, X. 2007. *Social Assistance in China: The Minimum Living Standards Guarantee Scheme.* Beijing: Institute of Social Development and Public Policy, Beijing Normal University, Beijing.

## APPENDIX A

# Pension Needs for Nonwage Rural and Urban Citizens

## Introduction

This appendix outlines an approach to promoting widespread pension coverage for rural and urban residents who are outside the wage employment sector. It first discusses the development of the Chinese rural pension system to date, including major new initiatives, and then provides a proposal for a national pension scheme for rural and urban nonwage residents that draws from ongoing experience in China and internationally. The New Rural Pension Scheme (NRPS) program announced by the State Council in 2009 (and operational in over 60 percent of rural counties by early 2012) represents a major and welcome push toward the rapid expansion of pension coverage with the aim of full geographic coverage by 2013.[1] The approval of a national scheme for urban residents in mid-2011 designed along similar lines to NRPS completes the national framework for expanding pension coverage and for eventual integration of rural and urban resident schemes. Many of the design features of the new schemes reflect lessons from China and other countries. Together, they form a solid base for further development—not only for rural citizens but also for uncovered segments of the urban population. The proposal in this appendix is consistent with the principles of the new schemes as outlined by the State Council.

This appendix is divided into six sections. It first discusses the rationale for a pension system that covers the rural and urban nonwage population; this discussion was informed by an analysis of elderly poverty and sources of support, and demographic trends, as well as international experience with pension expansion. The next section provides a brief summary of the history and lessons from experience with rural pensions in China, followed by a discussion of the 2009 NRPS and the 2011 Urban Residents Pension Scheme (URPS). The appendix then outlines the basic principles that should guide pension scheme design and briefly discusses the integration of urban and rural residents under a single residents' scheme.[2] The following section provides a proposal based on a longer-term vision for a national pension system for the nonwage rural and urban population with two main elements—voluntary individual accounts, in which participation is incentivized through a matching contribution from the government, and a Citizens' Social Pension (CSP) providing minimum subsistence to all uncovered elderly. This proposal draws closely from the design of the NRPS and URPS programs, although it has distinguishing features that seem worthy of consideration as the Chinese authorities continue to develop their pension system. Both programs and the proposed schemes are discussed in light of relevant international experience. The discussion then moves to transitional issues in the proposed pension system for the rural and urban nonwage population, including the interaction between individual accounts and the social pension. The final section provides conclusions.

## Rationale and Expectations

Existing analysis on China provides a solid rationale for greater public intervention in support for the elderly, particularly among the rural population. Table A.1 shows poverty rates by income and consumption measures between rural and urban elderly households. Poverty among the elderly is a much greater problem in rural than in urban areas. The China Urban and Rural Elderly Survey (CURES [2006]), which is a nationally representative sample of elderly, suggests that 19 percent of the rural elderly had consumption levels below the official poverty line, and 29 percent were below the higher "basic needs" line; meanwhile, only 6 percent of the urban elderly are below the "basic needs" line. The poverty gap measure, which provides a measure of the depth of poor households below the poverty line, also suggests a more severe problem in rural areas than in urban areas. Finally, the poverty severity measure picks up the

**Table A.1    Measuring the Poverty of the Rural and Urban Elderly**
*share of population under the poverty line (percent)*

|  | Income poverty | | | Consumption poverty | | |
|---|---|---|---|---|---|---|
|  | Head-count index | Poverty gap | Poverty severity | Head-count index | Poverty gap | Poverty severity |
| **Rural elderly** | | | | | | |
| Official poverty line | 19.6 | 8.3 | 4.4 | 19.2 | 7.5 | 4.0 |
| Basic needs line | 28.7 | 12.7 | 7.3 | 28.7 | 11.8 | 6.7 |
| One-dollar-a-day line | 30.3 | 13.1 | 7.6 | 29.2 | 12.3 | 7.0 |
| **Urban elderly** | | | | | | |
| Basic needs line | 5.4 | 2.0 | 1.3 | 5.8 | 2.7 | 1.8 |
| One-dollar-a-day line | 3.4 | 1.7 | 1.2 | 5.5 | 2.5 | 1.6 |

*Source:* Cai and others 2012.

effects of inequality among the poor and suggests that severe poverty is also a more serious problem in rural than urban areas.[3] Given the access that segments of urban elderly have to pension income as well as family support, it is not surprising that poverty is much higher among the rural elderly. However, it is important to note that more analysis is needed to disaggregate those segments of the urban population presently without pension support. It would be reasonable to expect that they may have a considerably lower welfare level than the average urban elderly citizen.

The rationale for public support for the rural elderly is particularly strong. Several factors underlie this rationale.[4] First, the rural elderly have been consistently poorer, suffered a higher incidence of chronic poverty, and have been more vulnerable than both working-age households and the urban elderly in China over time. Figure A.1 shows the incidence of poverty among rural households from the early 1990s to the mid-2000s. Households headed by older people are consistently the poorest in rural areas even as poverty head counts among all rural households have fallen sharply.

Second, projections for China show that (1) the demographic transition is accelerating and (2) aging and the growth of old-age dependency will be rapid and far more pronounced in rural than in urban areas.[5] Figure A.2 illustrates just how significantly the Chinese population will age between 2008 and 2030. The share of population over 60 years of age will double during this period. Moreover, the elderly population as a share of the population starts off higher in rural areas than it does in urban areas, and the gap only widens by 2030. Similarly, the old-age

**Figure A.1    Percentage of Poor Rural Households by Age of Household Head**

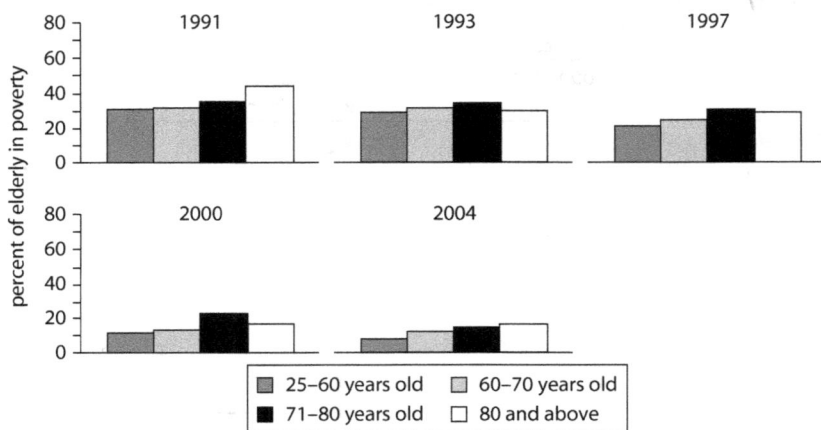

*Source:* CHNS various years. Poverty incidence is shown by age of the head of household.

**Figure A.2    Trends of Population Aging in Rural and Urban China, 2008–2030**

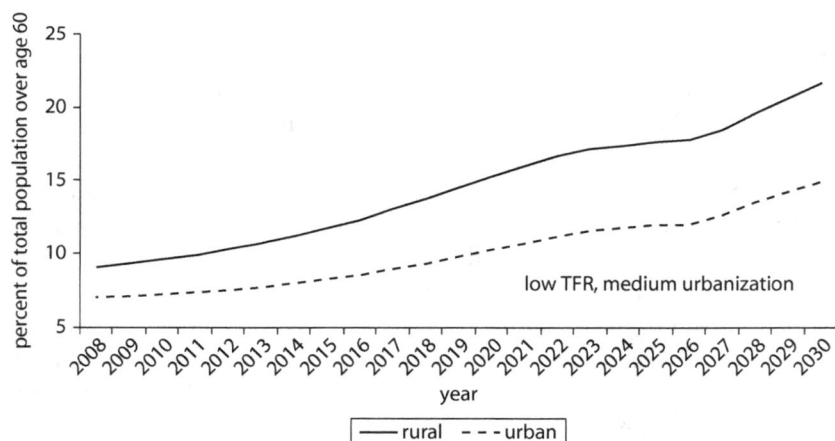

*Source:* Cai and others 2012.
*Note:* TFR = total fertility rate.

dependency ratio will more than double over the projection period, with the gap between urban and rural areas also growing wider by 2030 (see figure A.3).

Third, the sources of support for the elderly are highly dependent on families and labor income for those without pension support in rural and urban areas. Sources of support are also very different both between rural

**Figure A.3    Old-Age Dependency Ratios in Rural and Urban China, 2008–2030**
*percent*

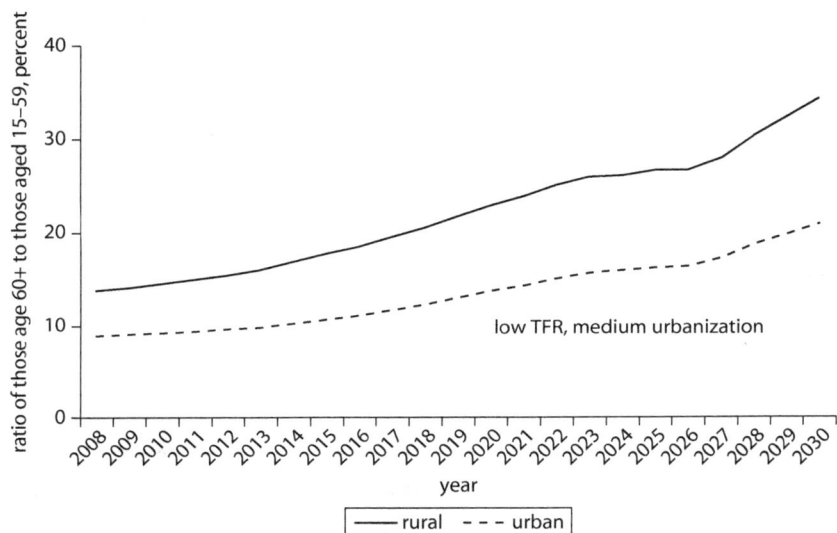

*Source:* Cai and others 2012.
*Note:* TFR = total fertility rate.

and urban elderly and between men and women. Although pensions are the single most significant source of support for the urban elderly, they remain a minor source of support for the rural elderly and are almost entirely confined to former civil servants, military, and village cadres. Even among the urban elderly, less than half cite pensions as their primary source of income; this share is just over a third for elderly urban women. In contrast, labor income is a much more significant source of support for the rural elderly and is the primary source of support for almost 38 percent of the rural elderly (see table A.2). The primary source of support changes sharply among the rural elderly during their sixties.

Although informal sources of support will remain important, they will come under increased pressure, particularly for the rural poor. The demand for family support is likely to become acute in coming decades as the old-age dependency ratio rises rapidly. Working-age adults will be under increasing pressure to support a growing population of urban elderly. Thus, the positive effects of rapid growth and rising incomes will be offset significantly by the growing resources required to provide for elderly well-being. In urban areas, analysis suggests that (1) private transfers are indeed responsive to elderly poverty in extended families but (2) the

**Table A.2    Primary Sources of Support for China's Elderly**

*percent*

|  | Urban | | | Rural | | |
|---|---|---|---|---|---|---|
|  | Average | Male | Female | Average | Male | Female |
| Labor income | 13.0 | 18.4 | 7.9 | 37.9 | 48.5 | 27.5 |
| Pensions | 45.4 | 56.9 | 34.6 | 4.6 | 8.1 | 1.3 |
| *Dibao* | 2.4 | 1.8 | 2.9 | 1.3 | 1.8 | 0.9 |
| Insurance and subsidy | 0.3 | 0.3 | 0.2 | 0.1 | 0.2 | 0.0 |
| Property income | 0.5 | 0.5 | 0.5 | 0.2 | 0.2 | 0.1 |
| Family support | 37.0 | 20.7 | 52.3 | 54.1 | 39.3 | 68.5 |
| Other | 1.5 | 1.4 | 1.6 | 1.8 | 2.0 | 1.7 |

*Sources:* National Bureau of Statistics 2005. Percentages indicate share reporting specified income sources as the most significant source of support.

private transfer response is insufficient to prevent elderly poverty where no or very low pension entitlements are obtained from the system and generally low retirement incomes.[6] Available evidence from rural areas also suggests that the risks of public transfers crowding out private transfers from family members are not as significant as is sometimes feared.[7] Both analyses provide a rationale for public sector intervention to support the elderly not already covered by pension arrangements.

Fourth, although savings patterns across China are generally high and remain positive even in old age, they are strongly correlated with household income; the rural poor, on average, are not saving.[8] Moreover, concerns have been expressed that many people are saving too much as a precaution against old age, health, and other shocks, thereby contributing to macroeconomic imbalances between saving and consumption. Figure A.4 shows savings rates of rural households across the income distribution in 2003 and 2007. Another comparison of interest is with urban savings behavior. Over the period 1978–2007, the rural household savings rate has been higher in most years than the urban rate, rising from 13 percent to 22 percent over the period and peaking at almost 29 percent in 1999. More volatility is seen around the trend in rural savings rates than for urban households, reflecting the greater variability of incomes in rural areas. In the early reform period, the rural saving rate rose to 22.9 percent in 1984 after successful implementation of the household responsibility system but dropped sharply with the economic recession in the late 1980s to the early 1990s. The savings rate then returned to an upward trend between 1995 and 1999 before leveling out at above 25 percent for four years and then dropping again between 2003 and 2006. The urban savings rate has fluctuated less around a

**Figure A.4    Rural Saving Rates by Income Quintile**

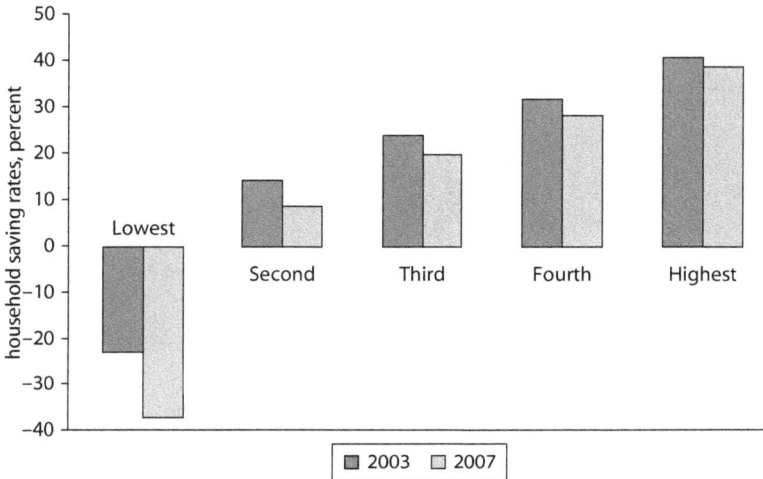

*Source:* China Rural Household Survey Yearbooks 2005 and 2008. Saving equals net income minus consumption expenditure.

consistent upward trend since the early 1990s and in recent years, has been higher than the rural savings rate. What is not yet known, in both cases, is the impact of the 2008–09 financial crisis on savings behavior.

In light of international experience, the government's plan to achieve full pension coverage by 2020 is ambitious, though its target of full geographic coverage for voluntary schemes by 2013 appears to be being realized.[9] Historically, pension coverage has tended to be closely correlated with a country's per capita GDP, largely because per capita GDP is correlated with the proportion of the labor force in the formal sector, overall levels of income, urbanization, and the shares of services and agriculture in GDP. Other factors include a history of state socialism, which, in some parts of the world, has left a legacy of relatively high coverage rates. Figure A.5 demonstrates the relationship between the coverage rates of contributory pension schemes and per capita income. Overall, less than 20 percent of the global labor force is covered by pensions—an average that masks massive variation. The rates of coverage in the former command economies are higher than global averages (based on their GDP per capita) as a result of the state's historical role as an employer. By comparison, China's coverage prior to the advent of the NRPS and URPS schemes was notably lower than one might have expected based on its per capita income. An important factor to consider

**Figure A.5    Pension Coverage Rate of Active Labor Force, Various Countries, Mid-2000s**

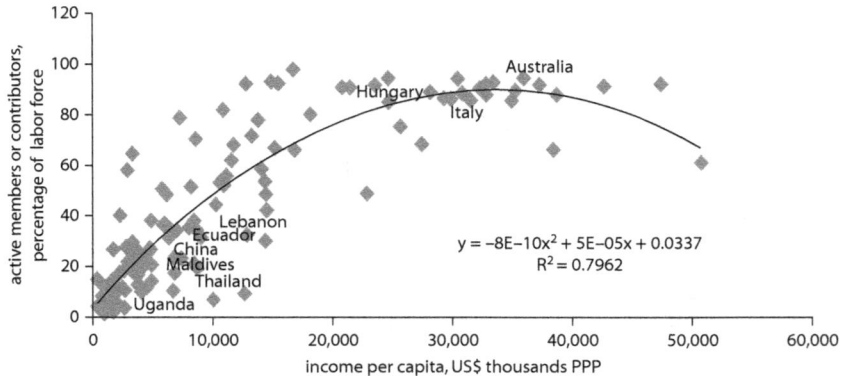

Source: World Bank forthcoming. China's coverage rate is for 2008.
Note: Coverage rate = contributing or participating members of working age as a percent of the employed labor force.

when weighing the evidence from international experience, however, is the historically low incidence in developing countries of state-subsidized social pension schemes and/or matching defined-contribution schemes (an issue that is discussed later in this appendix).

When setting goals for pension coverage expansion, another reference point is the status of coverage among OECD countries, the majority of which have had pension systems for decades, some dating to the nineteenth century. Despite this, very few have attained full coverage (see figure A.6), and the trend has been toward reduced coverage since the 1980s as rates of informal employment have grown.

As another point of reference, figure A.7 shows pension coverage rates among the economically active population in Latin America in the 1990s and 2000s. Coverage rates—even in solidly middle-income countries with mature pension systems—generally remain below 60 percent. A second important observation is that pension coverage among the economically active population does not always expand over time but can slip back (as in Ecuador and Costa Rica) or stagnate (as in Chile, Brazil, and Argentina). Experience in Latin America may point to the limitations in expanding pension coverage through funded defined-contribution schemes(which are popular in the region) in the absence of other incentives for informal sector workers to participate.

Although a country's circumstances, administrative capacity, and other factors are undoubtedly important, international evidence suggests that

**Figure A.6 Pension Coverage in OECD Countries**

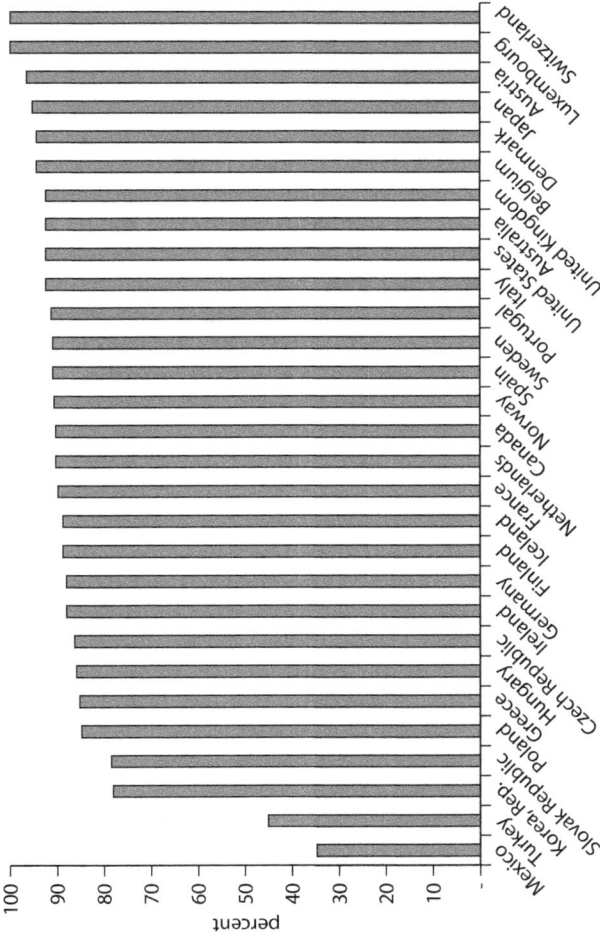

*Source:* Forteza and others (2009).

**Figure A.7    Coverage among the Economically Active Population, Latin America, 1990s–2000s**

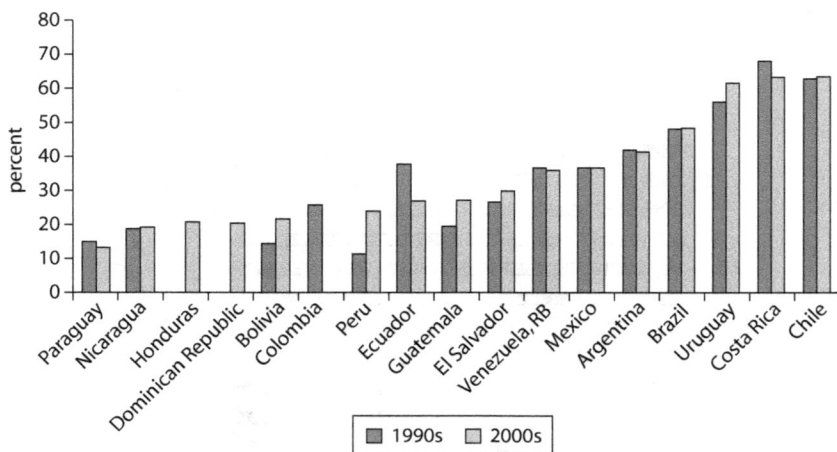

*Source:* Rofman and others 2008. Argentina 1995–2006; Bolivia 1999–2005; Brazil 1995–2006; Chile 1996–2006; Colombia 1996–1996; Costa Rica 1995–2006; Dominican Republic 2006; Ecuador 1995–2006; Guatemala 1998–2006; Honduras 2006; Mexico 1998–2006; Nicaragua 1998–2005; Paraguay 1999–2006; Peru 1999–2006; El Salvador 1995–2005; Uruguay 1995–2006; Venezuela, RB 1995–2006.

achieving wide pension coverage at China's level of income is possible but will prove challenging and take time. In particular, agricultural and informal sector workers in low- to middle-income countries have historically been unusually difficult to bring into pension systems using the approaches employed in many developing countries. Many common factors contribute to the challenge, including (1) the administrative difficulty of reaching rural workers in low-capacity environments where work is often informal; (2) a lack of understanding and demand among rural and informal workers for pensions due to myopia, low financial literacy, and other factors; and (3) a general lack of financial incentives from governments to induce participation. This underscores the need for innovative approaches that focus on participation incentives for informal and rural sector workers.

## China's Experience with Rural Pensions

This section outlines the evolution of the Chinese rural pension system over the last two decades with a particular focus on recent provincial pilot schemes that have informed the design of the NRPS.[10] This evolution can be categorized into three main phases (1) an initiation and expansion phase from 1986 to 1998, (2) a contraction and stagnation phase from 1999 to 2002, and (3) a renewal phase from 2003 to 2009. A new and exciting phase began in 2009 with the initiation and rapid expansion of the NRPS. Each phase is discussed in turn below.

### *Initiation and Expansion of Rural Pensions: 1986–1998*

The initial exploration of rural pensions was set out in the 7th Five Year Plan (1986–1990), which noted that "efforts should be made to study how to establish a rural pension system, launch and gradually expand pilot schemes in line with economic development." (State Council 1986). This was built upon through county-level pilots led by the Ministry of Civil Affairs (MOCA) in the Beijing and Shanxi provinces, which emphasized mixed financing responsibility between government, collectives, and individuals, with most of the responsibility falling on individuals. This was followed in 1991 by (1) the State Council issuing Document No. 33, *Decision on Establishing a Unified Basic Old Age Insurance for Enterprise Employees*, which designated MOCA to take the lead on rural pensions and (2) MOCA launching pilots in five counties of Shandong province.

There was a clear policy push in the early 1990s to expand rural pension schemes. The various pilots contributed to a major policy document in 1992 from MOCA: *Basic Scheme for Rural Pension at County Level* (referred to hereafter as *Basic Scheme*). This was elaborated in a subsequent policy document in 1995,[11] which outlined a set of basic principles for rural pension schemes while allowing for variations in specifics by localities:

- Schemes were to be voluntary, mainly financed from individual contributions, supported by contributions from collectives at the level of villages and townships, and supported by preferential government policies (for example, tax relief for collectives on contributions). The Basic Scheme set retirement ages at 60 for both men and women, although it was not uncommon in the practices that emerged to set 55 as the retirement age for women.
- Following the lead of the urban pension system reform, schemes were to be based on funded individual accounts.
- Individual contributions were to range from 2–20 RMB monthly with a matching of 2 RMB by the collective.
- Elderly farmers were entitled to receive a pension until death. In cases where they lived less than 10 years after retiring, any balances remaining in their individual accounts could be inherited.[12]

- Investments of accumulated contributions were to be placed in bank deposits and national bonds; no direct investments were otherwise allowed. Although portfolio rules mandated investment in low-return investments, the system in practice also committed to a guaranteed rate of return.
- Administration was to be by the local bureau of Civil Affairs, and administrative costs would be covered from contributions (with a cap of 3 percent set subsequently).
- The oversight and regulation of the scheme was to sit largely with the implementing agency (that is, the MOCA at the county level), subject to the internal controls of the MOF and internal auditing.

As a result of this policy initiative, coverage of rural pensions expanded significantly during the 1990s with programs established by the end of 1998 in 31 provinces and 2,123 counties (just under three-quarters of all rural counties). This was also the high point of coverage prior to the 2009 national pilot, with 80.25 million rural workers participating and more than 600,000 pension beneficiaries. However, concerns soon began to emerge about the operation of local schemes and the lack of a sound governance framework; the Asian financial crisis in 1997 served to underscore the need to rethink the program.[13] Responsibility for rural pensions was subsequently switched from MOCA to the then Ministry of Labor and Social Security (MOLSS—now MHRSS) in the 1998 administrative restructuring.

### Contraction and Stagnation: 1999–2002

As a result of concerns about the effectiveness and sustainability of rural pension schemes, a sharp policy shift occurred in the late 1990s to limit their expansion. The change in the official position on rural pensions was reflected in the 1999 State Council declaration that China was not yet ready for universal rural pensions and that counties should (1) cease expansion of schemes; (2) rectify the operations of existing schemes; and, where possible; (3) transfer schemes to the management of commercial insurers. By 2001, the shift in policy stance contributed to a sharp decline in coverage to just under 60 million participants, with the number stabilizing in the low to mid-50 millions through 2007 in roughly 1,900 counties. Despite this contraction, new participants continued to enter the system and accumulated funds from existing schemes continued to increase, more than doubling from 2000 to more than 41 billion RMB in

2007. The number of pension beneficiaries approached 4 million by 2007 as existing schemes matured (see table A.3). The variability of indicators over time is noteworthy, especially during the 1990s.

The development of the rural pension system during this phase was characterized by deficiencies that undermined the achievement of policy objectives, including the following:

- *Coverage was highly imbalanced* geographically, with four coastal provinces (Jiangsu, Shanghai, Shandong, and Zhejiang) accounting for approximately 45 percent of total participation and 64 percent of total accumulations. Poorer regions, in contrast, generally failed to attain significant penetration.

- Although the policy indicated that participation was voluntary, *local level authorities in many cases mandated participation* in the face of disinterest from farmers.

**Table A.3    Rural Pension Indicators, 1993–2007**

| | No. participants (million) | | | | | |
|---|---|---|---|---|---|---|
| Year | Total year end | New participants | New participants employed in township enterprises | Counties | No. recipients (million) | Accumulated fund (billion RMB) |
| 1993 | | | | 1,100 | | 1.48 |
| 1994 | 34.84 | | | | 0.17 | 2.70 |
| 1995 | 51.43 | | | | 0.27 | 5.95 |
| 1996 | 65.94 | | | | 0.32 | 9.95 |
| 1997 | 74.52 | | | 2,100 | 0.61 | 13.92 |
| 1998 | 80.25 | | | 2,123 | | 16.62 |
| 1999 | 80.00 | | | | | |
| 2000 | 61.72 | 1.84 | 1.51 | 2,052 | 0.98 | 19.55 |
| 2001 | 59.95 | 3.12 | 0.92 | 2,045 | 1.08 | 21.61 |
| 2002 | 54.62 | 4.13 | 0.67 | 1,955 | 1.23 | 23.32 |
| 2003 | 54.28 | 2.24 | 1.40 | 1,870 | 1.98 | 25.93 |
| 2004 | 53.78 | 3.97 | 0.37 | 1,887 | 2.05 | 28.50 |
| 2005 | 54.42 | 2.34 | 0.29 | 1,990 | 3.02 | 31.00 |
| 2006 | 53.73 | | | 1,905 | 3.55 | 35.40 |
| 2007 | 51.71 | 3.06 | 0.19 | | 3.91 | 41.20 |

*Sources:* Bulletins of Ministry of Civil Affairs (1993–1997); Ministry of Labor and Social Security (1998–2007); Yearbook of Labor and Social Security (2001–2008).

- *Matching contributions from collectives were often not made* and their incidence was highly skewed toward a small number of richer provinces. The privatization of Town and Village Enterprises in the 1990s contributed to the lack of employer matching. As a result, 98.5 percent of matching contributions were concentrated in only five provinces (the four coastal provinces noted above, plus Beijing).

- At the local level, concerns were expressed about the concentration of matching funds for cadre members rather than for all scheme members.[14]

- Compared to the urban scheme, where administrative costs are borne by the government, *the 3 percent administrative fee on rural schemes was deducted from farmer contributions*, which was considered inequitable.

- *In many schemes, benefits were unable to be paid in full*, with at least 200 counties canceling schemes and contributors being unable to recoup their contributions. Even when benefits continued to be paid, they were frequently significantly lower than expected due to low returns on accumulations. Low returns were partly due to a preponderance of investments in bank deposits with very low rates of interest. The reluctance to invest in higher-return government securities was exacerbated by localized problems with fund management. As examples, Beijing and Hebei lost significant amounts of invested accumulations through the bankruptcy of fund management companies entrusted to invest in government securities.

- *Supervision of schemes was weak.* The MOLSS figures for the end of 2000 indicate about 20 percent of accumulations had been invested in unauthorized assets, including real estate, stocks, enterprise bonds, and nonbank financial agencies. Although the intent of local implementers may have been to increase returns and meet guaranteed return directives, their failure to abide by investment guidelines indicates significant issues in regulation. This was in part a structural problem because local implementers were under the direct authority of local governments, but the scheme, in principle, was under the bureau at a higher level.

- *Significant volatility was seen in the ratio of guaranteed rates of return, interest rates on investments, and inflation; this contributed to significant negative real returns* on accumulations in some periods and the reverse in others (see table A.4).

- *Pension benefits were very low*, with average pension at about 85 RMB per month in 2007. Moreover, benefits were highly variable across provinces and individuals. A general lack of confidence in schemes also resulted in very low contributions in excess of the minimum by farmers. For example, where farmers chose to contribute 2 RMB per month, their estimated pension after 15 years in nominal terms would have amounted to about 10 RMB per month.[15] Taking into account inflation and administrative costs, their real benefits would have been even lower.

- *The planned transfer of administration to labor bureaus was not undertaken in a timely manner* (or at all in some areas) with 350 counties not having transferred management by 2007.

### Renewal: 2003–2009

Renewed impetus toward a new rural pension system emerged in late 2002 with the CPC Congress, which resulted in new guidelines from MOLSS in 2003.[16] This was followed by (1) opinions of the Central Party Committee (CPC) and the State Council at the end of 2005, which were part of the wider commitment on "Building a New Socialist Countryside," and (2) the 2006 plenary meeting of the 16th CPC, which committed to universal social insurance coverage by 2020. This was enshrined in the new Law on Social Insurance, which underwent two readings in 2009 and was approved in 2010. Between 2003 and 2009, some growth of rural pension schemes was seen, with more than 300 counties in 25 provinces establishing new schemes by the end of 2008.

**Table A.4    Rates of Return on Accumulations and Bank Deposits versus Inflation Rate, Various Years**

*percent*

| Indicator (%) | 1991.1 | 1993.5 | 1994.1 | 1997.1 | 1998.1 | 1998.7 | 1999.7 | 2007.1 |
|---|---|---|---|---|---|---|---|---|
| Interest rate for accumulation | 8.80 | 8.80 | 12.00 | 8.80 | 6.80 | 5.00 | 2.50 | 3.15 |
| Interest rate: one-year bank deposit in bank | 8.64 | 9.18 (10.98 at July) | 10.98 | 7.47 | 5.67 | 4.77 | 2.25 | 2.52 (4.14 year end) |
| Inflation rate | 3.40 | 14.70 | 24.10 | 2.80 | −0.80 | −0.80 | −1.40 | 4.80 |

*Source:* Wu 2009.

The rural pension schemes established during this period fall broadly into three types: (1) social pooling plus individual accounts, (2) flat universal pensions in combination with individual accounts, and (3) individual accounts only. In addition, the schemes differed in terms of the financing role of government at the accumulation and payout stages. As a result, effectively five variants were in existence by 2009 when the national rural pension pilot program was announced (and into which such schemes should eventually be merged):[17]

- Flat pensions plus individual accounts with government financing at the payout stage only. Under this variant, individual contributions went to individual accounts while the government financed flat pensions from general revenues. The most notable example of this model was Beijing after 2005. This was taken a step further in 2009 with revision of the scheme to expand coverage of the rural pension to urban residents not covered by work-related urban schemes.[18]

- Flat pensions plus individual accounts with government financing: (1) by matching contributions to individual accounts and (2) at the payout stage through the financing of flat pensions from general revenues. This model was seen, for example, in Baoji in Shaanxi province after 2007 (a city where 74 percent of the population are farmers) and in Qian'an in Hebei province. In large measure, this model was the precursor to the new national rural pilot design.

- Individual accounts with social pooling, with government financing during the accumulation phase. This model is similar to the urban employee pension system but with lower contributions and lower benefits. This model was typically implemented in regions with high urbanization rates and good fiscal positions, such as Suzhou in Jiangsu province after 2003 and in Qingdao in Shandong province.[19]

- Individual accounts combined with social pooling with government financing: (1) by matching contributions to individual accounts and (2) during the payout phase. This model was implemented in richer prefectures such as Zhongshan and Dongguan.

- Individual accounts only with government matching for contributions to such accounts. This is the simplest design, although it lacks risk pooling of any form. This model was implemented in Yantai in Shandong province after 2005 (a city where 58 percent of the population are farmers) and in Hangshou in Zhejiang province.[20]

In addition to the above common models, other experiments with rural pensions were conducted, including the "land for pensions" schemes. Wen Jiang county of Chengdu city, for example, allowed farmers to enter the urban pension system under the so-called *two give-ups* approach, whereby farmers relinquish the management rights on their land and the use of the land on which they dwell in exchange for a pension. Similar approaches were taken in Chongqing and within Guangdong province prior to the expansion of the national pilot. Finally, schemes even in 2012 continue to be under implementation for specific subgroups of farmers, particularly farmers whose land has been expropriated and migrant workers in urban areas. This approach is common in areas experiencing rapid urbanization (even in less developed provinces such as Ningxia) and offers entitlements in the urban system as partial compensation for expropriated land.

The discussion above suggests that there was a rich history of experimentation with rural pensions in China in the lead-up to the 2009 national pilot. This is not surprising given the wider commitment of the Chinese authorities to balanced development and development of a rural social protection system. From this experience, various patterns and issues emerge, as is discussed below.

(1) *Voluntary with incentives.* In policy terms, all schemes were voluntary, relying on a mixture of incentives to encourage participation. At the same time, a feature in some schemes (for example, Suzhou and Baoji) was the system of so-called family binding whereby the pension eligibility of older contributors close to retirement age is determined by whether his or her spouse and all adult children contribute to the new system. Opinions differ among local commentators on the merits of this feature, though it has been adopted in the national pilot.[21] Apart from this feature, the local rural pension schemes in the 2000s were incentive-driven through the subsidy mechanism although the extent to which any program with sufficiently strong support from the local administration is truly "voluntary," has been debated. The incentive-based approach resulted in high coverage in various pilots. For example, Beijing's participation rate rose from 37 percent to 85 percent following an increase in the local subsidy level, while in Suzhou—where government contributions constitute 60 percent of

the combined total—participation reached 99 percent. The experience in Baoji was a 68 percent participation rate among all farmers, rising to 92 percent for farmers over the age of 45.

(2) *Retirement ages and contribution requirements.* As noted, the prescribed retirement age under the former Basic Scheme was 60 for both sexes, and participation started at age 20. This varied at both ends under the local pilot schemes—with the entry age for participation as low as 16 in Beijing and 18 in Baoji (although it remained 20 in places such as Yantai), and the retirement age set at 55 for women and 60 for men in Beijing, at 59 for both sexes in Yantai, and with no upper-age limit in Baoji. A clear issue here for localities seeking to integrate urban and rural systems was the retirement ages in urban systems, which are typically 55 for women and 60 for men.

Widespread practice in local pilots was that 15 years of contribution history were needed to qualify for full benefits (similar to the urban old-age insurance scheme), with the obvious exception of individual account-only schemes where minimum contribution periods are irrelevant. However, some schemes recognized the transition issue and had special treatment for those above age 45. For example, Baoji allowed those over 45 to have a full pension if they contributed until age 60; those over 60 were also entitled, subject to "family binding" (a feature adopted in the NRPS). Some schemes also made provisions for the lump-sum payment of contributions by those without a full contribution history—in some cases at the point of retirement (for example, Beijing and Zhuhai) and in others during the accumulation phase. Other schemes allowed older cohorts to continue to make contributions for up to five years after reaching the normal retirement age.

(3) *Financing models and sustainability.* A key feature of all the local pilot schemes in the 2000s was significant public subsidies, either on contributions to individual accounts, or during the payout phase, or both. This represented a major shift and recognition by central and local authorities that some form of matching was necessary to incentivize participation by rural populations.[22] Box A.1 provides information on the experience of India in this regard. This experience has also been addressed in part in the Chinese literature, and

**Box A.1**

**Rajasthan's Vishwakarma MDC Pension Scheme**

In 2007 the government of Rajasthan, India, introduced an MDC scheme for 20 categories of low-income workers, almost all of them in the informal sector. To be eligible, workers must be residents of Rajasthan, aged between 18 and 50, and not covered by any other provident fund arrangement supported by the government or an employer. Workers who contribute 100 rupees (just over $2) per month for at least 10 months each year will be provided a 1,000 rupee annual match on their contribution, financed by the state government. An annual interest rate is paid on the combined accumulation, which is announced each year and equivalent to the rate of return on the formal sector provident fund (about 8 percent per annum in 2008). This has been designed to provide a benefit at retirement just above the poverty line. At 2010 interest rates, a 30-year-old worker who contributes for 30 years would receive a monthly pension of about 2,000 rupees at retirement at age 60. The scheme does not allow early withdrawals of accumulations. Account holders are provided with an annual account statement. Internet-based individual accounts are opened for each worker in the scheme, and a computer-generated passbook is provided within 30 days, which contains a scanned photo image and the enrollment form of the account holder. The individual is issued a unique identifier at the point of registration using an application called the Social Security Solution (*sCube*), which allows for portability of the account and for the worker to make contributions at any point in the state. *sCube* allows online and offline data entry using a variety of options and requires only a half day of training to operate. A strong emphasis is placed on raising awareness of members before and following enrollment using short films, pension comics, interactive pension calculators, and other approaches.

*Source:* www.iimp.in.

general recognition exists of the need for public subsidies to support rural pension schemes.[23]

Although the large majority of public subsidies have come from general revenues, experiments have also taken place with partial funding from dedicated revenue streams. Zhuhai city pioneered this approach beginning in 2006 by allocating land transaction revenues to total no less than 15 percent of overall contributions to finance a reserve fund for incremental pensions and for those who had exhausted their individual account accumulations.[24]

A major and still unresolved issue was the fiscal sustainability of different local scheme designs. Looking at a national scheme, simulations based on government spending ranging from 1 percent to 2.5 percent of general revenues have been conducted using different system parameters. These analyses indicate that a broad-based rural pension system should be fiscally affordable and sustainable in the aggregate.[25] Earlier reports using the government's own projections indicated a cost of 1.8 percent of fiscal expenditures (about 66 billion RMB) in 2008 for the central government's portion. However, more work is needed. For example, rural mortality tables on a sufficiently disaggregated basis are needed and can be generated from census data. More importantly, clarity is needed on the financing responsibilities of different levels of government and the variable capacity of subnational levels to meet them.[26]

(4) *Contribution rates and benefit levels.* As one would expect, there was substantial variation in local pilots in their structure, absolute levels of contributions, and benefit levels. Most local schemes designated a range on the contribution rate made to individual accounts, often linked to average wages or rural incomes. Baoji had a range of 10–30 percent of average rural income (and planned to lower the base to 5 percent), whereas Beijing had a much wider range—from 9 percent of average rural incomes to 30 percent of average urban wages. Suzhou appears to have been an exception in this regard, with a flat contribution rate and base for all contributors (10 percent of either the rural average income or one-half of the average urban income). Interestingly, at least one Chinese scholar has raised the idea of farmers being allowed to make some contributions in grain—although no such example was found in research for this report—while others have proposed allocating grain subsidies paid to farmers to rural pension schemes.[27]

With respect to benefits, the practice is emerging of paying close attention to the *dibao* level and fiscal sustainability when setting benefits for the flat pension portion of schemes. The general rule of thumb appears to be that flat pension benefits should be at or slightly above the average *dibao* threshold in the locality. Adding funded benefits is anticipated to take total pensions notably above the *dibao* level. This may vary upward according to local fiscal capacity (for example, Beijing set its flat pension portion at 35 percent of rural average income). For the individual account portion of schemes, the calculation of the payout in local schemes varied. For Beijing and Baoji, for example, the individual account benefit was calculated by dividing the amount in the account at retirement by 139 (the same method used in their urban schemes—which reflects the combined assumptions of a notional life expectancy at age 60 and an assumed drawdown interest rate of 4 percent; this has also been adopted by the new national rural and urban pilots). Although the approach has been similar elsewhere, the actuarial factor used in the calculation has varied (for example, Zhuhai used a factor of 180, whereas in Suzhou it was 120). Such variable practice strongly suggests a need for work on rural mortality tables, ideally at a disaggregated level, to ensure that this portion of the benefit is not exhausted too early or, more likely, if urban mortality rates are being used, exhausted too late.

(5) *Institutional issues.* The experience of local pilots in the 2000s with respect to both scheme administration and fund management demonstrated a degree of continuity, but also the shortcomings in scheme regulation. Overall administration of local schemes remained with the Social Security Bureau, with roles also for villages (collection of contributions and in many cases payment of benefits), townships (consolidation of collections, approval of benefits, and registration), and counties (for general oversight and scheme design). A general improvement also appears to have taken place in computerization of scheme information systems. Within this general administrative structure, a variety of local innovations in administration were found. For example, Suzhou farmers have been able to make contributions directly through banks rather than village officials, and post offices (including mobile facilities) have been used in areas with lower banking penetration. Allowance has also been made in some schemes for the seasonality of farmer incomes, so that schemes such as Baoji made collections only once a year in July or August.

With respect to fund management, the Basic Scheme resources had been managed at the county level; local pilots after 2003 have remained similarly managed. Some researchers have suggested the city level as the appropriate level for fund management; others have proposed the provincial or even national levels.[28] What is clear is that portfolio rules have continued to be very conservative and remain so in the national pilots. Some researchers have proposed establishing reserve funds to cover low rates of return although such funds are more typically used to address fluctuations in returns or the exhaustion of benefits due to longevity in funded systems. The concept of a reserve fund is, in principle, attractive, and actual practice, in places such as Zhuhai, suggests interest.[29] The more significant concern going forward is the regulation of the funded portion of the new national schemes. As seen, this was a significant weakness of the old schemes, and even in the mature urban schemes regulation continues to be an area where the capacity of the system remains stretched.

(6) *Portability between schemes.* A range of transition policies existed for local schemes initiated in the 2000s. The first type of transition is from old to new schemes in the same locality. Local practice differed, with areas such as Beijing allowing portability of funded accumulations from old to the new schemes, and others, like the province of Hunan, stipulating that participants must close their accounts in old schemes before starting afresh in new pilot schemes. The second (and ultimately more important) issue is portability between rural and urban schemes (or migrant worker schemes located in urban areas where these exist). This will be critical to reaching the government's stated goal of an integrated social security system by 2020. The ease with which this can be done has varied according to scheme design and the compatibility of rural pilots with existing urban schemes. In Suzhou, for example, there was a simple 2:1 rule for farmers wishing to transfer their social pooling rights from the rural to urban scheme; this was easily done in Suzhou because the rural contribution base was exactly half that of the urban system. In Beijing, provisions were also made for portability, although this is only done at the point of retirement. If a former farmer accumulated enough years in the urban system at retirement, he or she would enjoy an urban pension (with an allowance for lower rural contributions), whereas his or her urban contributions would be credited to the rural pension scheme if the accumulation period in the urban system was less than 15 years. In principle in all schemes, the funded portion of schemes is easily made portable.

(7) *Interface of pensions and social assistance.* The relationship of local rural pension schemes to various social assistance benefits also merits consideration. The most interesting example is *wubao*, a social welfare benefit that guarantees an "average" standard of living for people in the so-called *three no's* category (no income, no labor capacity, no sources of family support) in which the elderly appear to be significantly overrepresented.[30] In some areas, such as Suzhou, *wubao* recipients had their individual account contributions refunded. For rural *dibao*, there can be receipt of both pension and *wubao* because *dibao* is a household level benefit, which can result in total household income falling below the local *dibao* line even if a pensioner is in a new scheme. Finally, pensions from local schemes have had no effect on the receipt of the supportive allowance for following family planning policy, although some Chinese researchers have proposed integrating the programs through the use of the family planning subsidy as an additional subsidy toward individual pension contributions (once participants are past child-bearing age).[31]

## Looking Ahead—The New Rural Pension Scheme

Renewed attention to rural pensions has shifted to high gear with the announcement in 2009 of a national New Rural Pension Scheme, which started in late 2009 and aims to achieve full geographic coverage, originally no later than 2020 but in more recent government pronouncements by 2013.[32] The diverse experience with rural pension schemes at the subnational level outlined above has offered important lessons for policy makers at the national level, which are reflected in significant measure in the design of the national pilot. The guiding principle of the pilot is *basic insurance and wide coverage with flexibility and sustainability.* The pilot started in 10 percent of counties nationwide in late 2009, with an initial aim of full geographic coverage in rural areas by 2020. However, the schedule has already been accelerated with a target of 23 percent of counties to be included by the end of 2010, over 60 percent of counties covered by early 2012, and the expectation that all counties will covered by 2013. Initial experience with take-up has been positive, with more than 36 million contributors enrolled in the first few months of implementation by the Chinese New Year 2010 and about 13.4 million people already receiving pensions. This gives an estimated national participation rate of about 50 percent with local participation rates as high as 80–90 percent in some areas, particularly those such as Baoji that already had more mature preexisting pilots. Participation has continued to expand rapidly, with around 250 million contributors by early 2012 and around 100 million people receiving pensions under the new scheme. Some key features of the design are the following:

- Participation by rural workers is voluntary.

- All rural residents over 16 years of age are eligible to participate if they are not already covered in a basic urban scheme.

- Participants become eligible for a pension at age 60.

- The scheme provides for individual pension accounts with matching contributions and a basic flat pension for workers who, in the mature system, will have contributed for 15 years. The initial value of the basic pension under the scheme is 55 RMB per month, which can be topped up by local governments at their discretion from their own revenues. Individual accounts have a rate of return equal to the one-year deposit interest rate of the People's Bank of China; benefits are computed by dividing the accumulation at age 60 by 139 (as is done in the urban scheme). The indexation procedure for the basic pension is somewhat vague—to be set in accordance with "economic development and changing prices."

- For those over age 60 at the time the scheme is introduced, they can receive the basic pension benefit provided their children are contributing to the scheme (that is, "family binding"). For those with less than 15 years left before reaching age 60, they should contribute during their working lives and can then make lump-sum contributions to make up any shortfall of contributions for the vesting requirement of 15 years of contributions.

- Financing of the scheme comes from a combination of (1) central subsidies to support the basic pension (in full for central and western regions and 50 percent for eastern regions); (2) individual contributions (ranging from 100 to 500 RMB annually at the choice of the worker); (3) a partial match on the individual contribution by local governments of at least 30 RMB per year (independent of the contribution level chosen by the worker) or at a higher rate as shall be determined; and (4) collective subsidies, which are encouraged but not mandated, with no level specified. During the first months of implementation, the practice of contributors was most commonly to choose the 100 or the 500 RMB contribution levels. At the same time, some provinces and counties have allowed for considerably higher contribution levels of up to 2,500 RMB from farmers in some coastal areas.

- Fund management for individual account accumulations will begin at the county level, with the aim to shift this to the provincial level as quickly as is feasible. Supervision of funds would be by local offices of the MHRSS.

The overall approach of the new pension pilot reflects lessons from international experience and significantly improves on earlier rural pension schemes. The matching of individual account contributions—the so-called *matching defined-contribution* (MDC) approach—sensibly recognizes the need for incentives for rural workers to participate in pension schemes. In addition, the introduction of a basic minimum benefit echoes the practice of various developed and developing countries that have introduced social pensions for the elderly although the linking of eligibility for the basic benefit to individual account contributions represents an important difference in approach. Finally, the role of central financing reflects lessons from other areas of social policy in China, including health insurance and *dibao*, which have clearly demonstrated the need for central subsidies to lagging regions if the equity objectives of coverage expansion are to be realized.

Although the objectives and broad design features of the rural pilot program have much to recommend them, various issues in the program's design may benefit from further consideration and closer evaluation as the scheme is implemented. Addressing these issues could help improve incentives, equity, portability, and fund management. The following four issues are discussed further below:

- Contribution levels, the degree of subsidy, and participation incentives
- Benefit eligibility and levels
- Fund management for the individual account part of the scheme
- Portability of benefits and system "dovetailing."

With respect to subsidies to incentivize participation, the current match of 30 RMB against the minimum 100 RMB annual contribution is low when compared to emerging practices for MDCs in developing countries (where a 1:1 match is more common). The flat match also acts as a weak incentive for making contributions above the 100 RMB minimum, although it has merit from an equity perspective. A further complicating factor is that the assurance of a basic pension after the vesting period of contributions acts as a significant incentive to participate. Overall, there is no international consensus on the appropriate matching rate in MDC schemes. Thus, it will be important to monitor the pilot to see whether the 30 RMB match is sufficient, both in incentivizing participation at the basic 100 RMB contribution level and in terms of incentivizing higher individual contributions. This is a question that can only be answered empirically. The initial limited evidence from survey data suggests that there is significant concentration at the lowest contribution rate. According to a 2010 survey in Chengdu, for example, 46 percent of participants from pilot counties chose the lowest contribution rate of 100 RMB/year while only 8 percent chose the highest rate of 500 RMB/year (Wang and others 2011). A survey on pilot counties in Anhui Province also shows that more than two-thirds of participants chose the lowest contribution rate (Luo 2011)

The discussion of subsidies and incentives also raises the issue of the appropriate balance between *ex ante* subsidies (the matching of individual account contributions) and *ex post* subsidies (the provision of a basic pension benefit) in the program. Although the current emphasis on the *ex post* subsidy has the advantage of simplicity, it is less attractive in terms of a mobile rural population. Once the system matures, rural workers who enroll in an urban scheme upon migration would not benefit as greatly from the incentive effect of the *ex post* subsidy under the current design, where portability of the basic benefit entitlement remains unclear. This may be an important consideration with an increasingly mobile and urbanizing population. Increasing the *ex ante* subsidy by increasing matching would lessen this possible disincentive effect.

An obvious question raised by a shift in the balance of public subsidies from *ex post* to *ex ante* is its impact on the poverty alleviation objective of the basic rural pension. If greater public subsidies were shifted *ex ante*, maintaining a neutral fiscal impact would require a lower basic pension in a situation where the 55 RMB benefit is already below the rural poverty line and could reduce the basic benefit below the average *dibao* level, which has additional negative incentive effects. This could be dealt with in at least two ways. First, it may be possible to effect a partial benefit reduction of the basic benefit for individuals above a certain income threshold in order to protect the benefit level for poorer elderly people.[33] Second, the local level may be able to top up the basic benefit to ensure that it exceeds the local *dibao* level, though this could not be assured in areas that are fiscally strapped.

A second issue that merits consideration relates to fund management. The initial approach of allowing fund management at the county level has a range of drawbacks, including investment risk and the risk that funds are used for other pressing purposes, leaving accounts that are in practice "empty." Such localized management complicates the provision of portability of account balances for rural workers who move beyond their home counties. In addition, the demographic trends in rural areas suggest that a sizeable reserve fund will likely be necessary in the rural system, the management of which is best done at higher levels.

In addition to the drawbacks of subprovincial fund management, the use of the one-year deposit rate of interest as the rate of return for individual accounts is likely to prove problematic over time (as has been the case for urban schemes). Although very secure, such a low rate virtually guarantees a low individual account balance at retirement and thus weakens participation incentives for rural workers. Even given the appropriate desire to limit investment risk, other approaches which better balance risk and return on individual accounts would be worth exploring further (as, for example, Guangdong has started to do on a pilot basis with some of its urban system pension accumulations).

The following specific elements of eligibility for the scheme should be monitored and reviewed over time:

- *Retirement age of 60 years.* For the present, this is sensible in its alignment with the urban scheme. At the same time, the aging of China's population will demand the upward adjustment of retirement ages over time; this should be considered sooner rather than later by both rural and urban systems. A pressing need exists for reliable—and periodically updated—rural mortality tables to assess the appropriateness of the coefficient of 139 in the drawdown phase of individual account balances. The coefficient is aligned with that used by the urban system but should, in principle, be fine-tuned in line with rural mortality trends. Unisex life expectancy tables published by the World Health Organization for China indicate that life expectancy at age 60 is 19.1 years or 229 months, suggesting that the 139 figure is significantly too low.[34] This indicates that there is a substantial subsidy embedded in the annuity factor for the individual account pension of about 65 percent of the benefit amount.

- *Policies for vulnerable groups for whom local governments are expected to pay partial or full individual account contributions.* The State Council document leaves this issue open, referring to groups "with paying difficulties ... like those with serious disabilities." Given the importance of the principle of equity underlying this provision, it would be useful to develop a better defined common policy for persons for whom contributions should be made (and in what amounts). Apart from people with disabilities, for example, would adults in *dibao* households be included in this provision? Practice appears mixed, with some areas contributing on behalf of *dibao* households, in whole or in part, while other areas have adopted narrower categories of eligibility (though being in a *dibao* household appears to be the default trigger for the individual full subsidy in most areas visited by the authors).[35] It would also be useful to consider whether the central government should fund—or partly fund—such contributions, perhaps together with local authorities. Although central funding risks local level authorities gaming the system, it could presumably be controlled through clear guidelines on eligible populations and would obviate the risk that poor people in fiscally constrained localities are excluded.

- *Eligibility of workers with rural* hukou *who are resident in urban areas but not enrolled in the urban pension system.* In principle, the new scheme allows them to participate and to receive local and central subsidies even when resident in cities. It will be useful in monitoring implementation to see how this plays out and to study the policy interactions with emerging URPS schemes. There is some evidence of such behavior from urban household surveys in major capitals in 2010 (Giles and others 2011). Although the central subsidy should, of course, not be affected by the current residence of workers (rather than *hukou*), the incentives are questionable for local authorities to (1) match individual account contributions and (2) top up the basic pension benefit for workers with local rural *hukou* who are not currently resident in the rural locality.

- *The policy anticipates but does not clearly address the portability of pension rights under the new scheme.* This is an important issue and should be addressed soon. Portability of vested rights and individual account balances—both across rural areas and between rural and urban schemes—is important given China's increasingly mobile labor force. The recent national document on the portability of rights within the urban old-age insurance system suggests that the issue has been recognized. Ensuring that portability (both in policy and in practice) in the new rural scheme is aligned with emerging practices in the urban scheme is essential if the new scheme is to achieve its social security and labor market objectives. In practical terms, this will require the rapid development of systems to reliably transfer information and funds across localities.

The implementation of the scheme will face four key challenges (on which MHRSS is already focusing) (Dorfman and others 2012):

- *The first relates to capacity at local levels, particularly at the county level and below.* The massive and very rapid expansion of the system will place demands on local-level implementation and delivery capacity. These demands will present real challenges in many areas, particularly in terms of service delivery for participants and beneficiaries. The intention of the government is to introduce rural social security service centers at least down to (and ideally below) the county level. However, existing staffing ratios imply service loads in an expanding system well above those that one would typically observe internationally for similar schemes. At the same time, interesting experiences are emerging from initial partnerships with the banking sector that are helping to spread the administrative burden of managing client contributions and basic recordkeeping (for example, Guangdong province has a general service agreement with the Postal Savings Bank, which collects contributions, maintains individual pension accounts, and is the vehicle for direct payment of pensions).

- *The second relates to the information systems required to support the new program and to link it to related programs such as New Cooperative Medical Scheme and other localities.* The government's stated intention is to extend the systems to grassroots levels, although this presents challenges for both the capacities of the systems and the training of personnel. Moreover, it risks fragmentation of information systems if not closely managed (although the standardized software from MHRSS should help in promoting greater coherence than has been observed in urban schemes). The standard software has allowed in some provinces the direct management of system-wide recordkeeping at the provincial level by the Social Insurance Administration under MHRSS.

- *The third relates to the penetration of financial and banking services in rural areas and the impact of implementing the scheme on payment systems and the systems of collections for contributions.* MHRSS is working actively on this issue in cooperation with national banks for better rural coverage (one example of such a partnership is with the Postal Savings Bank noted above), but even banks with wide coverage do not presently have branches at all townships (an estimated 7 percent of townships did not yet have a bank in 2009). This may be an area where exploring roles for nonbank financial institutions and relying on mobile banking merit further exploration.[36]

- *The fourth relates to the question of the level of contribution matching for individual accounts across counties (which raises issues of equity).* The obvious challenge is avoiding a situation in which poor counties fail to match individual account contributions (resulting in lower accumulations for the poor), while still maintaining enough local interest in the scheme to encourage accountability at the county level. Initial experience suggests that different balances being struck. In some provinces (for example, Inner Mongolia and Ningxia), the province has been financing the match, whereas in others (for example, Shandong), the aim is to have matching entirely financed by counties.

As stated earlier, the NRPS has many positive and innovative features. At the same time, although the scheme relies on a broadly sensible design and represents a milestone in social policy in China, the issues discussed above identify scope for improvement and further refinement of policy parameters if China's objectives are to be fully attained. In addition to the NRPS, the national government introduced a URPS in mid-2011 (State Council 2011). The URPS shares almost the same design as the NRPS, with exactly same basic pension level determined by the central government, the same financing design, and the same matching contribution provided by local authorities. The scheme aims to provide minimum voluntary pension savings arrangements to cover the unemployed, other urban workers without employment contracts, and urban retirees without alternative sources of retirement income. Significantly, it is only open to those with local urban *hukou,* so that migrant workers from rural or other urban areas are not eligible to participate in their city of residence but only their area of *hukou* registration (whether rural or urban). Survey evidence from selected major cities in China for 2010 confirmed that a proportion of migrant workers reporting participation in pension schemes were in fact contributing to schemes in locations other than that of their surveyed residence (Giles and others 2011). One characteristic that is distinct for the urban scheme is that contribution tiers can range up to 1,000 RMB/year.

As with the rural scheme, the URPS comes on the back of considerable experimentation with urban residents' schemes at the sub-national level during the 2000s. In cities with sufficient fiscal capacity, the expansion in local schemes was based on a design with a combination of an individual account and a basic pension. In some cases (for example, Hangzhou), individual account contributions were matched by local authorities, whereas in others (for example, Beijing), no such match was used. In richer areas, such schemes had often already been merged with ongoing rural schemes to achieve an integrated residents' pension scheme, in numerous cases with benefit levels that are equivalent between participants with urban *hukou* and those with rural *hukou* from the prefecture. Like the NRPS, such initiatives seem to offer promise as vehicles for expanding pension coverage to the nonwage sector and for promoting the vision laid out by policy makers of rural-urban integration.

In light of emerging experience with rural and urban residents' pensions, the following section reviews some core design principles. The section that follows outlines a proposal for pensions for rural and urban nonwage populations, which shares both the goals of the NRPS and the URPS and some of their key features while offering some points of variation in policy parameters that may be worth considering as China continues its efforts to achieve rapid coverage expansion.

## Pension System Design Principles

Both in China and internationally, there is consensus that a pension scheme should satisfy the following criteria:

- *Adequacy*—The benefit levels it provides should be sufficient to perform the most basic function of promoting security in old age.
- *Broad coverage*—The system should provide basic protection to the vast majority of workers and retirees, offering the possibility of saving for retirement and life-cycle consumption smoothing, including for those without stable incomes.
- *Sustainability*—The system needs to be designed to make it robust in the face of shocks and demographic trends (the latter is of special concern in China, as was noted earlier).
- *Affordability*—The system should be affordable by the government, individuals, and employers, both in a strict financial sense and, more

broadly, at a level that does not inhibit labor market efficiency and the economic competitiveness of enterprises.

- *Multilayered*—While perhaps not as axiomatic as the principles above, international experience strongly points to the benefits of diversification of risks during the accumulation and decumulation phases of a pension system, thereby contributing to benefit predictability.

Apart from these principles, a further consideration for a pension system for rural and urban nonwage populations is the future integration between urban and rural pension systems and the issue of portability. Although "integration" is unlikely, at least in the foreseeable future, a common design framework is useful to facilitate portability between systems. Equalization of benefits between rural and urban areas is one principle worth pursuing. As has been well documented, mass migration to urban centers has taken place in recent decades, with estimates of the so-called floating population at about 150 million workers, of whom roughly two-thirds were migrant workers from rural areas.[37] In recent years, these workers have also tended to stay for longer periods in their destination location, with about two-thirds of migrant workers remaining resident for three or more years. This reflects the long-term trend in the labor market toward greater urbanization; in 2011, China became more than 50 percent urban. In such cases, the need for workers to have their pension accumulations and entitlements move with them—or be "totalized" between different locations so that they enjoy their cumulative benefits from different locations at retirement—is increasingly important.

## Proposal for a National Pension System for Nonwage Populations

This section proposes an integrated basic two-pillar pension system for rural and urban nonwage populations that borrows significantly from the design of the current rural and urban residents' pilots, while suggesting some adaptations that may increase the strengths of the system over time. The two pillars proposed are the following:

- *A Voluntary Individual Retirement Insurance Scheme (VIRIS)* along the lines of the national *NRPS and URPS*. It would be an integrated scheme covering rural nonwage workers and urban residents. The VIRIS scheme would be voluntary, with contributions made on a monthly, quarterly, biannual, or annual basis. Individual contributions would be matched with a governmental subsidy. The matching subsidy would be based on a national framework allowing for a minimum match, which could be supplemented from local finances. The scheme would be fully funded, with a rate of return guaranteed by the central authorities to reduce the risk to contributors of having "empty" accounts.

- *A Citizens' Social Pension (CSP)* to ensure a basic level of income support for the rural and urban elderly who are unable to meet basic subsistence needs from contributory pension sources. A key principle of such a benefit would be that it should be set nationally in a common way based on a proportion of the regional average wage (for urban residents) or the regional average per capita income (for rural residents), thus providing a comparable level of income support above a basic subsistence level (proxied by the *dibao* threshold or poverty line in rural areas).

The combination of these two pillars shares a similar set of objectives with the current NRPS and URPS, although with less stringent eligibility criteria for the CSP relative to the basic pension in NRPS and URPS. The proposed structure would primarily seek to provide an enhanced safety net for the elderly with inadequate or no participation in the urban old-age insurance scheme at a stage in their lives when they will have decreasing capacity to generate income and, hence, to mitigate old-age poverty. Second, it would provide incentives for nonwage rural and urban people to save during their working lives for their retirement. Third, it would provide greater uniformity of pension arrangements across space, thereby facilitating the aggregation of pension savings and labor mobility between rural and urban areas.

A key starting point for design of any pension system is the target benefit level that the system would aim to provide retirees after a lifetime of work and long period of contributions. The target benefit level should consider the combined pension from both an individual's account and the social pension, as well as anticipated voluntary family savings. Policy makers should consider how the target benefit level might vary across cohorts and among persons with different contribution histories. The target benefit level could be the poverty line or some other threshold, such as the *dibao* threshold or the *dibao* threshold plus some amount, to ensure incentives to contribute. The target benefit level should in principle be indexed or set relative to per capita income. Options for the relative contribution of the VIRIS and the CSP to achieving this targeted level of income replacement are discussed later.

Following the lead of the individual account design in the NRPS and URPS, the proposed model for the VIRIS is an MDC scheme whereby nonwage rural and urban worker contributions to individual accounts are incentivized by a matching contribution from government.[38] The contributions would be voluntary and flat, as in the NRPS and URPS, but benchmarked against average urban wages and rural incomes in the area. Benefits would take the form of an annuity for those with adequate accumulations. As with the NRPS and URPS, the objectives of the VIRIS would be to (1) provide a uniform framework for pension savings for people in the nonwage sector in rural and urban areas, including those migrating to urban areas and rural areas where they do not have *hukou*, (2) subsidize a minimum savings level as a means of prefunding future retirement benefits, and (3) support labor mobility through a uniform framework.

The proposed approach is motivated by the same concerns as the current individual account portion of the NRPS and URPS. First, the nature of work for nonwage and variable employment relationships makes it difficult to mandate participation. Second, the uncertainties and volatility of nonwage income generates high levels of precautionary savings among households primarily dependent on such income. Thus, creating incentives for such workers to lock up their savings in a pension scheme is likely to be necessary. Third, an individual account accumulation creates the opportunity to craft rules for selectively using accumulations during people's working lives in the face of specified shocks.[39] Finally, keeping the design simple—a flat rate contribution and a 1:1 match with a standard subsidy from the central government to provinces, for example—facilitates implementation, is easily understood by farmers and informal sector workers, and supports fiscal planning and allocation. The following paragraphs discuss the design issues of the VIRIS in more detail.

### Design Issues in the VIRIS
*Voluntary participation.* Given the nature of nonwage employment, making the VIRIS voluntary is sensible for a variety of reasons, including (1) the volatility of nonwage incomes, (2) high discount rates among rural and urban self-employed and informal sector workers, (3) traditional mistrust of government savings schemes, and (4) a history of low or negative real rates of return on savings. In addition, it would seem advisable

to have flexibility on the periodicity of contributions within a year to allow for the specificities of rural and informal incomes and to facilitate access. Such an incentive-based approach (rather than mandated participation) has resulted in high coverage in the NRPS and URPS in recent years. A voluntary approach is also consistent with international practice.

*Matching subsidy.* Offering a matching subsidy in the NRPS and URPS represents a major shift and recognition by authorities that incentives are needed to attract the participation of rural and urban nonwage populations. The policy direction is also consistent with experience in many OECD countries and in middle-income countries such as Brazil and Mexico, as will be discussed further later. The need for incentives has been addressed in the Chinese literature, and the move toward public subsidies for rural pensions has generally been supported.[40]

Determining the appropriate rate of matching subsidies by the public sector (and, hence, the fiscal cost of the match) is not straightforward; the performance of the new schemes should be closely monitored to select the most appropriate match in the medium term. This will depend on several factors including available resources, the elasticity of take-up against different rates of matching (see figure A.8 for illustration of this relationship), and the interaction of the contributory system with other forms of public transfers for the elderly. Despite the widespread existence of matching fully funded pension schemes, virtually no robust evidence relates rates of matching with participation in different settings. Too low a match will create insufficient incentive for participation. Too high a match will create a fiscal burden that is larger than necessary.

A related question is whether the match should vary as a function of the level of individual contributions or should be flat, perhaps based on some share of average rural income or urban wages in the area. This involves a trade-off between equity and fiscal concerns, on one hand, and the relative strength of incentives to contribute above the minimum rate, on the other. The evidence on savings behavior in China suggests that concerns about incentivizing savings for retirement may be less acute than they are in many countries, thus strengthening the justification for focusing on the lower end of the income distribution that may be vulnerable in retirement.

Although no strong evidence exists to suggest an optimal MDC matching rate, simulations are instructive. Palacios and Robalino (2009) estimate that an MDC approach can be cost effective provided that (1) the take-up

**Figure A.8    Take-up Rate and Matching Contributions**

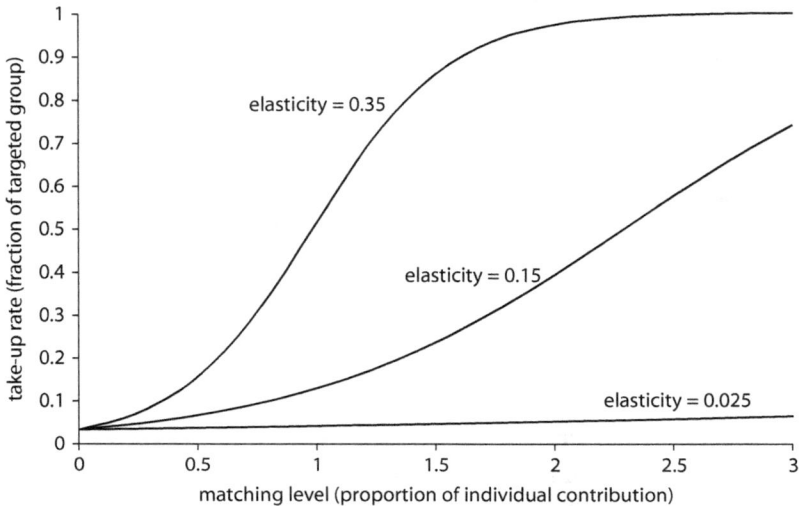

*Source:* Palacios and Robalino 2009. The take-up rate is defined by $TR=\exp(z)/(1-\exp(z))$, where $z=-3.45+b\times(0.05\times m)/0.5$, where $b/100$ is the take-up rate matching elasticity and $m$ is the level of matching. In this example, 0.05 refers to the contribution rate expressed as a share of average earnings and 0.5 is the income of the plan member relative to average earnings. The parameter $-3.45$ was calibrated to reproduce a take-up rate of 3 percent when $m=0$.

rate/matching elasticity is not too low (below about 0.15) and (2) individual contribution rates are not too low (below about 5 percent of average earnings). Overall, this study suggests that matching rates should not be below 0.5 and could aim to match 1.0 in contributions.[41] These findings must be interpreted with caution, however, as much of the evidence on matching comes from voluntary urban enterprise occupational schemes and the 401(k) experience in the United States, which may have limited international applicability.

General revenues are generally the preferred source of funding for the matching subsidy (and are the financing source for the NRPS and URPS) although experience exists in China and internationally of using earmarked revenues to provide partial funding. Brazil's rural social pension program, for example, is funded from an earmarked rural employer tax of 2 percent. In China, Zhuhai city pioneered the use of land transaction revenues, beginning in 2006, to finance a reserve fund for incremental pensions and for those who have exhausted the accumulations of their individual account.[42]

A clear decision should be taken on which level(s) of government (national, provincial, municipal or county) should finance matching contributions for individual accounts. The higher the level of financing, the lower is the risk that the matching contribution could be reduced or limited because of local fiscal circumstances. However, this must be balanced against the practicalities of matching in an environment where contributions will vary across and within provinces (and hence be potentially complex for the national government either to determine the matching funds, or to provide a flat match that would result in variable relative incentives across space). In an effort to finance a uniform national subsidy, the central government may place more weight on the flat portion of a future integrated scheme. In this light, it is recommended that matching funds come from the provincial level or below, with the central government contributing a minimum matching contribution.

Another important question is whether to mandate employers and collectives to contribute to matching individual contributions in cases where such an employment relationship exists. Although this may well be desirable in principle—and would provide closer parallels with the urban old-age insurance scheme—the experience of previous rural schemes suggests that it may not be realistic.[43] The NRPS allows for such contributions but does not rely on them to the degree that some schemes did in the past.

A final important question is how to set the *level* of contribution. Based on experience with the NRPS and the desirability of establishing a common social policy framework, it would be sensible to set contributions at a uniform percentage of the regional average rural income (for rural populations) and the regional average wage (for urban workers), subject to a national floor to ensure some minimum protection in old age. This already appears to be happening to some extent in the national rural pilot counties and urban resident schemes, although average contribution levels vary widely. These percentages should be based on simulations where contributions and retirement ages are varied, benefits are assumed to be indexed to inflation in retirement, and separate mortality tables are applied to rural and urban populations. The values chosen should be set such that they generate levels of income replacement that satisfy the social policy targets established by the authorities.

**Benefit amounts and payout.** Vesting requirements for individual accounts are probably unnecessary if such accounts are delinked from receipt of a basic benefit as suggested by this report.[44] However, the question remains whether a maximum age should be set at which people can begin to participate in the VIRIS. The arrangements used by previous local schemes are not particularly informative in this regard. Given this, the authorities might consider giving persons with small account balances at retirement a lump-sum payout rather than an annuity. More broadly, important questions exist regarding how to treat those who will not contribute long enough to generate a reasonable pension from their individual account and, hence, regarding the interaction between the individual account and the CSP (discussed further below).

As is the case for the NRPS and URPS, the benefit amount generated from individual accounts should be determined based on an individual's account balance at retirement. The formula for computing benefits for those who are in the scheme long enough to generate a reasonable pension must be determined. Of key importance are having current and accurate rural and urban mortality tables, preferably based on the 2010 census and on disaggregated data at least to the provincial level. As discussed earlier, significant variation has been observed in how benefits have been computed under previous rural pension schemes in China. Beijing and Baoji divided individual account balances at retirement by 139 for those retiring at regular age, Zhuhai used a factor of 180, and Suzhou a factor of only 120. Although 139 has been adopted by the NRPS and URPS (resulting from the combination of a conditional life expectancy at age 60 and an assumed drawdown period interest rate of 4 percent), this may need closer review as the schemes achieve wider coverage and mature. Currently the average mortality figures for China discussed above suggest that there is a substantial implicit subsidy in the current schemes. This could be addressed by use of updated and separate urban and rural mortality tables. As is the case for any funded scheme, the retirement age should be left to individual choice, although the age of eligibility for the CSP will influence individual decisions.

The key determinant of the real value of the VIRIS pension will be the rate of return earned on contributions during the accumulation phase. Figure A.9 presents a simulation of the benefit level from an individual account based on a total annual contribution of 360 RMB in present-value terms (just under three times the current minimum combined contribution from the individual plus a government match) and based on the assumptions that (1) the scheme is launched in 2010, (2) rural mortality remains unchanged, (3) the retirement age is increased (to age 65), (4) benefits are price indexed, and (5) other assumptions as

**Figure A.9    Stylized Example of Annuitized Monthly Benefits Based on Different Contribution Histories**

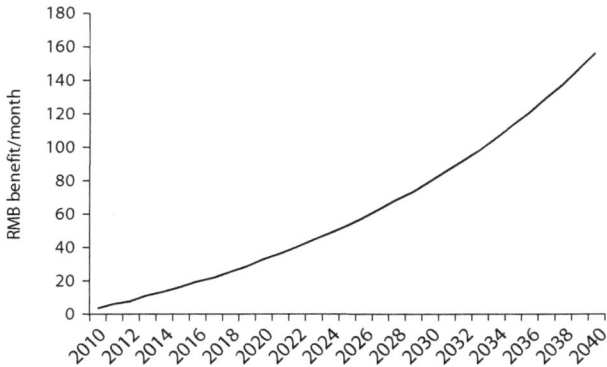

Source: World Bank estimates.

Note: Projections are in constant real terms. Key assumptions: (1) contributions of 30 RMB/month beginning in 2010, (2) retirement age of 65, male life expectancy (2008) remaining constant through the projection period, (3) real interest rate on account balances 5.0 percent, (4) price indexation, (5) the wedge between real rate of return and real wage growth is −1 percent over the first 10 years and 1 percent afterwards, and (6) the scheme begins in 2010.

described below the figure. The figure underscores the relatively modest individual account accumulation that will likely result under this set of plausible assumptions with a retirement age that is notably higher than that presently used in the NRPS and URPS. Of course, the national pilots' total replacement rates will not be based solely on benefits paid from individual accounts, but the example underscores the importance of ongoing consideration of the *total replacement rates* that the authorities will seek from their rural and urban residents' schemes and the contribution toward this level of income replacement that can realistically be expected from individual accounts under the current minimum required contributions and government match.

The other crucial determinant of benefits from the VIRIS is the assumed retirement age. In principle, any age could be chosen in a new scheme, but it is important not to make the age too low because doing so will reduce the levels of income replacement it can provide. To this end— and consistent with proposals for the urban scheme—an age of 65 years old has been assumed. A gradual transition to this retirement age should be undertaken over time, as is proposed in the other appendixes for the urban workers' scheme.

It may also be desirable in the medium term to permit account holders to borrow a portion of their VIRIS account accumulations at a specified interest rate and with legally binding repayment conditions. Eligible conditions might include the purchase of a home, certain types of health care costs, or educational costs for children. In some systems, including 401(k) accounts in the United States, such "borrowings" are repaid at a designated interest rate by the individual. In other schemes, loans simply reduce the total accumulated balance. Given the volatility of nonwage incomes and the economic conditions of residents who work outside the formal sector, the opportunity to borrow from one's individual accounts would be an attractive feature of the scheme; consideration should be given to how such a feature would be structured.

Rules for payouts would also need to be developed. The options include annuitization, phased withdrawal, and lump-sum payouts. Previous rural schemes have used phased withdrawal; this would be adequate for the foreseeable future, but authorities should look toward eventually providing annuities instead. The lump-sum option, however, is likely to be important for the transitional generation (as is discussed further below). Some previous rural schemes in China provided for the lump-sum repayment of contributions to those without full contribution histories. In some cases, the repayment was made at the point of retirement (for example, in Beijing and Zhuhai), and in others, during the accumulation phase. Others have also given older cohorts the option of continuing to make contributions for up to five years after reaching the normal retirement age.

***Notional or fully funded accounts for VIRIS?*** A bigger picture question on the proposed VIRIS is whether the funding of public subsidies for individual accounts should be actual or notional.[45] The issue of investment rules for the VIRIS is not simply one of likely rates of return. If investment of accumulations is restricted to bank deposits at fixed interest rates—as has been the case in urban and most pilot rural schemes to date—the more fundamental question becomes whether funded individual accounts or notional accounts are the preferred funding approach. The relative attraction of actual versus notional funding depends on a few key factors. The first is the investment rules (to include consideration of possible guarantees for rates of return) for the VIRIS. If investments are constrained to fixed interest deposits in public sector banks, the difference in risks between funded and NDC accounts is significantly reduced, yet the return may be insufficient for benefit adequacy. Second, the policy choices for the future of the urban system may be relevant, given the government's desire for greater harmonization of urban and rural pension systems over time. If the urban system moves to an NDC design in the future, the attraction of notional funding for subsidies on individual accounts is increased. Counterbalancing these factors, however, are two significant issues that are specific to the proposed VIRIS. First, one finds a lack of awareness among farmers and urban nonwage populations of the NDC concept and natural skepticism given past scheme performance on the promises of pension schemes that are not funded—"real money" would be a more intuitive concept for farmers and urban nonwage populations. Second, and even more importantly from a structural viewpoint, the demographic transition in urban and more particularly rural areas in the coming decades would argue against an NDC approach. On balance, therefore, it makes sense to pursue a fully funded approach to VIRIS.

***Investment rules, management, and the regulation of contributions.*** The rules governing the investment of accumulations will have important repercussions for the level of income replacement the VIRIS will provide. Experience thus far with rural and urban pension schemes in China suggests that this is a key vulnerability in terms of a scheme's ability to provide adequate benefits at retirement. At this point an appropriate governance and investment management framework for rural or urban residents' pensions is lacking. Low and volatile returns on contributions in rural pension schemes have been one of their greatest weaknesses to date, a vulnerability shared by China's funded urban schemes. The People's Bank of China requires investments to be made in one-year time deposits, which have generated low real returns over the past decade (on the order of 1–2 percent in the urban individual account system), far below both rural and urban income growth. At the same time, understandable reluctance is found on the part of policy makers to expose rural and urban nonwage populations to significant investment risk, given their general lack of financial sophistication and the underdeveloped state of governance.

An alternative—and in the view of this report preferred—approach would be for the central government to guarantee rate of return on the VIRIS accounts. This guaranteed rate could be set at the equivalent of the NDC rate of return in the proposed MORIS (that is, national GDP growth). This would offer a workable compromise between the competing objectives of security and the adequacy of returns.

Although it may be too complicated at this stage, an option for the future is to allow for different investment rules for different cohorts of workers participating in the VIRIS scheme. For older workers, having conservative investment rules make sense in terms of limiting exposure to market risk and volatility and their lower degree of financial literacy. However, for younger workers, the compounded effects of low rates of return on conservative investments rules are likely to be large, and their extended contribution histories will allow for the averaging of market volatility across their life cycle. The authorities might consider using age-based portfolio default rules that provide for more aggressive investment for younger contributors that gradually become more conservative over the life cycle to focus on preserving the value of accumulations at retirement.

Another question that merits consideration is whether a reserve fund is desirable. Such funds are more typically used to address fluctuations in returns or the exhaustion of benefits due to longevity. In principle, the concept of a reserve fund is attractive, and practice in places such as Zhuhai indicates interest within China.[46]

The management of funds in individual accounts and the appropriate level of the system for doing this merit consideration. Current pilot schemes and past practice have generally involved management at the county level. However, there are clear advantages in combining funds from localities into a single pot of money that can be managed at higher levels to generate economies of scale in fund management. Experience with rural pensions thus far cautions against localized management and investment of accumulations. A sensible option would be to have funds in rural individual accounts managed by the National Social Security Fund (NSSF), although considerable preparation would be required for the infrastructure to record and remit balances to NSSF and make transfers back to paying authorities as the system matures. More specifically, the new scheme could put the public subsidy for individual accounts into the NSSF and contributions in the Agricultural Bank of China, the Postal Savings Bank, or other suitable financial institutions, with a uniform interest rate announced nationally and recorded into individual account passbooks. Although the option of contracting out fund management to authorized asset managers might be considered in the longer run, this would require a much stronger regulatory and accountability framework than exists presently.[47]

With respect to the regulation of VIRIS, presently there is inadequate capacity; this has been an ongoing weakness of rural schemes in China.[48] In addition, existing capacity to regulate even urban schemes is stretched.

Thus, it would seem desirable to not create new institutions for regulating VIRIS, but rather to build upon and strengthen capacity in the existing urban old-age insurance institutions to expand to non-wage workers in rural and urban areas. This also raises the issue of critical mass in regulatory capacity.

***Portability between schemes.*** Transition issues will become important as the NRPS and URPS schemes mature. The first type of transition is from old to new rural and urban resident pension schemes within the same locality. Practices in China have varied, with areas such as Beijing allowing portability of funded accumulations from old to new schemes, and others like the province of Hunan stipulating that participants must close out their accounts in old schemes before starting afresh in new pilots.[49] The national schemes appear to allow transfers of balances from prior schemes. The second (and ultimately more important) issue is portability between rural and urban schemes. This will be critical to reaching the government's stated goal of an integrated social security system by 2020. The ease with which this can be done has varied according to scheme design and the compatibility of the national rural and urban residents' pilots with existing urban schemes. If a former farmer has accumulated enough years in the urban residents' or workers' systems at retirement, he or she will enjoy an urban pension (with an allowance for lower rural contributions), whereas his or her urban contributions will be credited to the rural pension scheme if the accumulation period in the urban system is less than 15 years. In principle the funded portion of all schemes is easily made portable. The MDC design adopted in the NRPS and URPS schemes—and also proposed here—has no social pooling in a strict sense, though how to allow for the totalization of contribution histories across space in the case of the NRPS and URPS would need further attention.

Having a funded portion in the VIRIS scheme may play a useful role for workers who move either to areas where they do not have *hukou* and/or across rural and urban areas. In principle, it should be straightforward to transfer balances from one scheme to another in the funded portion through totalization agreements between schemes. This raises the question, however, of whether to also consider the option of pooling VIRIS accumulations in the provinces and to combine fund management. Such an approach has merit, although it may require greater coordination than is possible in the short run.

The issue of portability raises a host of design and implementation questions that will need to be closely considered during the pilot phase of the VIRIS. When a worker moves, will the funds in his or her account move or will only his or her contribution records do so? How will the system account for accumulations in the rural system when workers move to the urban system? Finally, are pensions paid from various locations or from a single payment authority? These sorts of practical questions raise issues for recordkeeping, communication and information exchange between systems, and the exchange of account information. In principle, such practical questions should be capable of being addressed by standardized record-keeping and reporting formats for the NRPS and URPS schemes (which have been developed and is being disseminated by MHRSS). It would also require the harmonization of fund transfer and pension disbursement procedures. Again, some degree of centralization would be desirable to lessen administrative demands at the lower levels, although this might be at provincial level within national guidelines. These are issues on which elaborated guidance from the central authorities will be necessary over time.

Although many open questions remain—and will doubtlessly be revisited in light of implementation experience with the ongoing NRPS and URPS schemes—below is a summary of the proposed key features of the VIRIS (see figure 9):

- Voluntary, flat contributions by nonwage urban and rural residents
- Funded defined-contribution design
- Applied to all nonwage residents not covered by other schemes
- Contributions based on a percentage of regional rural per capita income and urban average wages matched with government subsidies with the option of making higher individual contributions above a minimum level. Where appropriate, the contribution benchmarks may be fully harmonized between rural and urban resident schemes where prefectures deem it desirable.
- Rate of return on accumulations = national GDP growth rate, with the interest rate guaranteed by the central government
- Portable accumulations
- Individual accumulation paid out as an annuitized benefit
- Reserve investment management at a provincial or national level.

### International Experience with MDCs
The proposed matching defined-contribution approach under the VIRIS is relatively new but is being explored in some developing countries.[50] Many OECD countries provide tax incentives to encourage workers and

employers to contribute to voluntary private pension schemes. Most OECD countries provide incentives for employer matching contributions by allowing tax deductions for employers on such contributions up to specified limits. In the United States, for example, the value of foregone tax revenue for such deductions is estimated to be about 1 percent of GDP. Evidence suggests that such programs increase participation, although the impact on savings is on its composition rather than its overall level. What seems clearer is that tax exemptions increase savings among low-income people and others with low savings rates.[51] However, given progressive tax scales in most OECD countries, subsidies tend to disproportionately benefit better-off workers. In any event, using tax exemption to subsidize pension contributions would likely prove less effective in developing countries where the poor are less likely to be in the tax net in the first place and where distributional concerns on the use of public subsidies may be more pressing. In China a tax exemption would be meaningless for the large majority of rural and urban nonwage workers because their incomes are below the minimum personal income tax threshold. This is the reason for preferring a direct match approach. This is precisely the option chosen by the Chinese authorities in NRPS and URPS and seems appropriate.

Experience with MDCs in developing countries is more limited, as suggested earlier. Noteworthy examples come from the Indian states of Rajasthan and Madhya Pradesh, both of which have MDC pension schemes in operation for certain categories of informal sector workers. The authorities provide a 1:1 match on contributions from the state governments under the schemes. Funds are invested by contracted asset managers with no guaranteed rate of return for contributors. The state of Andhra Pradesh started a similar scheme in 2009 targeted to women in self-help groups with a subsidy of about $10 equivalent per annum per person, which is expected to produce a pension just above the poverty line. The oldest such MDC scheme in India is in West Bengal, which has provided a 1:1 match for roughly 60 categories of informal sector workers since the early 2000s.

As is the case for all defined-contribution schemes, the design of MDCs requires two policy issues to be addressed: (1) how to handle the death or disability of contributors and (2) managing financial risk for contributors. With respect to the former, pure defined-contribution schemes do not, by construction, provide insurance against premature death or disability during the accumulation phase. As a result, it is common to purchase group life and disability insurance policies for contributors in the scheme. Such policies would cover the difference between the individual's account accumulation at the point of death or disability and the benefits paid under the policy in the event of death or disability. The premium is calculated based on actuarial statistics for the group. Managing financial risk is handled differently in different countries ranging from the imposition of conservative portfolio rules (as is the case in China presently) to guaranteed rates of return to transferring all risk to contributors (as is the case in the Indian schemes described above). Given the likely degree of risk aversion on the part of rural workers in China and its underdeveloped regulatory framework, offering a guaranteed rate of return, as suggested above, seems the preferred option for the medium term. Such guarantees, however, create an open-ended fiscal burden because of the indeterminate size of the contingent liability they create.

### Citizens' Social Pension

The CSP is proposed as an essential instrument for those workers under the MORIS or VIRIS schemes with insufficient work histories and account accumulations to support a basic level of subsistence in old age. The objective of the proposed CSP would be to ensure basic living subsistence for those elderly who are not covered by existing pension provisions or are unable to generate adequate retirement income from their contributions during their working age. This could be for a variety of reasons, including sickness, disability, or time out of the workforce (for example, for child rearing or study). The rationale for a CSP is to (1) provide a low level of support for the growing number of elderly with minimal resources to prevent them from falling into poverty in their old age and (2) reduce incentives for overly high precautionary savings before retirement. While an alternative option of an enhanced *dibao* benefit for the elderly poor was considered, the CSP approach was felt to be preferred for several reasons (see box A.2).

The proposed CSP would follow uniform design parameters nationwide, although benefits would reflect local characteristics (see table A.5). Provincial authorities would be held accountable for observance of the national framework. The amount of the benefit would be set as a percentage of the regional average wage in urban areas and rural per capita income in rural areas, with the objective of exceeding the per capita benefit under the existing *dibao* scheme. A "pensions test" would reduce the benefit by a proportion of benefits received from other pension arrangements for those aged 65 to 74. The pensions test would need to be designed to reward those who contributed to other pension schemes

**Box A.2**

**Alternative Benefit Designs to Protect the Elderly Poor**

Policy makers need to decide whether a benefit to protect elderly poor would be best delivered as (1) a *dibao* supplement within the existing *dibao* program or (2) a new standalone social pension.[a] Variants of the former approach can already be seen in some parts of China, either in the form of top-ups on *dibao* benefits for poor elderly people or the more generous interpretation of *dibao* thresholds.

Two alternatives were considered, including a *dibao* supplement (an "enhanced *dibao*") and a new standalone social pension (a "Citizens' Social Pension"). Both are discussed below. As discussed further, this report argues that the standalone approach may better accommodate China's specific requirements and institutional setting.

- *An enhanced* dibao *for the elderly poor.* This could be designed in one of two ways: (1) providing *dibao* households with elderly members a supplement to their *dibao* benefit for individual elderly members (probably a flat supplement for simplicity)[b] or (2) increasing the per capita dibao threshold for the elderly so that the amount of *dibao* benefits is increased. The first approach would offer the benefit of concentrating incremental resources on the poorest elderly, whereas the second approach would widen *dibao* coverage among the elderly poor.
- *A Citizens' Social Pension for the elderly.* Analysis of the current system suggests that undercoverage of the poor is a significant issue in *dibao*.[c] Given the importance of a universal basic income support, this report concludes that a separate old-age income allowance is justified. Such a benefit would be noncontributory, most likely with distinct administration. As with the *dibao* supplement, design questions exist that must be addressed, particularly with respect to means-testing (for example, which age groups should be subject to means-testing, what criteria should be used, and how the test should be structured and administered).

Means-testing could be applied to either alternative, and options include (1) *verified means-testing,* (2) *proxy mean-testing,* and (3) *pensions testing,* which considers only the value of pension income when determining eligibility. Variants of these three basic options are also possible (for example, verified or proxy means-testing from ages 65 to 70 and a pension test thereafter).

*(continued next page)*

**Box A.2**   *(continued)*

Deciding whether to modify the existing *dibao* system or to introduce a Social Pension as a mechanism for preventing poverty among China's elderly should take into account the following considerations:

- The administrative challenges of program delivery
- The complexity of the social protection system for applicants and beneficiaries
- The potential fiscal implications of the two approaches
- The issue of horizontal equity between the elderly poor and other groups of poor
- The implications for longer-run integration of the overall pension and social assistance systems between urban and rural areas and for migrant workers and
- Social acceptability.

In light of these criteria, this report proposes the creation of a CSP with uniform design parameters nationwide, although benefit levels and financing should be locally determined based on regional average wages and living standards (as is currently the case for the urban *dibao*) (see table A.5).

a. For a general discussion of the issues involved in using social pensions versus social assistance programs to address poverty among the elderly and for a simulation of the two approaches using data sets from selected developing countries, see Grosh and Leite (2009).
b. Policy makers would have to decide whether the supplement should be uniform at the national, provincial, or subprovincial level.
c. See Chen and others (2006).

**Table A.5    Citizens' Social Pensions—Proposed Parameters**

| Issue | Provision/parameters |
|---|---|
| Applicability | All urban and rural residents |
| Eligibility | Urban or rural elderly aged 65 and higher; for persons aged 65 to 74, pension income must not be in excess of an applicable threshold |
| Benefit level (before pension test reduction) | Benefit set as percent of regional average wage (urban areas) or rural per capita income (rural areas) |
| | Benefit set above *dibao* standard |
| | Partially reduced for other pensionable income (aged 65–74) |
| | No reduction for those aged 75+ |
| | Benefit indexation: two-thirds to prices and one-third to wages |
| Financing | Noncontributory |
| | Financed from general revenues |
| | Shared responsibility between central and subnational governments |
| Interaction with *dibao* | Social pension to be included in family income for purposes of determining eligibility for *dibao* |

*Source:* Author's compilation.

while simultaneously targeting those with the least income from all sources, to include other pension benefits. Given the objective of eventually increasing the retirement age to 65 for men and women under the proposed Mandatory Occupational Retirement Insurance Scheme (MORIS), this report recommends setting 65 as the minimum age for both men and women to qualify for the CSP. This is important from a labor supply incentive viewpoint and to maintain consistency with the proposed future urban pension policy. Such a benefit would be noncontributory and financed by some combination of national, provincial, municipal, and local resources.

The proposed CSP is broadly consistent with the design of the basic benefit provision under the NRPS and URPS. The adjustment factor for the pensions test could be set as high as 50 percent initially (to provide a strong incentive to contribute to the VIRIS) but if this is too high it will more than offset the match in the VIRIS. The actual adjustment factor should be adjusted on the basis of actual experience. A stylized example is provided in figure A.10 using a benefit level linked to rural individual minimum consumption and applying a 50 percent adjustment factor.

**Figure A.10   Stylized Example of CSP Pension Benefit Levels and Composition under Proposed Scheme**

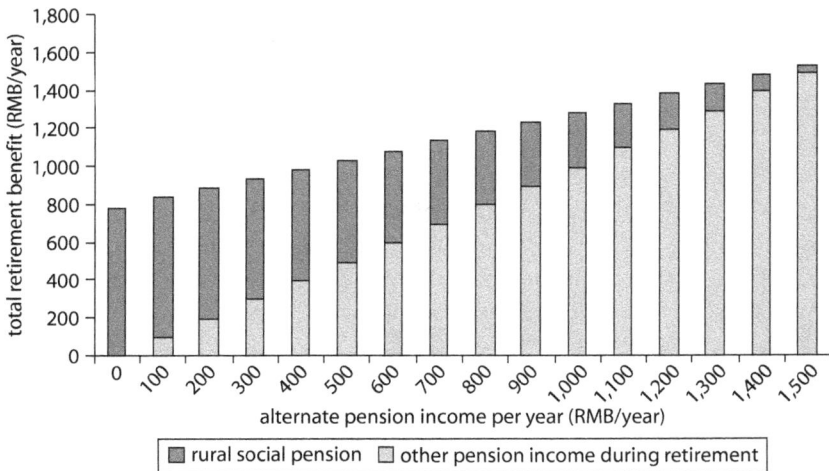

Source: World Bank estimates.
Note: Assumes CSP benefit of 788 RMB/year (2003 Ravallion-Chen rural consumption poverty level increased by the CPI from 2003 to 2009). In this example, CSP benefit is reduced by 50 percent of alternative pension income.

The CSP's value relative to the *dibao* threshold in different localities is an important design parameter. In this regard, the practice of the NRPS and URPS seems appropriate (that is, setting the CSP at a level above the *dibao* per capita threshold). This is important for incentive reasons, but— for fiscal reasons—it should not to be substantially higher. If the CSP is set too high, the incentive to contribute to the VIRIS will be weaker; if it is set too low, its poverty alleviation objective may be undermined. Under the NRPS, the central government has set the minimum flat benefit at 55 RMB monthly while allowing additional funds to be provided from subnational sources. This compares to a national average rural *dibao* threshold of 82 RMB in 2008, with a range from minimum of 26 to 267 RMB (or 11–41 percent of the national rural average wage). The *dibao* threshold rates suggest that closer attention is needed to the relative level of the CSP floor to align protections and incentives appropriately. Finally, pensions from NRPS and URPS and from the proposed CSP should not impact the receipt of the allowance for following family planning policies, although some Chinese researchers have proposed integrating the programs by using the family planning subsidy as an additional subsidy toward individual pension contributions.[52]

Key policy decisions that must be made include (1) the framework for the minimum CSP benefit level, (2) the benefit reduction applied to other pension income, (3) the approach to benefit indexation, (4) the qualifying conditions (to include age and residency), (5) the central, provincial, and local financing arrangements, and (6) the linkages to *dibao*.

Indicative cost estimates suggest that a CSP with a benefit set around the urban income poverty line would cost about 0.11 percent of 2010 GDP, rising to 0.31 percent of GDP by 2040 (see figure A.11). A rural CSP using the rural poverty line would cost around 0.11 percent of GDP in 2010 and stay relatively stable over time as a result of urbanization. These estimates will vary substantially with the benefit level, the growth in the benefit level, the level of urbanization, and the observed benefit reductions arising from the pensions test. The upward trend in cost projections reflects population aging and urbanization.[53] By comparison, by adopting a benefit level of about 28 percent of the urban average wage (the OECD average), the cost of the urban CSP would be 0.75 percent of GDP in 2010 rising to 2.1 percent of GDP by 2040 (see figure A.11). The costs presented above are indicative only; actual costs will reflect the specific parameters chosen. The fiscal burden would be quite manageable, assuming a modest supplement. For example, assuming an individual supplement of about half the average monthly *dibao* household benefit in

**Figure A.11    Indicative Cost Projections for CSP Benefits**

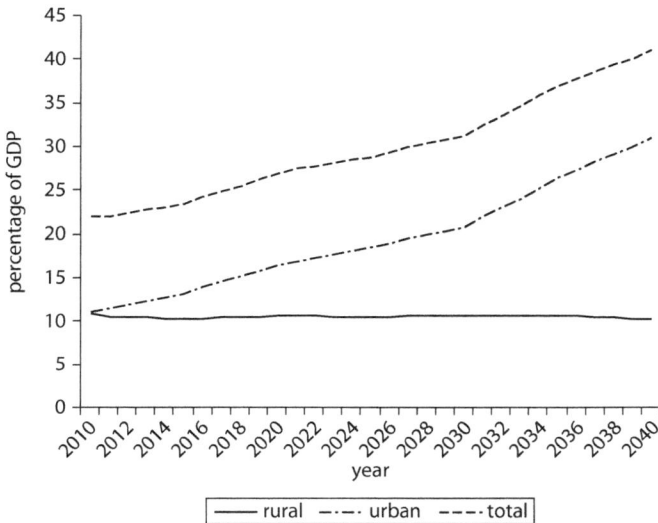

*Source:* World Bank estimates. Assumes (1) median variant urbanization 2010–2040, (2) total fertility rate of 1.8, and (3) the age distribution for the population over age 60 is the same as for the total population. The rural reduction due to pensions test and transition introduction is 5 percent in 2011, rising by 3 percent each year up to a maximum of 50 percent. The urban reduction due to pensions test is 40 percent in 2010, rising by 1 percent each year up to a maximum of 60 percent. The benefit level is assumed to grow at the rate of GDP.

2008 (or 70 RMB given that the average monthly benefit was 141 RMB), the incremental fiscal cost would be about 1.78 billion RMB, which is under 5 percent of total spending on urban *dibao* in 2008.[54] The biggest potential cost difference between the *dibao* supplement and a CSP would be if the benefit were to be made universal after a certain age. The cost of both approaches would rise as the population ages, but the fiscal burden of aging would be far greater for a CSP if it provided universal coverage beyond a certain age.

### International Experience with Social and Citizens' Pensions
Widespread experience is found with noncontributory social pensions in countries at all levels of income. The experience with reducing old-age poverty is generally positive, although issues of fiscal sustainability have arisen in lower-income settings. However, social pensions are providing to be an increasingly popular method for bridging the old-age coverage gap in pension systems.[55]

OECD countries have different approaches to social pensions, as is seen in table A.6.[56] About half of countries rely on a single approach to social pensions, the remainder rely on combinations of three basic approaches. The first is a *basic pension*—often called a *demogrant*—which is a flat benefit for the elderly awarded independent of income. Countries with basic pensions usually have some qualifying provisions, such as residency or contribution tests. A second approach is to provide a means or *"resource" tested social pension*, either through a separate program for the elderly or as part of a general social assistance scheme. Eligibility is subject to some form of means-testing, which can include income or income plus assets. The third approach is to establish a *minimum pension*, which is effectively similar to providing a resource tested pension in that it targets older people with lower incomes. The key difference is that only income from pension schemes is considered when calculating entitlement to a minimum pension. Consequently, someone with substantial income from nonpension sources can still qualify. In countries where a contribution history is required to qualify for social pensions, periods of unemployment and disability in many cases can be counted toward the qualifying period.

Among OECD countries, the replacement rate from social pensions ranges from 20 percent to 40 percent of average economy-wide earnings,

**Table A.6    Social Pensions in OECD Countries**

|  | Resource tested | Basic | Minimum |  | Resource tested | Basic | Minimum |
|---|---|---|---|---|---|---|---|
| Australia | X |  |  | Korea, Rep. | X |  |  |
| Austria | X |  |  | Luxembourg | X |  | X |
| Belgium | X |  | X | Mexico | X |  | X |
| Canada | X | X |  | Netherlands | X |  |  |
| Czech Republic |  | X | X | New Zealand | X |  |  |
| Denmark | X | X |  | Norway | X |  | X |
| Finland |  |  | X | Poland |  |  | X |
| France | X |  | X | Portugal | X |  | X |
| Germany | X |  |  | Slovak Republic |  |  | X |
| Greece | X |  | X | Spain | X |  | X |
| Hungary |  |  | X | Sweden |  |  | X |
| Iceland | X | X |  | Switzerland | X |  | X |
| Ireland | X | X |  | Turkey | X |  | X |
| Italy | X |  |  | United Kingdom | X | X | X |
| Japan |  | X |  | United States | X |  |  |

*Source:* OECD 2007.

with a cross-country average of just under 30 percent (see figure A.12). In Japan, for example, the rate is as low as 16 percent, and in Portugal, it is well over 40 percent. Comparisons are complicated by the availability of general social assistance programs for the elderly. Over the last decade, various OECD countries have significantly reformed their social pension programs, although no clear directional trend is found. Some countries— including France, Ireland, Mexico, and the Republic of Korea—have introduced (or increased the basis for) minimum pensions. Others— including Germany, Japan, and New Zealand—have cut earnings-related pensions with little impact on social pensions. Still others—including several Eastern European countries and Italy—have abolished minimum pensions altogether.[57]

As can be seen from table A.7, the most significant difference in design is whether noncontributory social pensions are universal, means-tested, or categorical in coverage. No definitive pattern by level of income exists in this respect. The broad distinction is sometimes drawn between social pension systems that are core elements of old-age security and those that are supplementary (either to contributory systems or to informal support systems). This can be shown in a shorthand manner by comparing the combination of coverage rates among the elderly and benefit levels relative to country income as is shown for selected developing countries in figure A.13.

With respect to the age of eligibility, experience also differs, but ages of between 65 and 70 are most common, as is shown in table A.7. The financing source for social pensions also varies across countries, although general revenues are most common. Brazil, in contrast, funds its social pension scheme from a 2 percent contribution from rural employers.

The impact of social pension schemes on alleviating old-age poverty in developing countries is generally positive although evidence is limited. Core schemes (found in Brazil, Bolivia, South Africa, Mauritius, Botswana, and Namibia) have been shown to reduce old-age poverty significantly while supplementary schemes have varied more widely in their targeting and their outcomes in terms of poverty reduction.[58] Evidence for other impacts from social pension schemes is even more limited, coming primarily from South Africa, Brazil, and Bolivia. The effects seem to be mixed. Positive effects may include permanent increases in income due to the investment of transfers, better health indicators, and higher school enrollment rates for children from pensioner households. Negative effects may include a reduction in labor supply on the part of other household members. The evidence is mixed on the reduction of family support to the elderly.

**Figure A.12    Value of Social Pensions as a Percent of Average Earnings in OECD Countries**

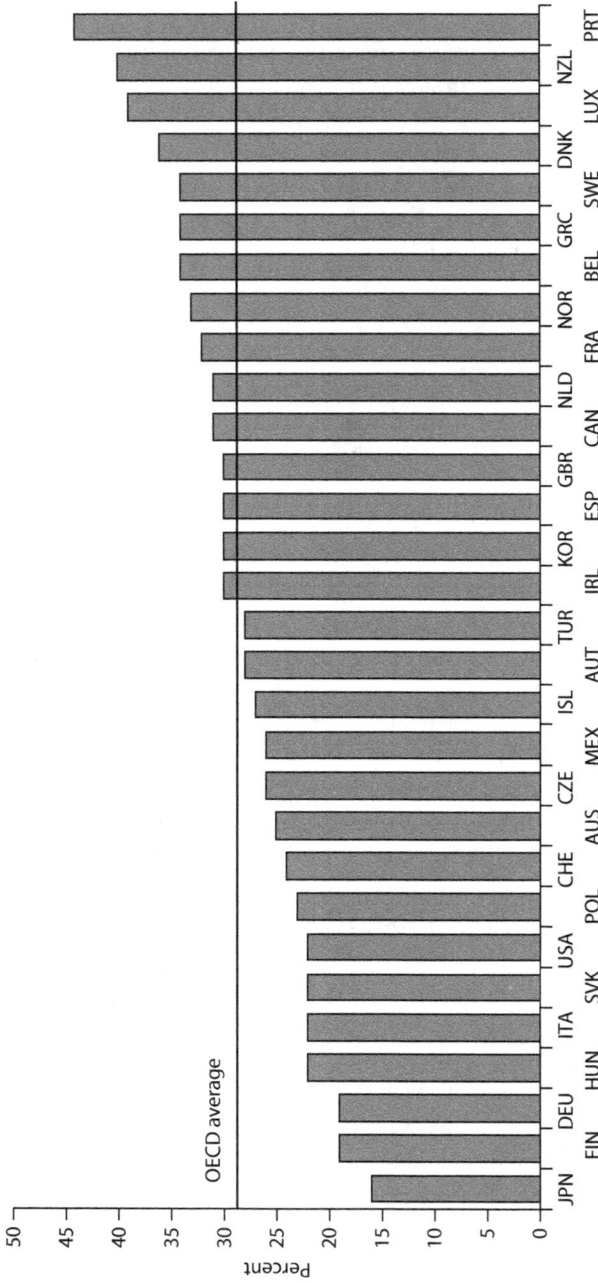

*Source:* OECD (2007).

*Note:* JPN, Japan; DEU, Germany; ITA, Italy; USA, United States; CHE, Switzerland; CZE, Czech Republic; ISL, Iceland; TUR, Turkey; KOR, Korea, Rep.; GBR, United Kingdom; NLD, Netherlands; NOR, Norway; GRC, Greece; DNK, Denmark; NZL, New Zealand; FIN, Finland; HUN, Hungary; SVK, Slovakia; POL, Poland; AUS, Australia; MEX, Mexico; AUT, Austria; IRL, Ireland; ESP, Spain; CAN, Canada; FRA, France; BEL, Belgium; SWE, Sweden; LUX, Luxembourg; PRT, Portugal.

**Table A.7 Examples of Noncontributory Pension Programs in Developing Countries**

| Country | Recent law | Type | Administration | Eligible at age |
|---|---|---|---|---|
| Argentina | 1993 | Means test | Ministry of Social Development | 70 |
| Bangladesh | 1998 | Means test | Ministry of Social Welfare | 57 |
| Bolivia | 1993 | Universal, but cohort restricted | Ministry of Economic Development | 65 |
| Botswana | 1996 | Universal | Department of Labor and Social Security | 65 |
| Brazil Social Assistance | (1974) 1993 | Means test | National Social Security Institute (INSS) | 67 |
| Brazil RMC/BPC Rural Pension | 1992 | Means test, basic contributory record | | 60 for men, 55 for women |
| Chile | 1980 and 1981 | Means test | Ministry of Development and Planning | 70 |
| Costa Rica | 1995 | Means test | Costa Rican Social Insurance Fund | 65 |
| India | 1995 | Means test | Ministry of Labor | 65 |
| Mauritius | 1976 | Universal | Ministry of Social Security and National Solidarity | 60 |
| Namibia | 1990 | Universal | Government Pension Fund (GIFF) | 60 |
| Nepal | 1995-6 | Universal | Ministry of Local Development | 75 |
| Samoa | 1990 | Universal | Labor Department and Accident Compensation Board | 65 |
| South Africa | 1992 (amended in 1997) | Means test | National and Provincial Departments of Social Development | 65 for men, 60 for women |
| Sri Lanka | 1939 | Means test | Provincial Department of Social Services | |
| Uruguay | 1995 | Means test | Ministry of Labor and Social Security and Social Welfare Fund | 70 |

*Source:* World Bank estimates.

**Figure A.13    Ratio of Social Pension to Per Capita Income Multiplied by Ratio of Number of Recipients to Number of Elderly**

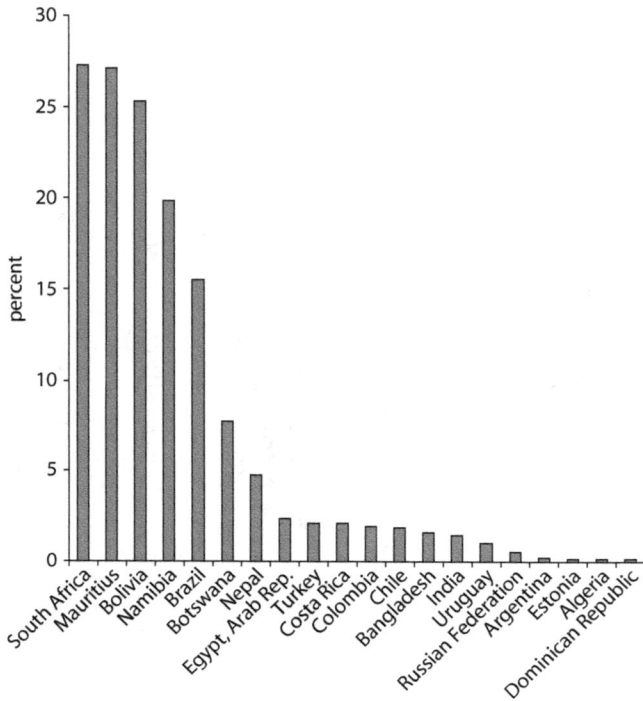

*Source:* Palacios and Sluchynskyy 2006.

Countries have also managed the interaction between social pension schemes and defined-contribution schemes in different ways. Chile serves as an interesting example. In its 2008 reform, Chile introduced a new *solidarity pension* with the objectives of (1) achieving universal pension coverage and (2) more effectively reducing old-age poverty. The *solidarity pension* also aims to better integrate the country's contributory system and the noncontributory system. The *solidarity pension* is targeted to men and women over age 65 (who are among the poorest 60 percent of the population) and is subject to a national residence requirement. For persons with no individual account accumulations, a universal basic pension is available. Those with a contribution history and individual account accumulations, however, are eligible for a top-up of their funded pension benefit subject to a ceiling on the combined amount. As a result, the top-up (known as the *solidarity contribution*) shrinks for persons with higher account balances. The withdrawal of the *solidarity pension* is designed to retain incentives to sustain higher contributions to the funded portion of the scheme. For those with higher income levels, they are permitted to supplement their individual account balances with voluntary contributions. Figure A.14 shows the scheme in graphical form. From a design viewpoint, the system strikes a useful balance between creating incentives to contribute and providing basic old-age protection for those with low or no contribution history (although concerns have been raised with the respect to its projected fiscal cost).

### The Interaction between Individual Accounts and the Social Pension and the Transitional Generation

A key policy decision relates to whether individual accounts and the CSP should be combined over time as the contributory system matures. The two broad options are (1) to retain the CSP for persons over a certain age to provide an income floor that is supplemented by benefits from individual accounts (if chosen, then questions must be addressed regarding the interaction between the CSP level and eligibility criteria and the contributory pension, as was illustrated in the case of Chile above) or (2) to gradually phase out the CSP as the contributory system matures, thereby having elderly poverty addressed through the regular social assistance program (perhaps, as is the case in some urban areas already, with an

**Figure A.14    Chile's System of Solidarity Pensions Introduced 2008**

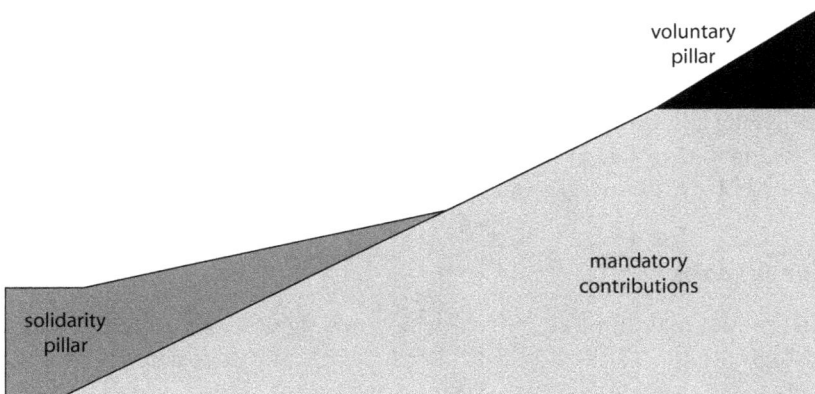

*Source:* Fajnzylber 2008.

elderly supplement on the *dibao* threshold or benefit level). This report recommends that the CSP should be retained even in the longer run although such a decision involves a pragmatic judgment of the social assistance delivery system and its ability to ensure that the elderly poor are protected.

In either case, a targeted benefit level from the combination of the CSP and individual accounts must be established, ideally falling between the poverty line and the average wage. The specific target should depend on the fiscal envelope and social policy decisions relating to work incentives as people age. The target should be indexed over time against prices or per capita incomes (or some combination of the two). This report recommends that indexation policies be aligned with those proposed for the urban old-age insurance scheme (two-thirds price indexation and one-third wages). This should be sufficient to meet poverty alleviation objectives.

Policy makers must decide how to handle those approaching retire-ment who will have insufficient time to contribute enough to their accounts to earn a reasonable pension. Special treatment is needed to manage this transition. The issue has been dealt with in a variety of ways under previous rural pension pilots in China, and various schemes have special treatment for persons above age 45. Baoji, for example, allowed persons over age 45 to receive a full pension if they contributed until reaching age 60; those over 60 were also entitled, subject to "family bind-ing." This is the same approach adopted in the NRPS and URPS. Some schemes also have provisions for the lump-sum payment of contributions by those without a full contribution history, in some cases at the point of retirement (for example, Beijing and Zhuhai) and in others during the accumulation phase. Others have older cohorts continue to make contri-butions for up to five years after reaching the normal retirement age.

One option for dealing with the transitional generation (defined, for example, as persons over age 50 in the year they start contributing) is to notionally credit their accounts with full individual and matched contribu-tions for all the years in which they did not contribute assuming a standard age of entry into the scheme of somewhere between 20 and 25 years old.

## Conclusions

The proposal outlined above clearly borrows significantly from the design of the current NRPS and URPS, while suggesting adaptations that may increase the strengths of the system over time. It could be used either as (1) the architecture for a future integrated national pension system for nonwage populations in rural and urban areas in China or (2) a list of issues and options that the government should consider as it expands the current schemes for rural and urban workers over time. In either case, the proposal provides only a general framework that would need to be elaborated to be operationalized. However, it does strike a reasonable balance between concerns for elderly welfare, fiscal demands, and labor market impacts. The discussion above is preliminary in nature and intended to provide a *big picture* overview of what a national policy framework might look like. How some of its proposed parameters and features might sensibly evolve from the national NRPS and the URPS is a subject for further discussion. However, a compelling rationale is seen for public intervention in the welfare of the elderly not already covered by urban pension systems, and the national NRPS and URPS demonstrate the commitment of the authorities to achieving their goal of universal social security coverage this decade.

## Notes

1. See *Guiding Suggestions of the State Council on Developing New Rural Pension Scheme Pilot*, Document No. 32 of the State Council, September 2009.
2. The term "residents" in China has a specific meaning in the context of social insurance, because of how being a "resident" is defined in reference to a person's *hukou* (household registration) status and type of employment. In this report the term "residents" refers to all rural workers (except local officials) and nonworking population, and to self-employed, informally employed, and nonworking populations with local *hukou* in urban areas. Residents are contrasted with "workers," who would be covered within the urban workers' old-age insurance scheme.
3. The poverty severity index relies on the Foster and others (1984) measure of poverty using a sensitivity parameter of two.
4. See Cai and others (2012) for a detailed empirical analysis of the welfare of rural elderly.
5. Ibid.
6. See Cai and others (2012) for a detailed analysis of these issues using the China Urban Labor Survey carried out by CASS in 2001 and 2002.
7. See Cai and others (2012) for an analysis of private transfers to the elderly in rural areas.
8. See Cai and others (2012).
9. See Forteza and others (2009).

10. This section draws from the World Bank Policy Note on rural elderly welfare (Giles, Park, and Wang 2012) and a background paper written for that report (Wu 2009).

11. In October 1995, the State Council redistributed a circular of MOCA on "Further Improving the Rural Pension Insurance."

12. The pension benefit calculation formula was $(0.008631526) \times$ (accumulation in individual account).

13. See Liang (1999), Ma (1999), Ping (2002), and Shi (2007) for a discussion of the shortcomings of previous rural pension schemes.

14. See Peng (1996) for examples of massive differences in the matching of cadre and farmer contributions under local schemes.

15. See Wang (2000).

16. See MOLSS, "Notice on Seriously Improving Work on Current Rural Pensions."

17. For detailed descriptions of the systems of Beijing, Baoji, Yantai, and Suzhou, see Wu (2009). For a detailed discussion of the Baoji pilot rural pension experience, see Zhang and Tang (2009).

18. See "Notice of Guide on Construction of Rural Social Pension of Beijing Government," "Provisional Method for New Rural Social Pension," and "2009 New Pension Scheme for Both Rural and Urban Residents."

19. See Suzhou, "Provisional Methods for Rural Pension" (2003).

20. See Yantai Municipal Government, "Provisional Method on New Rural Pension Insurance" (2007).

21. See Zhang and Tang (2009) who argue that such a system will encourage family disputes, whereas Sun (2006) considers such a system to be a pragmatic and innovative approach to addressing persons with short contribution histories.

22. For a comprehensive discussion of recent experiences with "closing the coverage gap" through the extension of pension systems to rural and informal sector populations, see Holzmann and others (2009) and Palacios and Robalino (2009) on the framework for matching defined-contribution schemes.

23. See Lin (2006) for European, Commonwealth, and low-income countries; Gong (2006) for Japan; Su (2007) for Korea, Rep.; and Zheng (2007) and Leisering and Gong (2002) for a general discussion of the subsidy approach.

24. See Zhuhai City, "Transitional Pension Method for Farmers and Land-Expropriated Farmers," as is described in Wu (2009). On similar lines, Wang (2006) has suggested that income from the auction of land use rights and resources from state-owned assets should also be used for such purposes.

25. See Dong (2008) and Chen (2004). The assumptions underlying these simulations merit note. For example, Chen, used a projection model based on data

from Jiangsu province and assumes that one-quarter of the increase in general revenues would be needed for rural pension subsidies to support a universal pension for men and women at age 60 and 55, respectively. Assuming this represents 2.5 percent of general revenues, a universal farmers' pension of 825 RMB annually could have been provided in 2010.

26. See Chen (2004) and Qin (2007) for approaches for allocating financing responsibility among levels.

27. See Mi and Yang (2008) on the grain payment proposal, supported by a survey in Anhui province that found that about one-fifth of rural respondents would prefer to make contributions in grain. See Zhan (2004) and Lu (2004) for proposals for the allocation of farmer grain subsidies.

28. See Lv (2005), Liu (2003, 2007), and Wang (2004).

29. See Zhang (2006) regarding a reserve fund proposal. See Lv (2005) for proposals for higher return portfolio options.

30. See World Bank (forthcoming) for a discussion of social assistance benefits in rural areas. There were roughly 5.3 million *wu bao* recipients nationwide in 2007.

31. See Yang (2007), Mi and Yang (2008), and Yang, C. (2007).

32. See "Guiding Suggestions of the State Council on Developing New Rural Pension Scheme Pilot," Document No. 32 of the State Council, September 2009.

33. An illustration of this approach from Chile is provided in the section that follows on international experience.

34. See http://www.worldlifeexpectancy.com/your-life-expectancy-by-age.

35. The possible coverage of *dibao* household contributions raises second-order questions for how to subsequently treat rural pension income in the *dibao* eligibility determination process because the marginal cost of pension receipts could easily outweigh benefits once both the loss of the *dibao* benefits and the attendant noncash benefits that attach to *dibao* receipt are taken into account.

36. See Pickens and others (2009).

37. See World Bank (2009).

38. See Palacios and Robalino (2009) for a discussion of MDCs, model and design questions, empirical evidence, and theoretical framework.

39. In some areas of China, existing pilot schemes also allow use of the accumulation as collateral for loans for business activities. Although this is an interesting approach, it suffers from obvious social policy risks if the share of accumulations pledged is not capped at a reasonable level. Moreover, such an approach is not common internationally.

40. See note 23 above.

41. See Palacios and Robalino (2009).

42. See Zhuhai City, "Transitional Pension Method for Farmers and Land-Expropriated Farmers," as described in Wu (2009). On similar lines, Wang (2006) has suggested that income from the auction of land use rights and resources from state-owned assets should also be used for such purposes.

43. Localized examples can be found of collectives in urban areas that have solid revenue bases from the rental of collective land to factories or for other users that may be able to provide significant matching.

44. The urban scheme does have a 15-year vesting period, which should be considered.

45. See Holzmann and Palmer (2006) for a comprehensive review of NDCs.

46. See Zhang (2008) regarding a reserve fund proposal. See Lv (2005) for proposals for higher return portfolio options.

47. Examples from other countries are found of contracting arrangements that offer the benefits of competition among asset managers while limiting the number of asset managers to ensure a critical mass of funds and generate economies of scale in fund management (for example, the Indian New Pension Scheme and a handful of funded pillar schemes in Latin American, Europe, and Central Asia). However, most of these countries have more developed regulatory and accountability frameworks than exist at present in China.

48. See Wu (2009) and Cai and others (2012).

49. See http://www.hnwqb.gov.cn/news/szws/2009/0405/17004.html.

50. This section draws on Palacios and Robalino (2009).

51. See Engen and Gale (2000) and Benjamin (2003).

52. See Yang, J. (2007) and Mi and Yang (2008).

53. These figures assume a benefit level of 1,200 RMB per year (about 4.1 percent of the projected urban average wage) beginning in 2010.

54. See Liu (2009) for expenditure and benefit figures for *dibao*.

55. See Palacios and Sluchynskyy (2005), Asher for middle-income countries, and Barrientos for on lower-income countries in Holzmann and others (2009). The terms "social" and "citizens'" pensions are used interchangeably in the discussion that follows.

56. See Pearson and Whitehouse (2009) for a discussion of social pensions in high-income countries.

57. See ibid. details of the effect of these pension reforms on net replacement rates by earnings level.

58. See Kakwani and Subbarao (2005) on African schemes, Barrientos on four developing countries, and Palacios and Sluchynskyy (2006) for an international overview.

# References

Benjamin, D. J. 2003. "Does 401(k) Eligibility Increase Saving? Evidence from Propensity Score Subclassification." *Journal of Public Economics* 87: 1259–90.

Cai, F., J. Giles, P. O'Keefe, and D. Wang. 2012. *The Well-being of China's Rural Elderly and Old Age Support: Challenges and Prospects.* Directions in Development Series. Washington, DC: World Bank.

Chen, Y. 2004. "Rural Pension: Design and Argument for a New Scheme." *Academic World* 5.

Chen, S., M. Ravallion, and Y. Wang. 2006. "*Dibao*: A Guaranteed Minimum Income in China's Cities?" Policy Research Working Paper 3805, World Bank, Washington, DC.

China Health and Nutrition Survey (CHNS). Various years. China Center for Disease Control and Prevention and the Carolina Population Center, University of North Carolina at Chapel Hill. http:www.cpc.unc.edu/projects/china.

China Urban and Rural Elderly Survey (CURES). 2006. "China Urban and Rural Elderly Survey Micro-Data." Unpublished report, China Research Center on Aging, Beijing.

Dong, K. 2008. "Establishing a Universal Pension Scheme in Rural Areas." *China Youth News*, July 16.

Dorfman, M., D. Wang, P. O'Keefe, J. Cheng. 2013. "China's Pension Schemes for Rural and Urban Residents," in *Matching Contributions for Pensions: A Review of International Experience*, edited by R. Hinz, R. Holzmann, D. Tuesta, N. Takayama. Washington, DC: World Bank.

Engen, E., and W. Gale. 2000. "The Effect of 401(k) Plans on Housheold Wealth: Differences across Earning Groups." NBER Working Paper No. 8032, National Bureau of Economic Research, Cambridge, MA.

Fajnzylber, E. 2008. "Extending Pension Coverage: The Chilean Perspective." Presentation to World Bank Pension Core Course, Washington, DC.

Forteza, A., L. Lucchetti, and M. Pallares-Miralles. 2009. "Measuring the Coverage Gap." In *Closing the Coverage Gap: The Role of Social Pensions and Other Retirement Income Transfers*, ed. R. Holzmann, D. Robalino, and N. Takayama. Washington, DC: World Bank.

Foster, J., J. Greer, and E. Thorbecke. 1984. "A Class of Decomposable Poverty Measures." *Econometrica* 52 (3): 761–66.

Giles, J., A. Park, and D. Wang. 2012. "Expanding Social Insurance Coverage in Urban China." World Bank Policy Note. World Bank, Washington, DC.

Gong, X. 2006. "Rural Pension System and Its Lessons in Developed Countries." *Journal of Central Finance University* 6: 6–9.

Grosh, M., and P. Leite. 2009. "Defining Eligibility for Social Pensions: A View from a Social Assistance Perspective." In *The Role of Social Pensions and Other Retirement Income Transfers: Closing the Coverage Gap*, ed. R. Holzmann, D. Robalino, and N. Takayama. Washington, DC: World Bank.

Holzmann, R., and E. Palmer. 2006. *Pension Reform: Issues and Prospects for Non-financial Defined Contribution Schemes.* Washington, DC: World Bank.

Holzmann, R., D. Robalino, and N. Takayama. 2009. *Closing the Coverage Gap: The Role of Social Pensions and Other Retirement Income Transfers.* Washington, DC: World Bank.

Kakwani, N., and K. Subbarao. 2005. "Aging and Poverty in Africa: The Role of Social Pensions." World Bank Social Protection Discussion Paper Series. No. 521, World Bank, Washington, DC.

Leisering, L., and S. Gong. 2002. "Policy Support for Social Security Reform under the Tenth Five Year Plan: Old-Age Pensions for the Rural Areas—From Land Reform to Globalization." http://www.adb.org/Documents/Reports/PRC_Old_Age_Pensions/default.asp.

Liang, H. 1999. "Economic Analysis of Current Rural Community Security of China." Dissertation, University of Fudan.

Lin, Y. 2006. *Research on International Comparison of Rural Social Security and Its Lessons.* Beijing: China Labor and Social Security Publishing House.

Liu, C. 2007. "Improving Rural Pension Scheme Design." *China Finance* 6: 68–70.

Liu, X. 2009. Presentation to Chengdu Social Assistance Conference, Chengdu, 2009.

Liu, Z. 2003. "Reflection and Reconstruction of China Rural Pension." Hunan Business School of Hunan Normal University. *Management World* 8: 46–56.

Lu, H. 2004. "Innovation of Rural Social Pension Scheme: Produce for Social Security." *Seeking Truth* 3: 62.

Luo, Xia, 2011. "Empirical Study on the RPPP—Case Study on Sixian City of Anhui Province." *Social Security Studies* 1: 67–73.

Lv, J. 2005. "Current Situation of Rural Social Security and Analysis of Its Development Path." *Journal of Ningxia Communist School* 6: 47–49.

Ma, L. 1999. "Slowing Down Rural Pension." *Exploration and Debate* 7: 11–12.

Mi, H., and C. Yang. 2008. *Basic Theoretic Framework Research on Rural Pension System.* Beijing: Bright Post Publishing House.

Ministry of Labor and Social Security. Various years. *Yearbooks of Labor and Social Security (2001–2008).* Beijing: Ministry of Labor and Social Security.

National Bureau of Statistics (NBS). 2005. "One Percent Population Sample, Micro-Data." Unpublished report, NBS, Beijing.

Organisation for Economic Co-operation and Development (OECD). 2007. *Pensions at a Glance*. Paris: Organisation for Economic Co-operation and Development.

Palacios, R., and D. Robalino. 2009. "Matching Defined Contributions: A Way to Increase Pension Coverage." In *Closing the Coverage Gap: The Role of Social Pensions and Other Retirement Income Transfers*, ed. R. Holzmann, D. Robalino, and N. Takayama, chap. 13. Washington, DC: World Bank.

Palacios, R., and O. Sluchynskyy. 2006. "Social Pensions Part I: Their Role in the Overall Pension System." Social Protection Discussion Paper No. 0601, World Bank, Washington, DC.

Pearson, M. A., and E. R. Whitehouse. 2009. "Social Pensions in High-Income Countries." In *Closing the Coverage Gap: The Role of Social Pensions*, ed. R. Holzmann, D. Robalino, and N. Takayama. Washington, DC: World Bank.

Peng, X. 1996. "Township and Village Enterprises and Rural Social Security in the South of Jiangsu Province." *Shanghai Finance* 6: 31–32.

Pickens, M., D. Porteous, and S. Rotman. 2009. "Banking the Poor via G2P Payments." CGAP/DFID Focus Note No. 58, CGAP, Washington, DC.

Ping., C. 2002. "Establishing a Unified Social Security System Is a Shortsighted Policy." *China Reform* 4: 16–17.

Qin, Z. 2007. "The Urgency, Current Situation and Policy Recommendation on Building Rural Pension System." *China Economic Times*. http://finance. people.com.cn/nc/GB/61159/5611208.html.

Rofman, R., L. Lucchetti, and G. Ourens. 2008. "Pension Systems in Latin America: Concepts and Measurement of Coverage." World Bank Social Protection Working Paper Series No. 0616, World Bank, Washington, DC.

Rural Household Survey Yearbooks. Various years. *China Statistical Yearbook*. Beijing: China Statistics Press.

Shi, Y. 2007. "Analysis of Conditions for Establishing Rural Pension System in China." *Group Economics* 4.

State Council. 1986. "The 7th Five Year Plan for National Economic and Social Development of the People's Republic of China, 1986–1990." Document submitted to the Fourth Session of the Sixth National People's Congress, Beijing.

———. 2011. "Guiding Opinions on Piloting Social Pension Insurance for Urban Residents." State Council, Beijing, June 7.

Su, B. 2007. "Rural Pension Systems of Western Developed Countries and Its Lessons." *Current Economy* 12.

Sun, W. 2006. *Building and Perfecting the Institution of Social Security in Rural Areas*. Beijing: Social Science Academic Press.

Wang, D. 2006. "Construction of Pension System in Context of Coordinating Rural and Urban Development." *Theoretic Frontier* 15.

Wang, D., J. Chen, and W. Gao, 2011. "Social Security Integration: The Case of Rural and Urban Resident Pension Pilot in Chengdu." Mimeo, World Bank, Washington, DC.

Wang, G. 2000. "Defects of Current Rural Pension System and Reform Thinking." *Quarterly of Shanghai Academy of Social Science* 1: 120–27.

Wang, Z. 2004. "Preliminary Study on Rural Pension System." *Enterprises Economy* 9.

World Bank. Forthcoming. *Social Assistance in Rural China: Tackling Poverty through Rural Dibao.* Beijing: World Bank.

Wu, Y. 2009. "Rural Pensions Background Paper for World Bank Rural Elderly Report." Mimeo, World Bank, Washington, DC.

Yang, J. 2007. "Innovation and Selection of Financing Sources of Rural Social Security." *Developing Research* 2.

Yantai Municipal Government. 2007. "Provisional Method on New Rural Pension Insurance." Yantai, Shandong province, China.

Zhan, Z. 2004. "Feasibility Analysis of Utilizing Grain Subsidy to Build Rural Social Security." *Survey World* 2.

Zhang, L. 2006. "Issues of Rural Pension Fund Management and Its Policy Recommendation." *Rural Finance and Accounting* 7.

Zhang, S. 2008. "Making Best Use of Rural Pension Fund." *China Rural Credit Cooperation* 9: 20–21.

Zheng, W. 2007. "Reflections on the Dilemma of China Rural Pension System." *Insurance Research* 11.

Zhang, W., and D. Tang. 2009. "The New Rural Social Pension Insurance Program of Baoji City Shaanxi Province, China." http://www.helpage.org.

# A Notional (Nonfinancial) Defined-Contribution Design for China's Urban Old-Age Insurance System

Notional or nonfinancial defined-contribution (NDC) schemes have been adopted by various countries over the last decade and a half, with Italy, Latvia, Poland, and Sweden broadly following the same design but with some distinct features. Norway introduced an NDC-type scheme in 2011 and Egypt enacted an NDC scheme in 2010 with implementation envisaged for 2013, while Belarus is considering such a design. A full evaluation of the various experiences with NDC and similar schemes has recently been published (see Holzmann, Palmer, and Robalino 2012, 2013). This section summarizes the characteristics of these NDC schemes and the lessons learned thus far (see table B.1 for a summary of key features of country schemes).

NDC design architecture offers several attractive features including (1) a direct link between contributions and benefits and hence a reduction in labor market distortions, (2) strong incentives to work longer and retire later as life expectancy increases, and (3) a framework that provides easy portability of accrued benefit rights. Moreover, for countries with pay-as-you-go (PAYG) pension schemes, the introduction of an NDC scheme does not impose the high transition costs that result from moving to a funded system.[1] Together with the other elements of the proposed pension design architecture for China (which are discussed later in this report), the NDC design offers an attractive benefit and financing structure toward which the current and proposed pension schemes can converge.

This chapter discusses (1) the rationale for adopting the NDC structure in the proposed wage employment pension scheme in China, (2) the key design features that must be considered when introducing an NDC scheme, and (3) lessons from international experience.

## Rationale and Advantages of an NDC Scheme in China

The NDC design is an excellent mechanism for strengthening the linkage between individual contributions and benefits. It is an individual account system that operates on a PAYG basis and under the principle that what you paid in you get out, but not more; solvency is achieved by crediting only a notional interest rate that is line with the internal rate of return an unfunded system can afford to pay. The benefits are directly correlated with contributions, and so the system creates strong incentive to contribute and eliminates the temptation to shift the burden of pension promises to future generations by making the magnitude of those promises fully transparent. To operate effectively, however, an NDC scheme must be designed with respect for a handful of key principles, which are discussed later in this section (see also Palmer 2006a, b). The NDC design is attractive for the following key reasons:

- *NDC schemes tie benefits to contributions.* An NDC scheme directly links the contributions made by an individual (and those made on his or her behalf by employers) to the benefits he or she ultimately receives. Contributions accumulate in a notional account that grows at a notional interest rate consistent with financial sustainability. At retirement, the individual receives an annuity computed on the basis of (1) projected cohort life expectancy at the individual's age of retirement and (2) anticipated notional interest rates. The resulting direct correlation between contributions and benefits minimizes the incentive for workers to avoid formal sector employment and to retire early, which can be a problem in conventional defined-benefit schemes.

- *NDC schemes do not create hidden intergenerational subsidies.* Unlike traditional defined-benefit schemes—which often affect intergenerational transfers that can be difficult to value—the liabilities associated with NDC schemes are transparent and easy for policy makers to evaluate. Moreover, if the legacy costs associated with pension entitle-ments for current retirees and accrued rights of workers are financed from outside NDC schemes, contributors are not burdened with financ-ing the accrued rights of earlier generations.

- *NDC schemes are financially sound and sustainable by design.* An NDC structure is financially sustainable even when a population is aging because benefits are calculated on the basis of an individual's notional account balance and remaining life expectancy. Given that NDC schemes are financed on a PAYG basis (that is, revenues from current contributions are used to pay benefits to current beneficiaries), the financial soundness relies on the following two additional features: (1) *a balancing mechanism* accommodates deviations between assets and liabilities created by long-term demographic and other changes while (2) a *buffer fund* provides liquidity to accommodate sudden exog-enous shocks and temporary demographic shifts (for example, baby booms or busts, as discussed below).

- *NDC schemes do not create transition costs associated with a shift toward funded systems.* For countries with PAYG pension schemes, introducing an NDC scheme does not create transition costs (that is, the need to finance *both* the benefits paid to current retirees and to prefund the accounts of workers who have yet to retire). This double burden is faced by countries that have elected to move from unfunded to fully funded pension schemes. NDC schemes thus offer many of the advan-tages of funded defined-contribution (FDC) schemes thus while elim-inating the need to finance such transition costs. Moreover, if the contribution rate set to generate a targeted level of income replacement is below the steady-state contribution rate for the unreformed scheme, reform-induced transition costs will be much smaller than those involved in transitioning to a funded scheme.

- *Benefits under an NDC scheme automatically adjust in response to increasing life expectancy and other social-economic changes.* Increasing life expectancy is one of the key motivations for pension reform. NDC schemes offer several compelling strategies for addressing such changes. First, NDC schemes create an incentive for individuals to work longer and retire later as their life expectancy increases and the population ages. Second, NDC schemes enable the full separation of old-age risks from disability risks (which can—and *should*—be separately priced). Third, NDC schemes accommodate increases in female labor force participation and rising divorce rates by providing individual pensionable rights. By using a defined-contribution structure, traditional spousal survivor pensions can be accommodated under NDC schemes through higher individual account values and annuitized benefits, and the balances in accounts can be split as part of a divorce settlement.

- *NDC schemes are less dependent on capital markets than are funded schemes.* Although NDC schemes do depend on functioning and efficient capital markets in which to invest the assets of their buffer funds, the level of capital market development required to support an NDC scheme is substantially less than that required to support an FDC scheme, which depends on the capital markets to intermediate all of its assets.

These advantages notwithstanding, the NDC design does not obviate the need to finance the *legacy costs* associated with the unreformed scheme when moving to the new scheme (discussed below).

Beyond these advantages, other compelling reasons exist for adopting NDC schemes in light of the special needs and characteristics of China:

- *NDC schemes can accommodate regional heterogeneity and support portability.* The NDC framework accommodates variation in contribution rates across individual pension schemes while still providing full portability of accrued rights (which are represented by the value of notional account balances) across geographic areas (that is, among counties, cities, and provinces). Full portability of accrued pension rights for migrating workers can be achieved by creating a framework for combining notional account balances in different locations across an individual's working life.

- *NDC schemes provide a convenient framework for converting existing schemes.* The NDC framework provides a mechanism for valuing pension rights from diverse schemes on a common basis. For example, one can calculate the value of accrued pensionable rights for active workers in the urban old-age insurance system (be it *middle men* or *new men;* see figure C.1 for an explanation of these terms), civil servants, and PSU workers and then credit this (*notional*) value to the initial balance of each individual's notional account. Once introduced, the rules of a new

NDC scheme would apply to all future earnings. Past service credit is thus captured using standardized rules through the calculation of notional account equivalents. Differences in benefit accruals among public sector institutions or other entities before the implementation of the reform would thus be fully reflected in individual account balances at the time of conversion. Such an approach can even be applied to workers close to retirement because accrued rights can always be converted into initial notional account balances, regardless of the nature of those rights.

- *NDC schemes support current consumption, labor, and enterprise competitiveness.* By reducing contribution rates, the total cost of labor is reduced, and that supports business and labor competitiveness. At a household level, the resulting reduction in the amount of income that must be set aside as savings for retirement can then support additional current consumption.

- *NDC schemes can support redistribution.* Redistributive features of the current basic scheme (*Social Pooling*) can be replicated under an NDC scheme by allocating a share of contributions with the same nominal amount credited equally to all notional accounts. Combined with the contributions based on the individual wages, this will effectively increase replacement rates for lower-income workers without sacrificing portability.

- *NDC schemes can support the gradual integration of urban and rural schemes.* NDC schemes can support the integration of defined-contribution rights accrued by rural workers and migrants at any point. Contributions and accumulations under the NRPS and URPS, for example, could be aggregated with notional accumulations under the proposed MORIS. This could be particularly useful for migrant workers.

- *NDC schemes in emerging economies may offer higher returns (and, therefore, benefits) than equivalent funded defined-contribution schemes.* In China, as in several other emerging economies, wages have historically grown at a rate that has greatly exceeded the rate of return earned on investment portfolios, particularly those invested primarily in low-risk, fixed-income securities. Low financial account remuneration leads to low benefits and replacement rates. As has been the case for China's funded individual accounts in its urban old-age insurance system, when the rate of return on individual accounts is lower than the rate of wage growth, individual replacement rates grow more slowly, resulting in low effective rates of accrual. A key advantage of NDCs is that the return on contributions is established under a framework at the outset, and workers are not subject to market risks (as is the case with FDC schemes). Because the notional interest rate is linked to GDP and, hence, to real wage growth, reasonable levels of income can be expected for a given contribution rate.

- *NDC schemes are consistent with China's macroeconomic developmental objectives.* Although an FDC design requires that contributions be made both to pay current retirees and to invest to fund the cost of future benefits, NDC schemes would not channel contributions to increased national savings. Furthermore, reducing the contribution rate by explicitly financing legacy costs outside the pension system will support business and labor competitiveness. At a household level, reducing the income that must be set aside as savings for retirement would support additional consumption.

- *NDC schemes can accommodate the eventual introduction of funding.* An NDC scheme, once implemented, permits the easy conversion to partial or full funding once (1) the financial markets are capable of providing adequate returns at reasonable risk to investors and (2) the budgetary and macroeconomic preconditions for financing transition costs have been met. Once these conditions have been satisfied, a share of contributions can simply be diverted from individual notional accounts to individual financial accounts and invested.

## Proposed Technical Design for an NDC Scheme

Five technical issues demand special attention when designing and implementing an NDC scheme in China. NDCs are a relatively new approach to pension design. Consequently, countries that have implemented NDC schemes are still refining their technical features (for a discussion of international experience; see the next section). The World Bank recommends that the design of a Chinese NDC scheme follow the conceptual *spirit* of the NDC design paradigm but select technical parameters that are (1) tailored to China's special needs and circumstances and (2) capable of supporting experimentation and subsequent refinement.

## The Notional Interest Rate

The notional interest rate is the rate applied to remunerate notional account balances during the accumulation phase and often co-determines the annuitized benefit at retirement along with life expectancy. It is also often used as the basis for indexing benefits in disbursement while maintaining long-term financial equilibrium.[2]

The basic principle that determines the notional interest rate—and drives its subsequent adjustment—starts with the balancing condition that applies to any pension scheme translated into the NDC framework. This principle can be stated as follows: *Pension liabilities must be less than or equal to the pension assets to ensure financial sustainability*:

$$
\begin{aligned}
\text{pension liabilities } (PL) &\leq \text{pension assets } (PA) \\
\text{pension liabilities } (PL) &= \text{balance of the notional accounts} \\
&\quad + \text{present value of benefits} \\
&\quad \text{in payment (disbursement)} \qquad \text{(B.1)} \\
\text{pension assets } (PA) &= \text{financial assets } (FA) \\
&\quad + \text{pay-as-you-go PAYG} \\
&\quad \text{assets } (GA)
\end{aligned}
$$

where financial assets $(FA)$ = the market value of any investments held by the pension fund and PAYG assets $(GA)$ = the present value of future contributions minus pension rights accruing to these contributions (that is, for a positive PAYG asset the implicit remuneration of contributions must be below the market rate of interest/marginal product of capital).

To guarantee equilibrium, the following condition must hold:

$$PL_t \,(1 + i^*) = FA_t \,(1 + r) + GA_t \,(1 + a) \qquad \text{(B.2)}$$

with $i^*$ representing the internal rate of return (or notional interest rate), $r$ = the market interest rate, and $a$ = the growth rate of the financial asset.

Solving for $i^*$ and simplifying:

$$i^* = \frac{FA_t}{PL_t} r + \frac{GA_t}{PL_t} a + \frac{FA_t + GA_t - PL_t}{PL_t} \qquad \text{(B.3)}$$

where $i^*$ is the sustainable growth rate of liabilities; that is, the rate at which the individual account balances and the pensions in payment can grow while keeping the system financially sustainable. Changes in the PAYG asset and financial asset ($GA$ and $FA$) and their growth rates ($r$ and $a$) need to be reflected in $i^*$.

No straightforward mechanism is available for estimating a sustainable notional interest rate over multiple generations, and so a *proxy notional rate* is required—such as the growth rate of the contribution base, wage base, or GDP—and a *balancing mechanism* is needed to correct for deviations.[3] If one assumes steady-state conditions and overlapping generations, the notional interest rate ($i^*$) would represent the *internal rate of return* that an unfunded scheme can deliver. Although such an internal rate of return should approximate the growth of the covered labor force and labor productivity, empirically the growth rate of the covered labor force and labor productivity does not guarantee financial sustainability. Thus, the use of both a proxy notional interest rate (such as the national growth rate of GDP) and a balancing mechanism are recommended.[4]

Two elements of population aging are treated differently under the proposed NDC framework:

- *Aging from below* is the process by which decreasing fertility rates gradually increase the proportion of the aged relative to the rest of the population (as is the case in China). Aging from below manifests in lower labor force growth over time as smaller numbers of children age and enter the labor force. However, over the same multigenerational period, the number of current and future retirees has already been established by patterns of fertility in generations past. Any pension system, including one with an NDC design, needs to be sustainable across all generations—even in the face of rapidly declining labor force growth and expanding elderly populations. As such, financial sustainability in China will require the adjustment of the notional interest rate through a *balancing mechanism* to accommodate this *long-term pattern of aging from below*.

- *Aging from above* refers to growth in the elderly population resulting from increases in life expectancy. This leads to an increase in labor force growth *to the extent that withdrawal from the labor market is delayed*. If individuals live longer but continue to retire at the same age, of course, then *aging from above* will have no impact on the labor force. The most important financial consequence of *aging from above* is the duration of retirement benefits resulting from increased life expectancy at retirement. *Aging from above* needs to be addressed through the best possible estimation of conditional cohort life expectancies at retirement. Of course, such estimates will inevitably be inaccurate *ex post*. Addressing such inaccuracies forces two policy options: (1) retirees can bear the risk of changes in mortality at retirement (in which case, the annuity factor should be periodically revised—most likely reducing benefits by the degree to which projected life expectancy increased faster than anticipated) or (2) workers and retirees can share the risk by adjusting the *balancing mechanism* applied to the notional interest rate and annual indexation.

China's current and projected real wage growth and anticipated coverage growth suggest that the rate of growth in covered wages and the rate of growth of GDP will diverge. Hence, the choice of the notional rate of return that best approximates the most sustainable internal rate of return (that is, the choice that will require the smallest balancing mechanism) should be determined through simulation that captures the most likely scenario of future development.[5] The availability and reliability of data should also be considered when determining the basis for the notional interest rate.

### Life Expectancy at Retirement

An accurate estimate of life expectancy at retirement is crucial in determining the annuity factor under an NDC scheme to ensure that the payout during the withdrawal phase approximates the notional account accumulation at retirement. It is essential to attain actuarial balance both for individuals and for the system as a whole. Life expectancy at retirement, along with projected notional interest rates, is used as the basis to translate accumulated (notional) account balances into an annuitized benefit stream payable until beneficiaries die. If projected life expectancies are too low, pension benefits will be too high relative to accumulated contributions. This distorts retirement decisions and jeopardizes system sustainability. If projected life expectancies are too high, pension benefits will be too low. This reduces social welfare. Life expectancies at different retirement ages (that is, *conditional* life expectancies) are based on mortality rates estimated for every cohort in a particular region in a particular year. As life expectancy for almost all cohorts is increasing throughout China (as it is throughout most of the world as a consequence of generally decreasing mortality rates at all ages), conditional life expectancies tend to underestimate how long individuals at retirement age can actually be expected to draw a pension because their life expectancy does not reflect further increases in life expectancy that might occur after they retire.[6] This suggests that the annuity factors used to compute benefits should employ cohort estimates of remaining life expectancy based on projected survival probabilities that take into account projected improvements in mortality at ages above the retirement age. Because there is lack of international consensus surrounding projected mortality improvements (see Alho and others 2013), the World Bank suggests that conditional life expectancies should reflect *past* improvements in life expectancy for each cohort that retires. If in the future greater consensus is found over the pace of future improvements in mortality, the methodology should be adjusted accordingly.

Another important institutional question for China is whether estimates for life expectancy should be based on national or provincial data, and urban or rural data. Material differences exist in life expectancy at retirement between different provinces and between urban and rural areas. These differences would materially impact benefit levels. Moreover, if benefits were to be calculated using different annuity factors from different life expectancies in different provinces, individuals would have an incentive to relocate to locations with lower life expectancies to maximize their benefits. Finally, material institutional challenges are encountered in acquiring robust life expectancy data on a provincial level in China. Because of these factors, the World Bank recommends the use of one life expectancy for all rural and urban schemes using conditional life expectancies that incorporate projected improvements in mortality, as was discussed earlier.

### Balancing Mechanism

The objective of the *balancing mechanism* is to ensure solvency of the scheme (that is, that projected long-term revenues are adequate to cover long-term expenditures over a period of, for example, 80 years). The balancing mechanism serves to preserve long-term financial sustainability of the NDC system. Because the contribution rate is fixed, ensuring long-term actuarial balance can only be achieved by (1) adjusting the notional interest rate, (2) adjusting the indexation of benefits in disbursement, or (3) providing government or other subsidies. *The balancing mechanism should follow a methodology codified in the design of the scheme and should automatically adjust the notional interest rate, the indexation of benefits in disbursement, or both.*

Adjusting the notional interest rate through a balancing mechanism reduces future initial benefits and thus improves long-term sustainability.

Because it has little short-term impact, it cannot correct for an imbalance between revenues and disbursements. This must be remedied through a buffer fund (as is discussed below). Adjusting benefit indexation has an immediate impact on cash flows but is more limited in terms of restoring long-term sustainability.

Critical to the efficacy of the *balancing mechanism* is the methodology for estimating the PAYG asset ($GA$) and for addressing short-term fluctuations in the financial asset ($FA$). The PAYG asset should be estimated periodically (at least initially every two to three years) using established actuarial methods that reflect long-term trends inter alia in covered employment, wages, and GDP growth. Once methodologies have been established and all variables have been estimated—to include the PAYG asset ($GA$),[7] the value of the pension liabilities ($PL$), and the value of the financial asset ($FA$)—the implicit rate of return can be estimated directly, thereby avoiding the use of GDP growth as a proxy for the sustainable notional interest rate. The better the estimator, the lower the probability of recourse to the balancing mechanism. Short-term fluctuations in the financial assets demand a judgment call and the development of clear valuation procedures for assets to avoid having short-term market fluctuations trigger the balancing mechanism.

The balancing mechanism must be supported by very clear rules regarding the level of deviation from financial balance that triggers adjustment. For example, the trigger for applying the balancing mechanism might be a deviation of the estimated pension liabilities ($PL$) from estimated total assets ($FA+GA$) by, for example, 10 percent in either direction. The rules must also address the phasing and timing of the adjustment. For example, they might be designed to reduce the liability-asset discrepancy to within 5 percent in five years. The parameters for such rules should be informed by stochastic simulation.

## Buffer Fund

Although the balancing mechanism ensures the long-term solvency of the scheme, it cannot guarantee short-term liquidity. Short-term liquidity requires a buffer fund with liquid assets to pay benefits even in the event of (1) a protracted reduction in contribution revenues and (2) an increase in benefit expenditures. Additionally, such a buffer fund may also be used for medium-term smoothing of the notional interest rate (that is, to prefinance an anticipated period of expenditures exceeding revenues due to a temporary demographic disequilibrium that might otherwise trigger a transitory application of the balancing mechanism).

*Bridging a temporary reduction in contribution revenues*—which generally results from a reduction in output, employment, or wages—while expenditures are maintained or even increased is crucial for any pension scheme. Reducing benefit levels in the face of a decline in contribution revenues is politically difficult, is suboptimal in terms of maximizing welfare, threatens the credibility of the system, and does not further the basic social policy objective of smoothing consumption over time.

*The size of a buffer fund needed to absorb exogenous shocks* depends on three factors: (1) the projected frequency and maximum depth of temporary declines in future contribution revenues, (2) the benefit protection objective in the face of revenue shortfalls (for example, to avoid cuts in nominal benefits or in real benefits), and (3) the government's degree of risk aversion (such as the probability that the benefit protection objective is not met should be less than, for example, 5 percent). A rule of thumb based on international experience suggests that a buffer fund should have 6 to 24 months of total expenditures of the pension scheme; the higher end of this range reflects the recent experience of countries in the wake of the recent global financial crisis.[8]

Although a buffer fund to bridge short-term liquidity requirements is an *essential* part of any NDC scheme, smoothing temporary demographic spikes—such as the aging bulge (as is being observed currently in the United States and, to a lesser extent, in Europe) or the effects of the one-child policy in China—is a choice. Sweden, for example, inherited a substantial reserve fund of over 30 percent of GDP from its legacy scheme and intends to use it for demographic smoothing for the aging bulge and beyond.

The methodology required for setting the parameters of the balancing mechanism, the indexation of benefits, and the size of the buffer fund will require considerable analysis, supported by long-term projections that anticipate a range of developmental scenarios and outcomes.

### Financing of Legacy Costs

Legacy costs refer to the cost of financing the implicit debt (that is, the present value of benefit promises to current beneficiaries and current workers before the implementation of the reform) over and above (1) the value of the PAYG asset (under the new contribution rate) and (2) the financial assets set aside to prefinance accrued rights. Legacy costs arise from three main sources: (1) old legacy costs due to prior reforms of the scheme (for example, from *old* and *middle men*), (2) new legacy costs attributable to reform (to include the shift toward a lower sustainable contribution rate), and (3) any accrued liabilities to date due to the inclusion of other schemes with cost-covering contribution rates above the sustainable new rate (see Holzmann and Jousten 2013 for details). Under NDC schemes, explicit financing for legacy costs from outside the pension system becomes a necessity because the contribution rate is fixed against a target replacement rate and an average retirement age. Additional resources, therefore, are needed to cover those pension promises beyond those directly supported by the NDC scheme. Although it is possible to retain a cost-covering contribution rate (for example, 30 percent) and to credit only a portion of collected contributions to the notional accounts of the reformed scheme, this would likely appear to participants to be an explicit tax and discredit the reform.

The sources of revenues selected to finance legacy costs should depend on their magnitude and timing. Very rough estimates presented in appendix C estimate (gross) legacy costs to be between 89 percent and 113 percent of GDP (for a chosen new contribution rate of 15 percent) and between 44 percent and 56 percent (for a chosen new contribution rate of 25 percent). The lower the contribution rate, the higher the legacy costs. The estimated legacy costs are attributable with a share of three-fourths to one-fourth to the urban old-age insurance system and schemes for PSU employees and civil servants, respectively. However, only about three-fourths of these (gross) legacy costs are additional budget outlays because most of the costs for civil servants and PSU are already borne by the budget. Very rough calculations suggest that a significant share of the legacy costs (net of government sector schemes) may be financeable by coverage expansion even if a low contribution of 15 percent is chosen. Even in such a scenario, however, the budget would need to cover initial financing requirements before the revenue effects of coverage expansion can be fully realized.

*To summarize:* Based on conceptual considerations and the experience of other countries with NDC schemes, if China were to adopt an NDC design for its urban old age insurance system, it is recommended that China take the following steps:

(1) *Establish an explicit balancing mechanism* to adjust the notional interest rate to ensure long-term stable structures and parameters
(2) *Index benefits on the basis of both the consumer price and GDP indexes* (subject to limits); this will result in smaller initial benefits but will offer room for reducing indexation without cutting benefits in real terms, if needed

(3) *Establish a buffer fund* with an explicit financing strategy to absorb short-term exogenous shocks and the medium-term effects of cash flow imbalances due to demographic spikes and

(4) *Estimate the legacy costs* of reform and *establish an explicit strategy for financing them*; over the long term, expanding coverage may substantially help reduce legacy costs, but fiscal support, such as transfers from the general government, will be required in the short term.

## Lessons from Countries That Have Implemented NDC Schemes

Four countries have thus far implemented NDC schemes (Italy, Latvia, Poland, and Sweden). In addition, Egypt enacted an NDC scheme in 2010 and Norway introduced an NDC-type scheme in 2011, while Belarus is considering the design. Other countries have either adopted main elements of the NDC design or have adjusted their own schemes to mimic those key elements. This section summarizes the characteristics of these NDC schemes and the lessons learned thus far (see table B.1 for a summary of key features of country schemes).

### Structure: Commonalities and Differences
**Context.** Three of the four countries that have introduced NDC schemes have also established some form of an FDC scheme and a noncontributory social pension scheme. In Italy, contributions to the FDC scheme are voluntary, whereas in Latvia, Poland, and Sweden they are mandatory.

**Contribution rates.** The total combined employer and employee contribution rates of funded and NDC schemes in Latvia, Poland, and Sweden are 20 percent, 19.52 percent, and 18.5 percent respectively, of which 14 percent, 12.22 percent, and 16.0 percent go to the NDC scheme, and 6.0 percent, 7.3 percent, and 2.5 percent go to the FDC scheme.[9] In Italy the rate is 33 percent (for employees), 20 percent (for self-employed), and 24 percent (for atypical contracts).

**Notional interest rate.** The choice of interest rate applied to the notional accounts and the annuity (benefit indexation) varies across countries and includes (1) the rate of growth of the covered wage bill, (2) per capita wage growth, and (3) GDP growth. Each country uses a different proxy for measuring the sustainable internal rate of return and for indexing benefits in disbursement.

**Table B.1  Key Design Features and Transition Modalities for NDC Schemes**

| Country (year of establishment) | Contribution rate (%) | Notional rate of return during accumulation phase | Post-retirement indexation | Reserve buffer fund | Explicit balancing mechanism | Initial capital |
|---|---|---|---|---|---|---|
| Italy (1999) | For employees: 33 | GDP growth | Price indexation | No | No | No initial capital: combination of old and new system |
| Latvia (1996) | 14 from 2012 | Growth in covered wage bill | Price indexation from 2011 growth | Gradually through surpluses | No: through indexation choice | Initial capital determined using service years and national and individual wages |
| Poland (1997) | 12.22 | Growth in covered wage bill | Price indexation including at least 20% of real wage | Gradually through surpluses | No: through indexation choice | Initial capital: present value of acquired rights as of December 31, 1997 |
| Sweden (1999) | 16.0 | Growth in per capita covered wages | Price indexation + difference between real per capita wage growth and 1.6% rate of return | Inherited from prior system | Yes: compares liabilities and assets | Initial capital using earnings history from 1960 when born 1938+ |

*Sources:* Chlon-Dominszak and others 2012; Palmer 2006b; World Bank pension database.

*Note:* DB = defined benefit; DC = defined contribution; GDP = gross domestic product; NDC = notional defined contribution.

*Buffer fund.* Two of the four countries have a buffer fund. Sweden inherited a major buffer fund from its pre-reformed scheme (over 30 percent of GDP at the time of reform). Poland has established a reserve fund through transfers from privatization assets and budgetary transfers that was used during the financial crisis to finance liquidity requirements of the pension system and for other purposes.

*Balancing mechanisms.* Only Sweden has an explicit balancing mechanism, but all countries have, in principle, balancing that adjusts the notional interest and annuity conversion factor to disequilibria of pensions assets and liabilities and changes in life expectancy.

*Recognition of acquired rights.* When moving to the new NDC scheme, three countries (Latvia, Poland, and Sweden) transformed acquired rights/contributions under the old scheme into an initial (notional) account balance that enables all active workers to be covered under the NDC scheme at the start of the reform. In Italy, only new entrants to the labor market after the reform was introduced are covered by the NDC scheme—individuals with 18 or more years of service credit at the time of reform remain under the old system. Workers who started contributing before the introduction of the NDC scheme in Italy will get benefits from both the old and new schemes.

### Preliminary Lessons

Overall, the introduction of NDC schemes has generally gone smoothly, and the schemes all enjoy strong political support more than 10 years after their introduction. The current crisis has created stress for all pension systems, and NDC schemes in these countries have similarly been affected. A recent stocktaking exercise for Italy, Latvia, Poland, and Sweden offers the following tentative lessons (see also table B.1):

- *Sustainability and labor market incentives.* Overall, the NDC schemes seem to meet expectations for financial sustainability and provide desired incentives for worker decisions regarding labor supply and retirement timing. Of course, significant differences are seen in the incentives in different countries that have established such NDC schemes depending upon the credibility of their reform efforts and the soundness of their implementation.

- *Political dimensions.* An NDC scheme is not a fool-proof approach and, therefore, needs to be carefully managed politically. As with other reforms, communication of the reform with stakeholders is as important in establishing political support as is the soundness of design, implementation, and administrative preparedness.

- *Recognition of acquired rights.* When moving toward an NDC scheme, it is important to place all active workers on a level playing field by transforming acquired rights into an initial notional account balance in the NDC scheme.

- *Target replacement rates.* The projected benefit levels of the reformed NDC schemes are lower than the schemes they replaced; however, they are still adequate by many accounts (for example, International Labour Organization standards). Overall, the mandatory system of these countries provides gross income replacement rates for persons with average incomes of 60–64 percent and net replacement rates of 75 percent in Italy, Latvia, and Poland. In Sweden, net replacement rates are approximately equal to gross replacement rates.

- *Financing of legacy costs.* Carefully considering the legacy problem and how to finance it is essential. Lacking an explicit financing mechanism and taxing the current generations of contributors and retirees, in addition to unspecified budgetary transfers, weakens the link between contributions and benefits and undermines the credibility of the scheme.

The recent financial crisis forcefully underscores the importance of having both a *buffer fund* and a well-designed explicit *balancing mechanism*, and subjecting both to comprehensive *stress testing*. All NDC countries without an explicit and built-up buffer fund (for example, all except Sweden) have been (or soon will be) obliged to take emergency measures to address crisis-induced fiscal shortfalls. In Latvia, measures include a temporary reduction of the contributions of the funded pillar to make room for the unfunded one; after a protracted debate, in Poland the contribution rate to the funded pillar was reduced from 7.3 to 2.3 percent in 2011, with a plan to raise it to 3.5 percent by 2018. It should be noted, of course, that such emergency measures were necessary for essentially all of the reformed pension systems in the former transition economies in Europe and Central Asia countries (see World Bank 2009). Even Sweden may need to revise its current balancing mechanism, which relies on a nonactuarial estimator for the PAYG asset, which is heavily influenced by the financial crisis and not long-term developments. In its current formulation it does not allow digging into the (huge) buffer fund, which has primarily demographic smoothing objectives and thus enforced a reduction in the annual benefit indexation in 2010.

## Notes

1. The introduction of a funded pension scheme in countries that have PAYG pension schemes results in transition costs as contributions from current contributors are diverted to funding and are, therefore, no longer available to pay benefits to current beneficiaries.

2. For the withdrawal phase, benefits can be indexed to changes in prices, to changes in wages, to the notional interest rate, or to some combination thereof. As a general rule, the higher the rate of indexation, the lower the initial benefit at retirement, and vice versa. If benefits are indexed at the notional interest rate, then both contributors and retirees are effectively sharing the burden (or the benefit) of a change in the notional interest rate. If another rate is selected, then typically benefits are readjusted periodically in accordance with an actuarial valuation reflecting changes in prices, wages, discount rates, and life expectancies. The current funded individual accounts use a common annuity factor of 139. Although this value was based on an assessment of these same variables, it should be periodically revised to reflect changing conditions.

3. An alternative—and technically more demanding—mechanism would be to immediately calculate the notional interest rate as the allowable growth of liabilities (this is the maximum rate at which the balance in individual accounts and pensions in payment can grow). Comparing total liabilities to total assets requires an approximation for the latter and an estimate of "contribution assets." Although such an approach is technically demanding, it is conceptually promising (see Robalino and Bodor 2009).

4. Under steady-state conditions, the notional interest rate will equal the growth rate of the contribution base ($gcb$), the growth rate of wage sum ($gws$), and the growth rate of GDP ($ggdp$). Under real-world conditions, however, these rates will diverge, at least temporarily, as a result of (1) the maturation of pension schemes that leads for many decades to an expansion in the number contributors (which results in $gcb$ being higher than $gws$, which will happen in China as a consequence of coverage expansion); (2) economic development, which typically leads to an increase in wages as a share of GDP (which results in $gws$ being higher than $ggdp$, which appears to be starting in China after a

sharp fall in wage/GDP share in the 2000s in the face of mass rural to urban migration); and (3) economic and demographic shocks, which can and do lead to material deviations from steady-state conditions for relatively long periods. Economic shocks that translate into changes in wages and employment are reflected in all three growth rates but in a manner that results in differentiated outcomes for contributors and beneficiaries as well as differentiated outcomes for short- and long-term financial sustainability. Demographic shocks, such as population aging, are also reflected in the rates but only partially and in a differentiated manner.

5. For a stochastic simulation comparing different proxies for the notional interest rate and the related stability of the balancing mechanism, see Robalino and Bodor (2009).

6. In high-income countries, life expectancy at birth has been increasing over the last few decades at approximately 30 months per decade. Life expectancy at age 60, however, has increased at about half this value. Consequently, the actual number of years someone aged 60 can be expected to live is underestimated by about two to three years (or 10–15 percent) when life expectancy at age 60 is applied at retirement and not subsequently adjusted over time.

7. See Robalino and Bodor (2009).

8. This rule-of-thumb is consistent with recent estimates generated by "stress tests" of the impact of the economic crisis on the pension scheme under alternative crisis scenarios using the World Bank's PROST (Policy Reform Options Simulation Toolkit) model for a synthetic European transition economy. Under a relatively rapid recovery scenario, the aggregated deficit of the pension scheme is four to five months of expenditures. Under a severe crisis scenario, the aggregated deficit is some 16 percent of GDP, or roughly two years of annual expenditures (see Hinz and others 2009).

9. The contribution rates for the funded scheme have been temporarily adjusted to create budgetary room in response to the financial and economic crisis (see Chlon-Dominszak and others 2012).

## References

Alho, J., J. M. Bravo, and E. Palmer. 2013 "Annuities and Life Expectancy in NDC." In *Nonfinancial Defined Contribution Pension Schemes in a Changing Pension World: Gender, Politics and Financial Stability*, vol. 2, ed. R. Holzmann, E. Palmer, and D. A. Robalino, ch. 22. Washington, DC: World Bank and Swedish Social Insurance Agency.

Chlon-Dominszak, A., D. Franco, and E. Palmer. 2012. "The First Wave of NDC Reforms: The Experiences of Italy, Latvia, Poland and Sweden." In *Nonfinancial*

*Defined Contribution Pension Schemes in a Changing Pension World: Progress, Lessons and Implementation,* vol. 1, ed. R. Holzmann, E. Palmer, and D. A. Robalino, ch. 2. Washington, DC: World Bank and Swedish Social Insurance Agency.

Hinz, R., A. Zviniene, S. Biletsky, and T. Bogomolova. 2009. "The Impact of the Financial Crisis on Public Pension Systems: Stress Testing Models of Mandatory Pension Systems in Middle Income and Developing Countries." Social Protection and Labor Department, World Bank, Washington, DC.

Holzmann, R., and A. Jousten. 2013. "Addressing the Legacy Costs in an NDC Reform: Conceptualization, Measurement, Financing." In *Nonfinancial Defined Contribution Pension Schemes in a Changing Pension World: Vol. 2—Gender, Politics and Financial Stability,* ed. R. Holzmann, E. Palmer, and D. A. Robalino, ch. 18. Washington, DC: World Bank.

Holzmann, R., E. Palmer, and D. Robalino, eds. 2012a. *Nonfinancial Defined Contribution Pension Schemes in a Changing Pension World: Vol. 1—Progress, Lessons, and Implementation.* Washington, DC: World Bank.

———. 2012b. *Nonfinancial Defined Contribution Pension Schemes in a Changing Pension World: Vol. 2—Gender, Politics, and Financial Stability* Washington, DC: World Bank.

Palmer, E. 2006a. "What Is NDC? to NDCs—Issues and Models." In *Pension Reform: Issues and Prospects for Nonfinancial Defined Contribution (NDC) Schemes,* ed. R. Holzmann and E. Palmer, 17–33. Washington, DC: World Bank.

———. 2006b. "Conversion to NDCs—Issues and Models." In *Pension Reform: Issues and Prospects for Nonfinancial Defined Contribution (NDC) Schemes,* ed. R. Holzmann and E. Palmer, 169–202. Washington, DC: World Bank.

Robalino, D., and A. Bodor. 2009. "On the Financial Sustainability of the Pay-as-You-Go Systems and the Role of Government Indexed Bonds." *Journal of Pension Economics and Finance* 8 (2): 153–87.

World Bank. 2009. "Pensions in Crisis: Europe and Central Asia Regional Policy Note." Human Development Sector Unit, World Bank, Washington, DC.

**APPENDIX C**

# Evaluation of Legacy Costs

## Understanding the Liabilities

Defining, forecasting, and planning for the financing of legacy costs for urban pension schemes in China is essential regardless of whether or not they are reformed. In any pension system, accrued-to-date liabilities should be matched by corresponding assets if the system is to be sustainable. The options for restoring sustainability include lowering benefits, delaying retirement, reducing the generosity of indexation policies, increasing contributions, and effecting budgetary transfers. In most countries, neither parametric nor structural reforms generally can reduce accrued-to-date liabilities significantly without reducing the accrued rights of current workers. Instead, reforms typically focus on shifting schemes toward financial sustainability in the future (that is, to reducing the actuarial deficit for future generations). This leaves an uncovered liability—generally referred to as the *legacy cost*—that must be financed regardless of reform.

Legacy costs can be broadly defined as the actuarial deficit of a reformed pension scheme. They arise from two sources, namely (1) costs associated with the unreformed scheme (which must be financed regardless of reform) and (2) costs created by the reform, such as reduced contribution rates. Examples of the former type in China include the move from higher benefits (for *old men* and *middle men*) to lower benefits for new entrants since 1997 (*new men*). (See figure C.1 for a definition of these terms.) The financing approach adopted has been to essentially retain the pre-1997 contribution rate, thereby burdening *new men* and some *middle men* with higher contribution rates than are necessary to finance their own benefits. Defined-contribution schemes tie future benefits to future contributions so that even though the resources contributed may be diverted to pay existing or future beneficiaries, a long-term balance between contributions and benefits is still required for sustainability. Under FDC and NDC schemes, contribution rates are fixed, and, by design, entitlements in individual accounts cannot be less than what is contributed without undermining the credibility of the scheme.

The significance of legacy costs for countries with large and growing elderly dependency ratios—including China—is that, unless these costs are adequately estimated and prudently financed, they can undermine fiscal stability and public credibility, the very purpose of reform. This chapter provides a conceptual framework for understanding legacy costs, then discusses the estimation of the liabilities of China's urban old-age pension system, and proceeds to estimate the pay-as-you-go asset, legacy costs, and phasing. It then explores the issue of financing legacy costs and the lessons of the Liaoning pilot and concludes by providing broad estimates and recommendations for financing legacy costs.

To design a viable long-term financing plan for legacy costs, the following steps are necessary:

- Estimate *accrued-to-date liabilities* of the reformed system; in China, this is complex because accrued rights reflect a variety of prior reforms as well as special ad hoc provisions
- Estimate *pay-as-you-go assets* and any financial assets and compute overall legacy costs as the difference from the total accrued liabilities
- Translate estimates for total legacy costs into annual cash flow requirements
- Establish a financing plan and identify budgetary and nonbudgetary resources to pay for the costs over time.

Reasonable but rigorous estimates of pension scheme liabilities, based on a clear understanding of their underlying composition, are essential to financing them. In China, estimating legacy costs is particularly complex because different categories of entitlements already exist as a result of the provisions of pilot systems and transition arrangements established over

**Figure C.1   China Urban Old-Age Insurance System: Categorization of Beneficiaries and Their Benefit Entitlements**

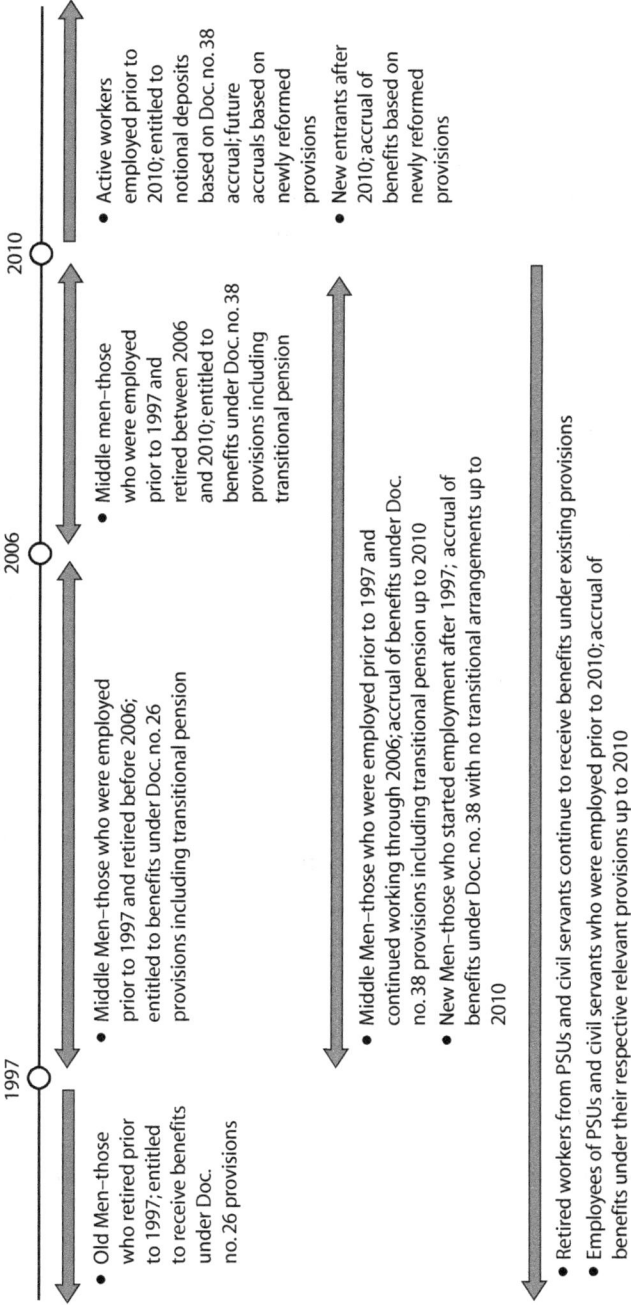

1997   2006   2010

- Old Men–those who retired prior to 1997; entitled to receive benefits under Doc. no.26 provisions

- Middle Men–those who were employed prior to 1997 and retired before 2006; entitled to benefits under Doc. no.26 provisions including transitional pension

- Middle men–those who were employed prior to 1997 and retired between 2006 and 2010; entitled to benefits under Doc. no.38 provisions including transitional pension

- Active workers employed prior to 2010; entitled to notional deposits based on Doc. no.38 accrual; future accruals based on newly reformed provisions

- New entrants after 2010; accrual of benefits based on newly reformed provisions

- Middle Men–those who were employed prior to 1997 and continued working through 2006; accrual of benefits under Doc. no.38 provisions including transitional pension up to 2010

- New Men–those who started employment after 1997; accrual of benefits under Doc. no.38 with no transitional arrangements up to 2010

- Retired workers from PSUs and civil servants continue to receive benefits under existing provisions

- Employees of PSUs and civil servants who were employed prior to 2010; accrual of benefits under their respective relevant provisions up to 2010

*Source:* World Bank compilation from relevant policy documents.
*Note:* PSU = public sector unit.

the last 15 years. If a different policy design were to be established, the liabilities associated with all entitlements accrued to the effective date of the new regime must be aggregated and treated as potential liabilities that must be financed. Regardless of how these liabilities are defined, the key is to formulate a methodology that is transparent and unbiased with estimates of magnitude based on generally accepted actuarial principles and consistent with macroeconomic forecasts. It is equally important that explicit decisions be made to ensure that any financing arrangement that emerges reflects a systematic process rather than the ad hoc negotiation with individual provinces.

If the authorities elect to introduce an NDC-based design for the old-age insurance system, it will be necessary to compute benefit entitlements based on past structural reforms and subsequent policy revisions and then translate such entitlements into initial NDC capital in accordance with internally consistent assumptions. Because of the highly decentralized nature of the existing urban old-age insurance system, a decade of different pilot provisions, varying degrees of economic development, and changing demographic conditions, it would be unrealistic to expect that any reformed regime could simply assume the burden of legacy liabilities without substantial computational analysis. To appreciate the underlying complexity, it is first necessary to appreciate the historical development of the urban old-age insurance scheme in China, including the key provisions of the 1997 reform and the policy changes initiated in 2005. The 1997 reform (promulgated by Document No. 26) created distinct groups of beneficiaries—*old men*, *middle men*, and *new men*—with different benefit entitlements. In 2005, Document No. 38 preserved the entitlements of those who had already retired as of 2005 but made further amendments to how benefits would be determined for *middle men* and *new men*, who would still be contributing to the system. With the reforms proposed in this report, the acquired rights of all three groups of beneficiaries would be preserved up to the effective date of the reform, and future service accruals would comply with the reformed provisions. Given this complexity, the liabilities established under the provisions of Document No. 26 and subsequently revised by Document No. 38 must be accounted for and financed separately to avoid undermining the sustainability of the proposed reforms.

Figure C.1 provides a schematic representation of the timeline, the categories of beneficiaries, and the basis of their entitlements. Boxes C.1 and C.2 provide a brief description of the key provisions of Documents

**Box C.1**

# Provisions under Document No. 26 of 1997

The following is a summary of provisions under the status quo as per Document No. 26:

- *Coverage.* Coverage under the old-age insurance program is applicable to all types of enterprises and their employees as well as to individual workers in urban areas.
- *Contribution rates.* Total contributions by enterprises are not supposed to exceed 20 percent of the contributory wage bill. Total contributions to individual accounts are set at 11 percent of wages. From a rate of at least 4 percent of wages in 1997, individual employee contributions were set to increase by 1 percent every two years thereafter until the contribution rate reaches 8 percent. Although the employee contribution rate was specified to increase to 8 percent of wages, the enterprise contribution rate was specified to decrease to 3 percent.
- *Contributory wage.* Employee contributions are subject to a minimum of 60 percent and a maximum of 300 percent of the local average wage. Those who earn less than 60 percent of the local average wage must contribute on the basis of an earnings level equal to 60 percent of the local average wage.
- *Retirement benefits.* Retirement benefits are determined based on each worker's status as of December 31, 1996. Workers who were already retired and were receiving pension payments in 1996 are referred to as *old men,* who continue to receive their pension entitlements in accordance with the preexisting defined-benefit formula in effect prior to the reform. Workers who started contributing after 1996 are referred to as *new men.* Their pension benefits consists of two parts: (1) a monthly basic pension equal to 20 percent of the last year's local average wage and (2) a monthly pension payable from the individual account derived by dividing the accumulated account balance at retirement by 120. Workers who were not yet retired in 1996 but were already contributing to the old-age insurance system in 1996 are referred to as *middle men.* Their pension benefits were to be determined on the same basis as the *new men,* but they were to be entitled to a transition pension based on the following formula:

$$(P \times A \times Q \times M) + K, \tag{C.1}$$

*(continued next page)*

**Box C.1** *(continued)*

where

$P$ = the accrual factor (typically ranging from 1 percent to 1.4 percent)

$A$ = local average wage for the year before retirement

$Q$ = an index of average contributory wage and calculated as $(X_1/A_1 + X_2/A_2 + X_3/A_3 + \ldots + X_n/A_n)/n$, where $X_1, X_2, X_3, \ldots, X_n$ represent the individual's contributory wage levels for the years 1996, 1997, 1998 through the year before retirement, and $A_1, A_2, A_3, \ldots, A_n$ represent the average local wage for the same years; and $n$ is the length of contributory service, that is, the years between the time individual accounts were first established (assumed to be 1996) through the year before retirement

$M$ = length of service before the establishment of the individual account; for the purpose of this projection, 1996 is assumed to be the year when individual accounts were established

$K$ = fixed amount of supplement (this amount varies by province and municipality and can range from 0 to 120 RMB per month); for the purpose of these projections, a monthly amount of 75 RMB was assumed.

In many provinces and municipalities, it is common practice to provide middle men who retired after 1996 with pension benefits that are the higher of (1) a pension determined using the calculation described above and (2) a pension based on the defined-benefit formula prior to the reform.

- *Pensionable wage.* The reference wage used in determining the basic pension is defined as the local average wage, including the wages of the *xia gang* workers in the year before retirement (*xia gang* workers—literally "step down from the post"—were those retained with partial or no pay in the process of SOE restructuring).
- *Normal retirement age.* Age 60 for men and age 50 for women in general (but age 55 for women who are in managerial positions).
- *Termination benefits.* Workers with less than 15 years of contributory service will not be entitled to receive any basic pension. Accumulations under the individual accounts will be refunded as a single lump sum.
- *Indexation of benefits.* Although Document No. 26 did not indicate a specific level of postretirement indexation, other State Council documents made reference to indexation based on some percentage of the increase in the nominal wage. However, Document No. 26 did not specify whether the pension amounts derived from the individual accounts would be subject to the same level of post-retirement indexation.

Nos. 26 and 38. To develop a viable financing plan, reasonable assumptions for determining previous entitlements to be applied towards the proposed NDC scheme need to be made with the following principles: (1) workers who are currently members of the urban old-age insurance system should receive all of their accrued past service as a notional deposit to their individual accounts, (2) civil servants and PSU employees should receive the same treatment, regardless of their past contributions, (3) workers entering the urban retirement system in the future should be subject to the newly reformed conditions and benefit formulas (although the retirement age would only gradually be increased to age 65 for men and women), and (4) the urban old-age insurance system should apply the same provisions throughout China, regardless of location. The basis for these constraints reflects many other contextual factors that lie outside the realm of this discussion on legacy costs.

*Past policy decisions contributed significantly to the current problem of legacy costs* in ways that could not have been anticipated by policy makers when the policies were designed. Provisions made before 1997, for example, made possible the liberal allowance of early retirement as a way to facilitate the reform of state-owned enterprises and to compensate for lower levels of income associated with hazardous occupations. This practice came to be seen as a convenient way of meeting the requirement to pay transition pensions to those with insufficient time to accumulate adequate accumulations in their individual accounts under the provisions made after 1997. These indirect consequences have greatly compounded the challenges created by the legal entitlements allowed in the past.

## Estimating the Liabilities of China's Urban Old-Age Insurance System

The aggregate liabilities accrued to date—which is the relevant measure of China's implicit pension debt for its urban old-age insurance system—is equal to the present value of pensions in disbursement and the present value of any acquired rights to future benefits. Although the liabilities of benefits in disbursement are typically simple to calculate, although in China, estimates must take into account various special provisions that will likely increase their cost. Likewise, under steady-state conditions, the present value of acquired rights is typically easy to estimate. In China, however, estimates are complicated by the fact that rights arise from three distinct groups and benefits.

Special provisions for old-age pensions were established to compensate low-income earners engaged in hazardous occupations and to honor the previous cradle-to-grave promises made to older workers who contributed during China's economic reform years. The retrenchment and restructuring of state-owned enterprises during economic reform contributed heavily to unfavorable pension system demographics. Pension funds traditionally relied on employment in state-owned enterprises for the bulk of their contributions. However, since the early 1990s, growth of employment in state-owned enterprises has fallen and has continued to lag behind employment in urban enterprises. This was accompanied by waves of early retirement as workers in their forties and fifties—who were unable, unwilling, or without the means to continue meaningful employment—were gradually displaced. In the absence of an adequate social safety net, this trend continued as workers opted for early retirement as a means to replace their lost income. Over time, early-retirement entitlements came to be seen as a kind of substitute for other forms of social benefits such as unemployment support, severance pay, and compensation for employees in bankrupt companies, as well as social subsidies for disabled workers and workers in hazardous occupations. Consequently the liabilities associated with paying for the benefits of these early retirees—many of whom are below the statutory retirement age—have come to be borne by existing and future generations of contributors in the form of higher contribution rates (in excess of what is required to pay for their own pensions).

The acquired rights of three distinct groups must be differentiated when estimating their related liabilities:

(1) *Rights acquired for new men* reflect, in principle, the pre-reform steady-state, so the computation of their associated liability should be straightforward (see box C.1). Provincial pilots, provincial differentiation, and changes in regulation, however, do not allow a simple application of homogenous rules but require a more differentiated approach (see box C.2).

(2) *Rights acquired under the transition rules and grandfathered benefits for old and middle men.* The liabilities associated with pension benefits committed to *old men* should be largely in disbursement and, hence, relatively easy to estimate. It will probably be more difficult to do this, however, for *middle men,* for whom special transition rules have been

**Box C.2**

# Provisions under Document No. 38

Subsequent to the conclusion of the Liaoning pilot program as guided by under Document No. 42, the State Council modified key provisions of Document No. 26 of 1997 by introducing Document No. 38 in December 2005, summarized as follows:

- The basic pension is determined at the rate of 1.0 percent for each year of contributory service (minimum of 15 years required) to be applied against the average of the last year's local wage and an index of an individual's average contributory wage over the contributory period.
- The new formula for determining the basic pension will help to reduce the incentive for workers to quit the system prematurely or to underreport their contributory wages.
- Individual accounts will be disbursed monthly based on the accumulated balance divided by the prescribed age-specific annuity factor at time of retirement.
- The actuarially imbalanced amortization factor of 120 for individual accounts has been eliminated and age-specific factors introduced that are now much closer to an actuarial equivalent factor (although there is room for improvement).
- As in the case of the Liaoning pilot, the total contribution rate to individual accounts was reduced to 8 percent of payroll. However, the account was to be *gradually* funded, starting from funding 3 percent of payroll from January 2006. Contributions to individual accounts were to be segregated from the social pooling component.
- The level of funding of individual accounts was to be gradual, beginning with a few relatively well-off provinces in 2006. By mid-2009, 13 provinces had migrated toward a partially funded individual account system.
- Future pensions were to be indexed to a certain percentage of average wage growth in the local economy over the last few years; pension adjustments have largely been provided as flat amounts depending on the existing level of pension payments.
- Specifics pertaining to the level of funding, financing responsibilities, the model of fund management, as well as the rights of provinces to introduce partial funding were not specified.

established. The accrued benefits for *middle men* from the 1997 reform up to the date when a new reform might be introduced follow closely those of *new men*.

(3) *Rights acquired by newly covered groups such as employees of PSUs and civil servants*, who are entitled to receive credit for past service. Under the reform proposed in this report, the definition of liabilities will also have to be extended to include past service liabilities for newly covered groups. Such past service entitlements would be determined based on past benefit provisions, years of service up to the conversion date to the newly reformed system, and wages effective at the time of conversion (regardless of whether prior contributions had been made). Because these liabilities are already financed through the general budget, however, estimating them only makes them explicit; they may not require an explicit source of financing.

*Reconciling the accrued liability with the determination of initial capital.* Although traditional actuarial methods can be used to calculate the acquired rights for each of these three groups for the purpose of computing their related accrued-to-date liability, the amount relevant for the legacy cost calculation will depend on the principles and timing ultimately used to commute these acquired rights into the initial capital that will be recorded in the individual accounts of the proposed NDC scheme. Different approaches can be taken, including (1) calculating initial capital based on the balances that would have accrued as a function of an individual's past wages and the notional interest rate as if the individual had been in the NDC scheme from his or her entry into the workforce (that is, estimation from below), (2) applying actuarial principles to determine the benefit to which an individual was entitled based on the rules of the prior scheme (that is, estimation from above), or (3) some combination of these two approaches. Once the process of commutation has been determined and initial capital has been awarded, the aggregate value of this initial capital plus the present value of benefits in disbursement constitute the overall relevant liability of the pension scheme—and the only computation that matters for the determination of the legacy costs.

## Estimating the Pay-as-You-Go Asset, Legacy Costs, and Phasing

The concept of a pay-as-you-go (PAYG) asset is a new but powerful tool for pension analysis. It is an integral component of a new conceptual framework that establishes a *balance sheet* for PAYG schemes in much the same way as is done for partially and fully funded schemes, thereby allowing the straightforward determination of a scheme's solvency. The asset side of the scheme balance sheet includes the PAYG asset, defined as the net lifetime tax of the current and all future generations (in other words, the present value of cash flows collected by the pension institution) plus any financial assets associated with the scheme. This net lifetime tax is the difference between the present value of contributions that this and all future generations will be expected to pay and the present value of benefits that it and future generations can expect to receive. If total assets (computed as the sum of the PAYG asset and any financial assets) are smaller than total liabilities (computed as the present value of all accrued to date pension rights of pensioners and workers), the scheme is insolvent, and the difference between the two represents an implicit unfunded liability that needs to be financed.

Although conceptually straightforward, it is less obvious how to accurately estimate the value of the PAYG asset, and so various options have been proposed. For systems near steady-state conditions (for example, the Swedish NDC scheme), the *pay-as-you-go* asset $(GA)$ is estimated as period contribution revenues $(C_t)$ times the turnover duration $(DT_t)$, the latter of which is approximated by the money-weighted average age of a retiree minus the money-weighted average age of a contributor (see Settegreen and Mikula 2009):

$$GA_t = C_t \times DT_t \qquad (C.2)$$

Another steady-state approach approximates the net assets of each cohort $Z(a, t)$ at age $a$ at time $t$ and aggregates net assets across current workers and future entrants (see Robalino and Bodor 2009). This estimate (in expectation value $E$) is then used to calculate the notional interest rate (that is, the implicit rate of return $[IRR]$). This approach performs better in stochastic simulations of the stability of the balancing mechanism compared with other approximations, such as average wage growth and GDP growth.

$$E(PA_t) = \sum_{a=f}^{L} N(a,t)Z(a,t) + \sum_{k=t+1}^{T} \sum_{b=f}^{L} \Delta N(b,k)Z(b,k), \qquad (C.3)$$

where $N(a,t)$ are the contributors of age $a$ at time $t$, $\Delta N(b,k)$ represents new entrants to the scheme of age $b$ at time $k$, $L$ is the length of contribution, and $T$ is the planning horizon.

Although such calculations under steady-state assumptions provide useful benchmarks for the PAYG asset, they are too crude for application to China given expected demographic changes, growth of the urban labor force, improvements in coverage, and changes in the relationship of (covered) wage growth and GDP growth over the coming decades. Such dynamic changes can be reasonably captured only by an actuarially based projection model that has the capacity to handle differences in benefit levels for various subgroups. One obvious choice would be the World Bank's Pension Reform Options Simulation Toolkit (PROST) model.

Calculating the PAYG asset for an NDC scheme is easier than calculating one for a defined-benefit scheme. For each individual and benefit cohort, the present value of contributions will, by definition, equal the present value of pension benefits if the notional interest rate is used as the discount rate. Hence, the key driver for computing the PAYG asset is the proper selection of notional interest rate, which depends on projected demographic development, coverage, patterns of wage growth, and the assumed discount rate. For China (as for other emerging economies), key assumptions for this sort of projection should be derived from a macroeconomic model that considers the transitional path of covered wage growth relative to GDP growth until a steady-state share of wages in GDP is ultimately attained. Computing the PAYG asset from such a projection model has the great advantage that the results can be crosschecked, because total legacy costs must be equal to the actuarial deficit (that is, the present value of future annual cash flow deficits) of the reformed system. If this is the case (presumably after some adjustments and recalibration), the resulting annual cash flow deficits represent the scheme's estimated annual financing needs (that is, the phasing of annual legacy costs). Given that the reform proposed herein assumes that the provincial authorities will bear responsibility for financing legacy costs, at least until national pooling can be implemented, the estimation of liabilities, the PAYG asset, legacy costs, and their annual phasing would need to be done for each of the provinces using a consistent macroeconomic framework and methodology. This is an ambitious but not impossible task.

## Financing Legacy Costs—Lessons from the Liaoning Pilot

The World Bank's evaluation of the Liaoning pilot provides an instructive example of how this process of estimating and financing legacy costs can be handled (World Bank 2004). For several years after the Liaoning pilot began, budgetary support was deemed adequate to cover the cost of high replacement rates from the old system, early-retirement pensions, as well as part of the transition costs. Contribution revenues were also used to pay for the cost of systemic design flaws. This led to higher than required contribution rates, which resulted in higher labor costs. Further analysis revealed that Liaoning's total implicit pension debt amounted to a staggering 153 percent of regional GDP in 2001 values, of which only 56 percent was the liability associated with the steady-state system, whereas 17 percent was due to systemic flaws, 4.3 percent was due to early retirement, and 23 percent was due to the transition benefit provision. If the system had been in steady state, it could have maintained positive net cash flow throughout the projection with a sustainable contribution rate of about 48 percent of payroll. The total financing gap was projected to be 206 percent of the 2001 GDP.

From an evaluation of the Liaoning pilot, it became clear that in the absence of a reduction in pension benefit payments, the shift to fully fund the individual accounts would result in an enormous funding gap in the social pooling portion of the system. During the pilot phase, Liaoning's pension expenditures were financed partly by the central government and partly by the local government. Budgetary transfers equivalent to between 1.0 percent and 1.4 percent of Liaoning's GDP allowed the accumulation of individual accounts to grow as designed and kept the pension system's overall budget balanced from 2001 to 2004. It appears that the financing requirement was made according to a clearly identified rule specifying the responsibilities of various levels of government. With the aim of covering the financing gap created by the diversion of contributions to individual accounts, the authority's plan was for the central and provincial governments to finance 3.75 percent and 1.25 percent of the estimated contributory wage bill, respectively. In reality, however, between 2001 and 2004, transfers were made in annual flat amounts. Although the overall budgetary transfer was significantly higher than the cost attributed to changing over to the reformed system, the method used for establishing the levels was unclear. Within the province, redistribution across municipalities was, in principle, facilitated by the Provincial Adjustment Fund according to a redistribution formula. Still, some of the main elements of the formula were not explicitly spelled out, thus leaving room for discretion.

For the period of the pilot that was evaluated, it was clear that the huge financial outlay created was largely due to the need to make up the difference between the replacement rates that the steady-state system could be expected to support and the replacement rates actually in place when the pilot was being implemented. Specifically, it was noted that although the proposed scheme's total replacement rate for a male worker at age 65 was estimated to be 48 percent (and that for a female worker at age 65 to be 43 percent), this was significantly lower than the average replacement rate of 88 percent observed in Liaoning in 2001. It should be emphasized that the focus here is *not* on how the Liaoning experiment went or to make a case for reproducing the Liaoning experience in other provinces. In fact, the final chapters on Liaoning's initiative to finance its pension reform have yet to be written. Nevertheless, a comprehensive and carefully documented study carried out by the World Bank provides valuable lessons learned for other pension financing initiatives that must deal with significant legacy costs.

Tackling legacy costs is not a theoretical exercise. Up to a point, the concepts and approaches presented in this document can help with the systematic preparation of a financing plan by pointing out important issues to consider, as well as by providing practical suggestions on how legacy costs can be addressed based on empirical studies. Yet, as this document has tried to show, most of the real work begins only once certain parameters have been defined and specific assumptions made. In other words, as much as the principles and frameworks can be used for reference, no substitute is available for high-quality actuarial projections and informed calculations for generating solid estimates and for contextualizing their requirements to guide decisions by policy makers.

## Broad Estimates of Legacy Costs, Their Phasing, and Suggested Financing

This section provides a simplified methodology for estimating the legacy costs of an NDC reform both for the urban old-age insurance system as well as for civil servant and PSU schemes effective January 1, 2008 (the date of the most recently available annual data).

### Legacy Cost Estimation Methodology
The starting point for the estimation is the pension system balancing condition suggested:

$$PL \leq PA. \qquad (C.4)$$

Equation (C.4) suggests that the present value of pension liabilities (*PL*) must be less than or equal to the present value of pension assets. Postreform, pension liabilities consist of the present value of pension benefits in disbursement (*PB*) and initial capital (*IK*) for all active workers (that is, the present value of accrued rights under the old system) for all schemes that are consolidated and integrated into the new scheme to include the urban scheme (*us*), schemes for civil servants (*cs*), and schemes for PSUs (*psu*):

$$PL = PB + IK \qquad (C.5)$$

with

$$PB = PB_{us} + PB_{cs} + PB_{psu}$$

and

$$IK = IK_{us} + IK_{cs} + IK_{psu}$$

Postreform, pension assets (*PA*) consist of financial assets (*FA*), the PAYG asset (*GA*), and legacy costs (*LC*) for each of the systems, which have been integrated with legacy costs as the residual. Written in the aggregate:

$$PA = FA + GA + LC \qquad (C.6)$$

Solving for legacy costs (*LC*) delivers an equation that can be used to estimate legacy costs for all three integrated systems separately or on an aggregated basis. To this end, a decomposition of changes in legacy costs from the unreformed scheme is employed because this generates insight into how to reduce legacy costs beyond explicit financing (see Holzmann and Jousten 2013).

$$LC = LC^u + \Delta LC = LC^u + \Delta PB + \Delta IK - \Delta FA - \Delta GA \qquad (C.7)$$

$$LC^u = \text{legacy costs of unreformed scheme}$$

### Preliminary Cost Estimates

A decomposition of equation (C.7) can used to estimate legacy costs by applying actuarial techniques and estimating the actuarial value of the unreformed and reformed components. This section proceeds using a simplified approach that requires only a few assumptions and proxies.

The reform should leave the financial assets and—with full commutation of acquired rights—the liabilities as well unchanged (that is, $\Delta FA$, $\Delta PB$, and $\Delta IK$ are all zero). In reality, of course, room is available to reduce legacy costs by reducing the liability (that is, by making $\Delta PB$ and $\Delta IK$ negative), for example, by changing indexation rules or by manipulating the discount rate when transforming acquired rights into initial NDC capital. The unreformed system also had positive legacy costs (that is, $LC^u > 0$) resulting from early-retirement rules and the commitments to *old* and *middle men* not covered under the steady-state contribution rate before reform. In our approach these old legacy costs are captured by applying the full cost covering contribution rate to the calculation of the (old) PAYG asset and its changes.

To estimate (gross) legacy costs, one needs (1) the cost-covering contribution rates for all three unreformed schemes $(CR^u)$, (2) the sustainable new contribution rate $(CR^r)$ that is chosen by the authorities in line with their targeted replacement rate, and (3) an estimate for the level of the PAYG asset for the unreformed scheme. For the latter, the balancing condition (of liabilities equal to assets) is used to estimate the implicit pension debt $(IPD)$ of the unreformed scheme. Under these simplifications, the following estimator for the legacy costs is obtained:

$$LC = \Delta LC = \Delta GA = IPD^u \times (CR^u - CR^r)/CR^u \qquad (C.8)$$

No recent estimates have been made for the implicit pension debt of the urban scheme, much less for that of civil servant and PSU schemes. However, one can use the relationship between implicit pension debt $(IPD)$ and the annual expenditure $(PEX)$. Under steady-state conditions, the ratio of $IPD$ and $PEX$ should be constant (about 30 to 35), whereas in maturing schemes the ratio can be much higher (even infinite).

The magnitude of this ratio can be motivated by the average number of years a retiree receives a pension (for example, 15) plus the average number of years the average worker has accrued rights (for example, 20 out of 40 years working) and cross-checked against estimated ratios of mature and immature schemes (see Holzmann and others 2004).

The estimated ratio in 2001 was roughly 60 for the urban old-age insurance system (this is the last available $IPD$ estimate for the urban system as is discussed in Sin 2005 and World Bank 2006). The estimated ratio for a more mature system in Liaoning would be 48. This provides a range of ratios with which to estimate the annual expenditure. The analysis below uses a range of 40 to 60 for the urban scheme, and 35 to 48 for civil servant and PSU schemes (which are believed to be more mature).

For the cost-covering contribution rate of the schemes, an older estimate of 35 percent for the urban scheme has been used (see World Bank 2006); the rate for civil servants (their scheme is noncontributory) and

PSUs has been estimated from their pension expenditures and overall wage bill providing similar levels. Applying these contribution rates to the low and high estimates of *IPD* gives us estimates for the legacy costs in table C.1.

The estimates vary, of course, as a function of contribution rate chosen for the new NDC scheme (15 percent, 20 percent, or 25 percent).

Table C.1 suggests the following:

- The IPD estimates for all three schemes amount to between 155 percent of GDP (low estimate) and 199 percent of GDP (high estimate). Although the expenditure share of state organ workers is somewhat larger, the assumed higher maturity of their schemes translates in a lower IPD share of roughly one-fourth of total IPD. This is translated into the legacy costs as the estimated cost covering contribution rates are broadly similar.

- *The wide range of estimated legacy costs results from the equally wide scenarios of steady-state contribution rates* for the new NDC scheme based on a similar range of target replacement rates. The lower the chosen contribution rate, the higher the legacy costs; but the absolute size of legacy costs under all rates is noteworthy. Choosing a contribution rate of 15 percent (which would result in an estimated replacement rate of about 40 percent at age 65 for men and women) would result in aggregate legacy costs of 89 percent (on the low end) or 113 percent of GDP (on the high end), respectively. These estimated costs are split between private and public sector schemes roughly by 3 to 1. In the case where a new contribution rate of 25 percent were to chosen (close to the estimated steady-state rate of the unreformed urban scheme of 27 percent) the total legacy costs would fall into the range of 44–56 percent of GDP.

- *These gross legacy costs do not fully translate into additional fiscal costs even if they were to be made explicit.* The current urban old-age insurance system, civil servants, and PSU schemes already receive government subsidies that are included in these estimates. These implicit and explicit subsidies are of particular importance for the public sector schemes that have not imposed contributions on participants (that is, civil servants) or imposed low rates of contributions to finance pension expenditures (PSUs). Perhaps as much as three-quarters of legacy costs for the civil service and PSU schemes are already financed by government

**Table C.1  Estimates of Legacy Costs under an NDC Reform**

| Estimates 2008 | Pension expenditure (% of GDP) | Implicit pension debt (% of GDP) | | Cost-covering contribution rate (%) | Legacy costs (low IPD estimate): new contribution rate % of GDP | | | Legacy costs (high IPD estimate): new contribution rate % of GDP | | |
|---|---|---|---|---|---|---|---|---|---|---|
| | | Low estimate | High estimate | | 15% | 20% | 25% | 15% | 20% | 25% |
| Contribution rate | | | | | 15% | 20% | 25% | 15% | 20% | 25% |
| Urban system | 2.46 | 118 | 147 | 35 | 67 | 50 | 34 | 84 | 63 | 42 |
| State organs | 0.34 | 12 | 16 | 36 | 7 | 5 | 4 | 9 | 7 | 5 |
| PSU | 0.75 | 26 | 36 | 34 | 15 | 11 | 7 | 20 | 15 | 9 |
| **Total** | **3.54** | **155** | **199** | | **89** | **66** | **44** | **113** | **85** | **56** |

Source: World Bank estimates.

revenues. More data would be needed improve the precision of the estimates. What is clear, however, is that delaying reforms of public sector pension schemes will not save fiscal resources; rather, it would make the costs more expensive on a present-value basis.

- *The estimated legacy costs for the urban old-age insurance system have a transitory and a transitional element.* The transitory element is the result of the 1997 reform that reduced benefits for *new men* (compared to *middle* and *old men*); this must be paid in any event. Currently it is financed through higher contributions by all workers (compared to what the *new men* can expect to receive in benefits). The transitional element will result from moving from a future (and higher) steady-state contribution rate under the unreformed scheme to the new (and lower) rate under the proposed NDC scheme. These additional costs are transition costs similar to those that result from moving from an unfunded to a partially or fully funded scheme. Hence a change from a 35 percent contribution rate to a 27 percent rate (the estimated steady-state contribution rate of the unreformed scheme) creates legacy costs already incurred by the system. A reduction of the contribution rate below 27 percent would create additional new and reform-induced legacy costs. The (average) estimated implicit pension debt of the urban system of 75 percent of GDP amounts to a very rough estimation of an inherited legacy cost of 30 percent of GDP and an estimated reform-induced legacy cost of 45 percent of GDP, assuming a new contribution rate of 15 percent is used.

### Anticipated Phasing of Legacy Cost Expenditures

Establishing the magnitude of legacy costs for a scheme and making them explicit is only the first step in estimating when costs will actually come due and how they should be financed.

The shape of legacy costs over time (that is, costs by year) is determined by the mechanism of transition employed from the old to the new schemes. If the transition is immediate (that is, all active workers are immediately transferred to the proposed new NDC scheme), then the legacy costs are front-loaded. The highest value will occur in the first year, gradually falling to zero and exhibiting a slightly convex curvature (see Holzmann 1998, figure 3.b). If the proposed new NDC scheme is restricted to new entrants only, then the legacy costs are back-loaded, rising from small values and peaking after roughly 40 years before gradually falling over the next 40 years (Holzmann 1999, figure 4.b). Shifting some current workers into the new scheme (for example, everyone below the age of 40) shifts the peak costs 20 years after implementation (Holzmann 1999, figure 5.b). Starting the reform from an actuarially balanced scheme, one obtains aggregate legacy costs that are the same in present value whether the move is slow or fast. However, if the unreformed system is actuarially unsustainable, then a delay in moving to the new scheme adds greatly to the overall fiscal costs.

If one supposes that legacy costs, net of existing ongoing existing government transfers, are, for example, 75 percent of GDP under a steady-state contribution rate of 15 percent, the initial annual costs would be slightly above 2 percent of GDP per year, declining to zero after all retirees with old commitments have exited the system (that is, potentially in 80 years or more). Most of the transition costs, however, would be disbursed in half this time.

Legacy costs need not be entirely financed by the government through general revenues. Partially reneging on acquired rights through the design of transition rules is one option for reducing legacy cost, and the magnitudes of savings are far from negligible. For example, under a 4 percent real wage growth assumption, moving from full to partial wage indexation can reduce implicit pension debt (and, hence, legacy costs) by a sixth.

The other promising (and realistic) option for China is to increase system coverage as a result of the better incentives offered by NDCs to join the formal sector, continued income growth as a proxy for increasing formalization, better enforcement, and further urbanization and growth of the urban labor force. From 1998 to 2008, coverage measured as a proportion of the urban labor force that contributes to the pension system increased from 39.2 percent to 54.9 percent (15.4 percentage points). This helped increase the reserves of the urban scheme from 0.7 percent to 3.3 percent of GDP (2.6 percentage points). Achieving a coverage rate of 90 percent by 2050 seems possible—and in line with international trends given the relationship between per capita income and coverage (see World Bank 2006). The increase in the urban labor force due to continued rural migration plus the increase in the coverage overall labor force should create a sizable cash flow because coverage increases reduce system dependency ratios below the old-age dependency ratios observed in the economy as a whole. If an increase in the retirement age takes place to hold the old-age dependency ratio constant, cash surpluses would be even larger.

A rough calculation suggests that system cash flows can co-finance the legacy costs by expanding coverage if a not too low new contribution rate is selected. To illustrate the magnitudes involved, a modeling exercise was performed that replicates the starting values of expenditures and revenues for 2008 for all three groups (employees of urban enterprises, civil servants, and employees of PSUs) integrated into an NDC scheme as well as their estimated legacy costs over a period of 80 years. The new NDC scheme is assumed to have a contribution rate of 15 percent or 20 percent, and various scenarios of coverage expansion are then simulated over the coming 40 years. Doubling coverage would result in full coverage under the urban scheme for a given labor force. An increase by 200 percent of contributors could result from an increase in the size of the labor force through further rural-urban migration and higher labor force participation. To keep things simple, demographic changes are ignored (de facto assuming that their impact is offset by high retirement ages and/or lower benefit levels). Figures C.2 to C.5 present the results for two contribution scenarios (15 percent and 20 percent) for both the gross annual deficit and legacy costs as well as their net values. For the latter, all legacy costs for government sector schemes are assumed to be already covered in the public finance domain.

Figure C.2 shows the gross annual deficits (that is, the annual cash flows of gross legacy costs) of the reformed scheme under different scenarios of coverage expansion for selected new contribution rates of 15 percent (figure C.2, top panel) and 20 percent (figure C.2, bottom panel). The kinks in the plots reflect the assumptions of the model with regard to the phasing of the legacy costs, the timing of coverage expansion, and its impact on revenues, but not on the overall size of the legacy costs. Smoother transitions would somewhat impact the curvature but would not change the overall magnitudes of the plots. The initial deficit of 2 percent and 1.5 percent of GDP, respectively, reflects the drop in contribution revenues from cost-covering rates of about 35–15 percent and 20 percent, respectively. The gradual fall (under constant coverage rates) reflect the phasing out of the inherited legacy and reform-induced legacy costs over an assumed period of 80 years in addition to financing the inherited legacy costs that are the same under both contribution rate scenarios. Increasing coverage leads to a much sharper fall as revenues increase but initially without related expenditures. Once this happens (after assumed 20 years), the decrease flattens out. Once coverage increase is stopped (after assumed 40 years), the deficit increases again till the

**Figure C.2    Phasing of Gross Annual Deficit under Different Degrees of Coverage Expansion and Contribution Rates**

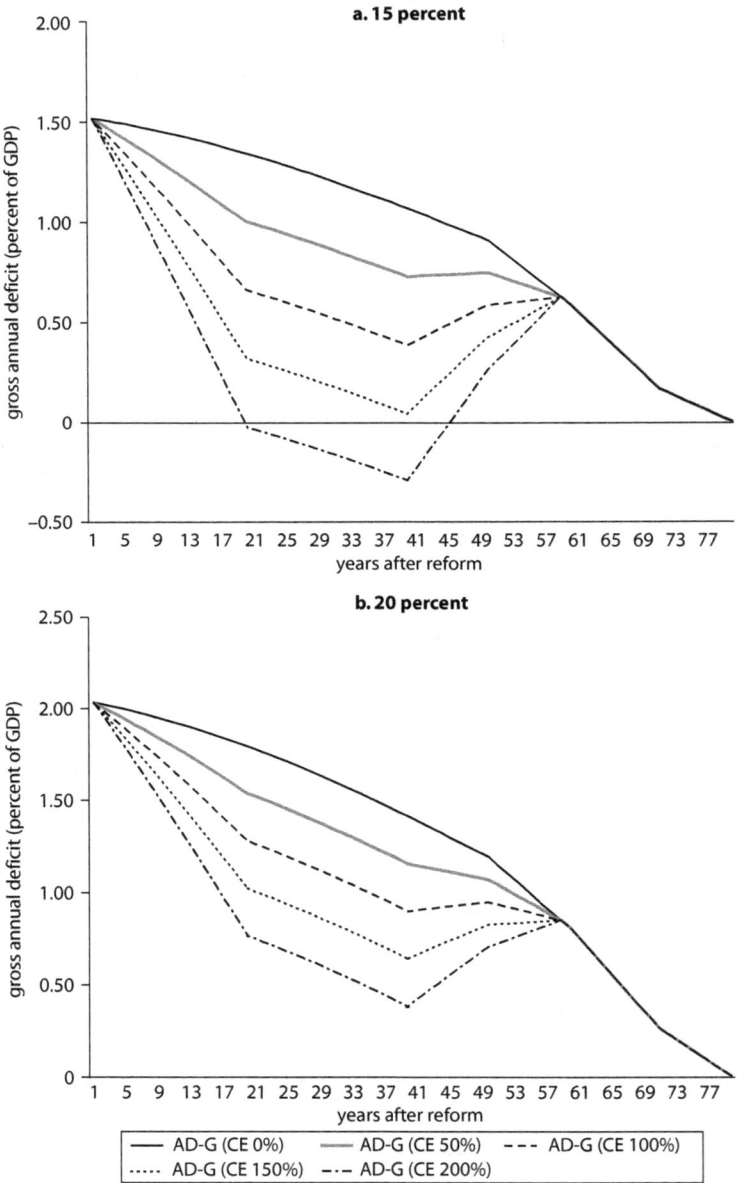

a. 15 percent

b. 20 percent

Legend:
— AD-G (CE 0%)          — AD-G (CE 50%)          - - - AD-G (CE 100%)
····· AD-G (CE 150%)       -·- AD-G (CE 200%)

*Source:* World Bank estimates.
*Note:* AD-G = gross annual deficit; CE = coverage expansion.

common deficit line is reach (after 60 years). From that point onward, any additional revenues are fully matched by additional expenditure so that the deficit time line is only driven by remaining legacy costs. The effect of the selected new contribution rate on the deficit profile is only on level, not on shape. With a selected contribution rate of 15 percent the gross deficit never turns negative; with the higher selected contribution of 20 percent, the gross deficit profile turns negative only under the highest coverage expansion scenario.

Figure C.3 translates these gross annual deficits into cumulative legacy costs in each year after the start of the reform. After 80 years, aggregated legacy costs stabilize for the baseline scenario because all inherited commitments will have been discharged. The aggregate amount is at 100 percent and 75 percent of GDP, respectively, depending on the contribution rate. The gross legacy costs, however, can get as low as 60 percent and 34 percent, respectively, for the highest coverage scenarios. The variations in the increases in coverage affect the magnitude of the gain in the reduction of gross legacy costs, amounting to about 10 percentage points of GDP for each 50 percentage point coverage increase under the lower contribution rate (15 percent) and about 13.3 percentage points of GDP for each 50 percentage point of coverage increase under the 20 percent contribution rate. A higher contribution rate has mechanically more leverage on coverage increase, but economically a higher contribution rate may not realize the same level of coverage expansion.

Figures C.4 and C.5 show the phasing of *net* annual deficits and *net* legacy costs. The net values assume that expenditures and revenues for government sector schemes are already in the budget. Hence, from a fiscal viewpoint, only the reform costs for the urban pension scheme will create new fiscal liabilities that must be covered. In the proposed NDC scheme, the *new* contributions and *new* expenditures for the now integrated government sector employees fully balance because neither legacy costs nor coverage expansion are assumed. In figure C.4, the net deficit starts out at 1.4 percent and 1.05 percent of GDP, respectively; the time profile under a different expenditure scenario follows the logic of the gross deficit. As under the latter, with the lower contribution rate (15 percent) the deficit never becomes negative but does so even under less drastic coverage expansion scenarios with a higher contribution rate (20 percent). Aggregating net annual deficits into net legacy costs, the plots in figure C.5 exhibit much lower overall costs and even result temporarily in cumulative surpluses under the scenario of 200 percent coverage expansion and with a selected contribution rate of 20 percent. Even

**Figure C.3   Phasing of Gross Legacy Costs under Different Degrees of Coverage Expansion and Contribution Rates**

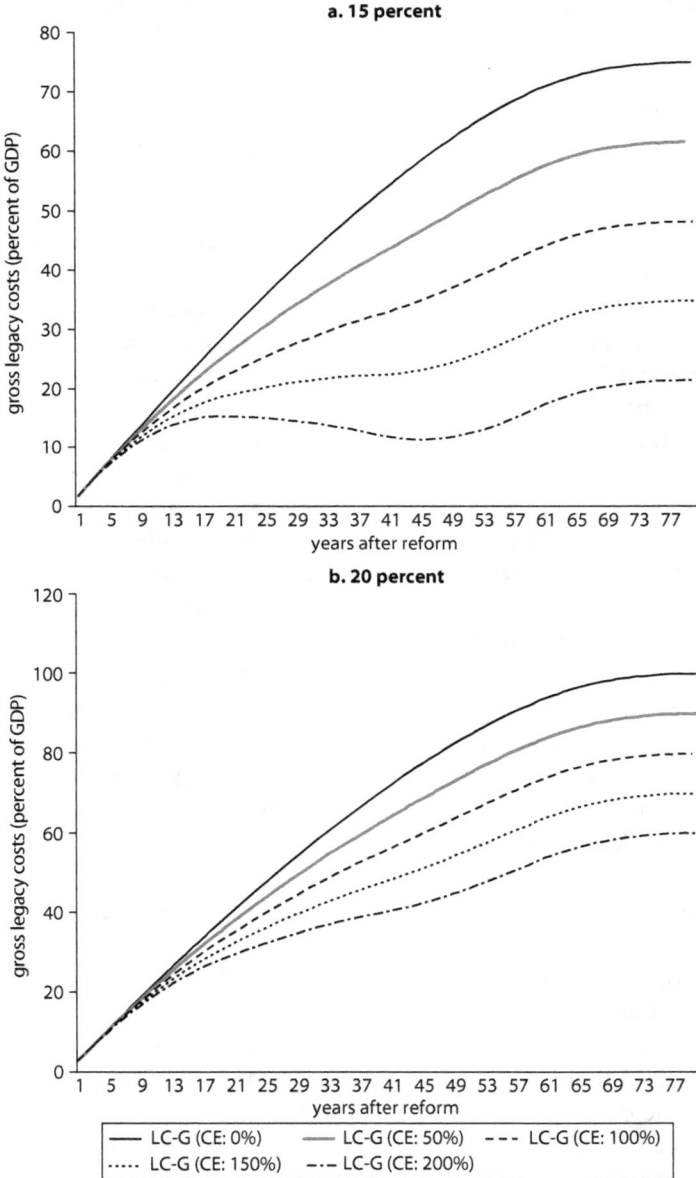

**a. 15 percent**

**b. 20 percent**

*Source:* World Bank estimates.
*Note:* LC-G = gross legacy costs; CE = coverage expansion.

**Figure C.4    Phasing of Net Annual Deficit under Different Degrees of Cover Expansion and Contribution Rates**

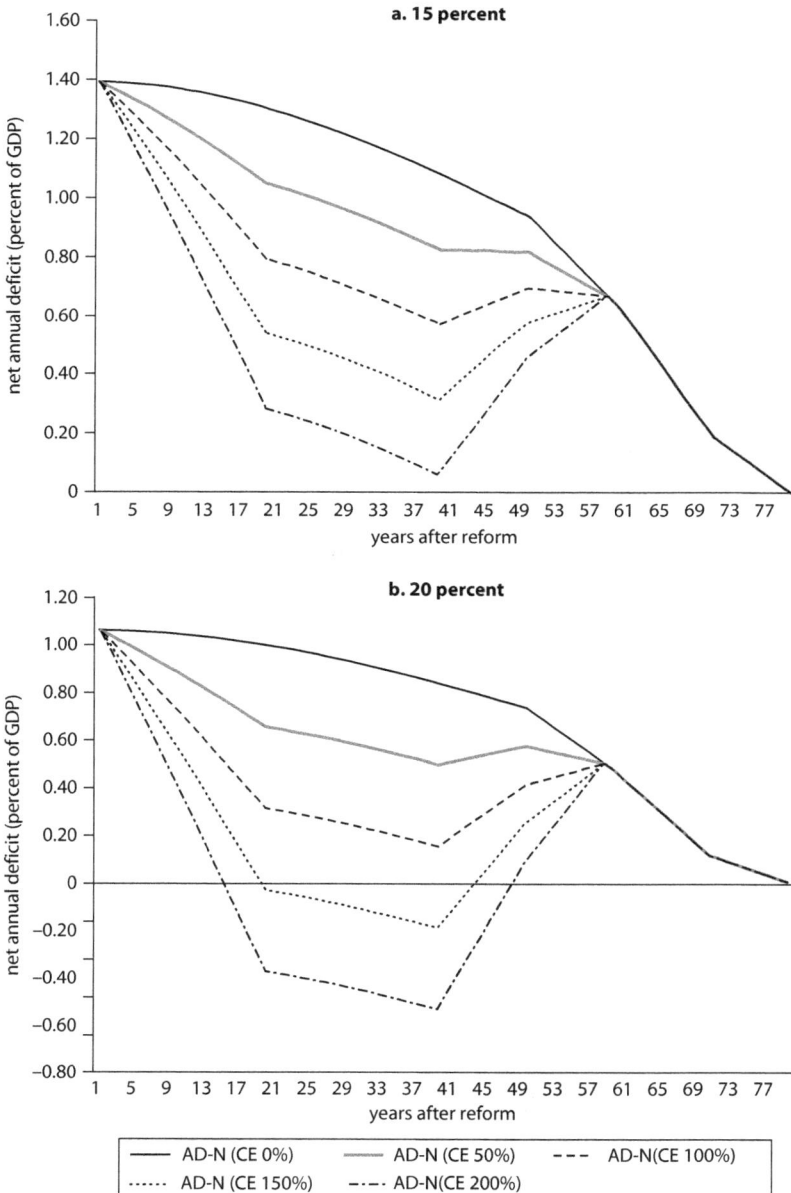

*Source:* World Bank estimates.
*Note:* AD-N = net annual deficit; CE = coverage expansion.

**Figure C.5    Phasing of Net Legacy Costs under Different Degrees of Coverage Expansion and Contribution Rates**

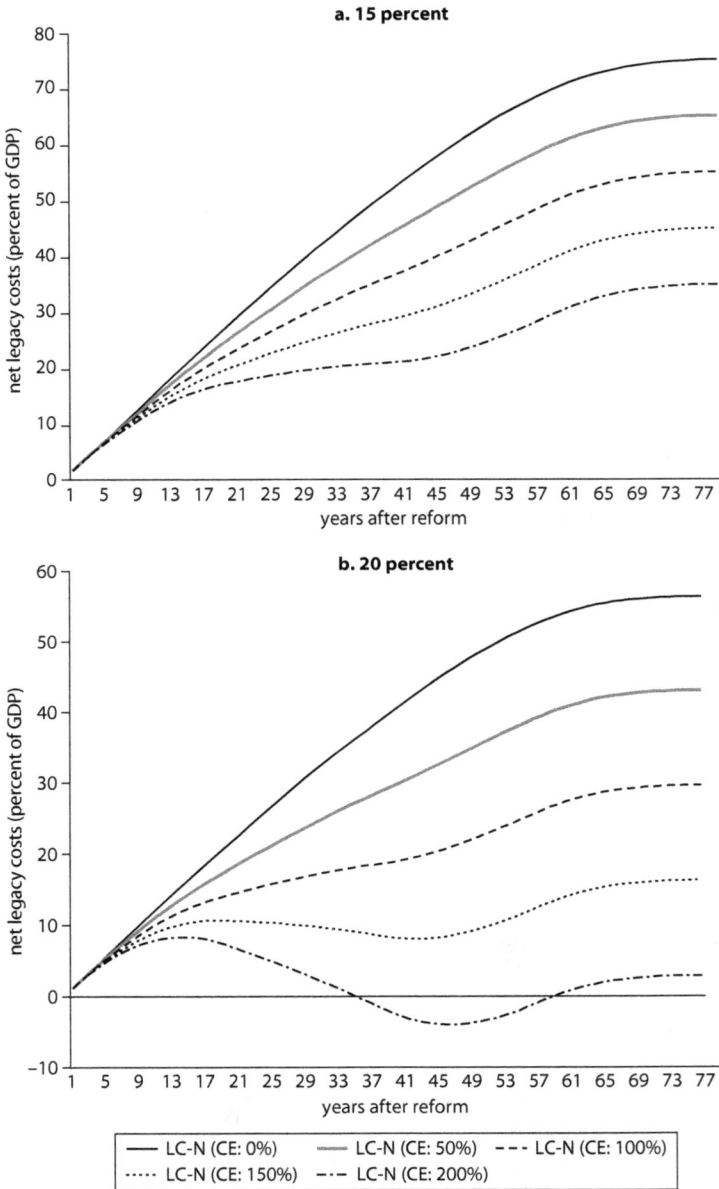

**a. 15 percent**

**b. 20 percent**

LC-N (CE: 0%)     LC-N (CE: 50%)     --- LC-N (CE: 100%)
····· LC-N (CE: 150%)     --- LC-N (CE: 200%)

*Source:* World Bank estimates.
*Note:* LC-N = net legacy costs; CE = coverage expansion.

if this optimistic level of coverage expansion were to be attained, some transitory financing of the costs may still be needed (as is discussed below).

For policy makers, the crucial conclusion that emerges from this analysis is the following: *Reform measures that reduce acquired rights and contribute to the expansion of coverage may reduce legacy costs substantially.* Doubling contributors alone over 40 years may more than halve the fiscally relevant net legacy costs to about 20–35 percent of GDP. Financing some 0.5–1 percent of GDP per annum over a period of 40 years from general revenues seems a surmountable fiscal burden. Of course, these estimates must be validated by actuarial study, but their broad magnitudes are unlikely to change significantly.

### Financing Strategies for Legacy Costs

The financing of legacy costs using general revenues transferred to the proposed NDC scheme raises numerous issues that merit further study. Below we give preliminary thoughts on the issue of estimation and disbursement and on budgetary financing:

- Conceptually, the use of budgetary transfers (on a monthly or annual basis) to the proposed NDC scheme should compensate the scheme for the lost revenues that will result from lowering the contribution rate to its equilibrium level and for honoring past commitments. Budgetary transfers should, of course, flow to the social security institution where revenue pooling takes place. If, initially, this is at provincial level, then estimations of legacy costs and transfers should be performed there. Although it is already methodologically complex to generate such estimates at the outset of reform, the challenge will become only more difficult as time passes and the counterfactual becomes increasingly blurred. Delay could create an incentive for the provincial authorities to game the process of estimation to maximize the size of the budgetary transfers irrespective of their underlying merit. This suggests that an initial estimation of the overall amount of provincial legacy costs should be conducted at the outset of the reform and a disbursement schedule should be established that extends, for example, for 40 years. The problem with such an approach is that the amount of budgetary support should logically fall over time if targets for coverage expansion are actually met. To sidestep this quandary, accelerated achievement of the government's stated goal of national pooling would be advisable.

- The fiscal resources for budgetary transfers to finance legacy costs must be identified. Some are already in place (for example, the payment of pensions from the general budget for retirees from the civil servant and PSU schemes). Most others will need to be financed through reduced public expenditures or higher general revenues. For the latter, choices are limited and should respect efficiency and equity considerations. Tax theory (as well as ex ante simulations and econometric studies) suggests that capital taxation is not a good solution because it risks reducing the long-term growth rate. Income taxes are also generally thought to be more distortional than consumption taxes (for example, value-added taxes). Although the use of a robust and simple value-added tax has proven viable in many countries of varying levels of per capita income (and is conjectured to be less distortive in terms of individual labor supply and savings decisions than, say, income taxes), some studies call for caution (see Holzmann and Jousten 2013 for additional references). For China, currently underexplored revenue sources include property taxes, environmental and "sin" taxes, and SOE dividends.

## References

Holzmann, R. 1998. "Financing the Transition to Multipillar." Social Protection Discussion Paper Series No. 9808, World Bank, Washington, DC. December.

Holzmann, R., and A. Jousten. 2013. "Addressing the Legacy Costs in an NDC Reform: Conceptualization, Measurement, Financing." In *Nonfinancial Defined Contribution Pension Schemes in a Changing Pension World, vol. 2: Gender, Politics and Financial Stability*, ed. R. Holzmann, E. Palmer, and D. A. Robalino, ch. 18. Washington, DC: World Bank.

Holzmann, R., R. Palacios, and A. Zviniene. 2004. "Implicit Pension Debt: Issues, Measurement and Scope in International Perspective." Social Protection Discussion Paper Series No. 0403, World Bank, Washington, DC.

Holzmann, R., E. Palmer, and D. Robalino, eds. 2012a. *Nonfinancial Defined Contribution Pension Schemes in a Changing Pension World: Vol. 1—Progress, Lessons, and Implementation.* Washington, DC: World Bank.

———. 2012b. *Nonfinancial Defined Contribution Pension Schemes in a Changing Pension World: Vol. 2—Gender, Politics, and Financial Stability* Washington, DC: World Bank.

Robalino, D., and A. Bodor. 2009. "On the Financial Sustainability of Earnings-Related Pension Schemes with 'Pay-as-You-Go' Financing and the Role of Government-Indexed Bonds." *Journal of Pension Economics and Finance* 8 (2): 153–87.

Settegreen, O., and B. Mikula. 2009. "The Rate of Return of Pay-as-You-Go Pension Systems." In *Pension Reform: Issues and Prospects for Nonfinancial Defined Contribution* (NDC) Schemes, ed. R. Holzmann and E. Palmer, 117–42. Washington, DC: World Bank.

Sin, Y. 2005. "China: Pension Liabilities and Reform Options." Working Paper Series on China, World Bank, Washington, DC.

World Bank. 2004. "Liaoning Pension System Assessment Report." Unpublished report, World Bank, Beijing.

———. 2006. *China: Evaluation of the Liaoning Social Security Reform Pilot.* Human Development Sector Unit East Asia and Pacific Region, Report No. 38183-CN, World Bank, Washington, DC.

## APPENDIX D

# Aging, Retirement, and Labor Markets

## Aging, Migration, and Labor Markets

The rapid aging of the population in China has raised concerns for elderly well-being, labor market participation, and old-age support, while, at the same time, (1) traditional familial support for the elderly has been declining and (2) the formal pension system is undergoing substantial transformation. Unlike many developed economies transforming into an aged society over a long time horizon, the pace of aging in China is so fast that its demographic transition will be complete in less than 40 years, but its income level is still low. China will, therefore, grow old before it becomes rich. Changes in demographic structure have important implications for the labor supply, pension schemes, old-age income support, fiscal sustainability, and long-term growth.

The shrinking of China's working-age population will pose numerous important challenges for the economy, two of which are (1) the need for a growing and increasingly skilled labor force in the face of a growing proportion of the population being lost to retirement and fewer new entrants because of declines in fertility and (2) the imposition of stress on the defined-benefit instruments in the urban old-age insurance system, which will face growing benefit expenditures amid slowing growth of contributions. *This appendix proposes the following three measures to address both challenges: (1) modify those pensions and labor market policies that discourage individuals from working longer, (2) remove financial incentives for early retirement, and (3) support policies that enable workers to strengthen their skills through a lifelong learning process.*

For countries with partially funded defined benefit mandatory pension schemes, one means of addressing the trade-off between fiscal sustainability and benefit adequacy in the face of population aging is to allocate a larger share of the increase in life expectancy to time spent working than to time spent in retirement by increasing the age at which individuals depart the labor market. This is a rational choice for individuals faced with the expectation of living longer and not being able to externalize the higher cost of their retirement. It is also the policy approach that guarantees the best actuarial balance between accumulated funds and accrued benefits under the given pension schemes.

Other options—such as encouraging greater migration, higher fertility, and faster productivity growth—that are frequently proposed to address the negative consequences of population aging for pension systems help on the margin, but by themselves are generally insufficient to restore sustainability in the face of a rapidly aging population. In China the existence of large-scale rural-to-urban migration and the extension of coverage to this working population will, to some extent, reduce the projected burden of old-age support and offset the effects of population aging in urban areas, but it will leave more serious aging problems in rural areas when young adults migrate to cities. Moreover, in the long run, the burden of urban old-age income support will increase when those covered young migrants reach their retirement age and begin claiming pension benefits.

This appendix examines the impact of population aging on labor markets and pension systems in China. It first investigates urban demographic trends by considering projected rural-to-urban migration. Second, it analyzes the effects of an increase in the retirement age on labor supply and dispels some of the myths surrounding labor market outcomes. Third, it explores the effects of an increase in the retirement age on the urban pension system. Finally, it proposes policy interventions to improve labor markets and pension systems in the face of population aging.

The World Bank's projections show the trend of China's overall population and illuminate the differences in the size of the aged populations in rural and urban areas, respectively (see figure D.1). In 2010 the total elderly population aged 65 and above was around 112 million. By 2020 this number will more than double. Between 2010 and 2040, the growth rate of the elderly population is projected to be 3.56 percent—a rate far

**Figure D.1    Aged Populations in Rural and Urban China, 2010–75**

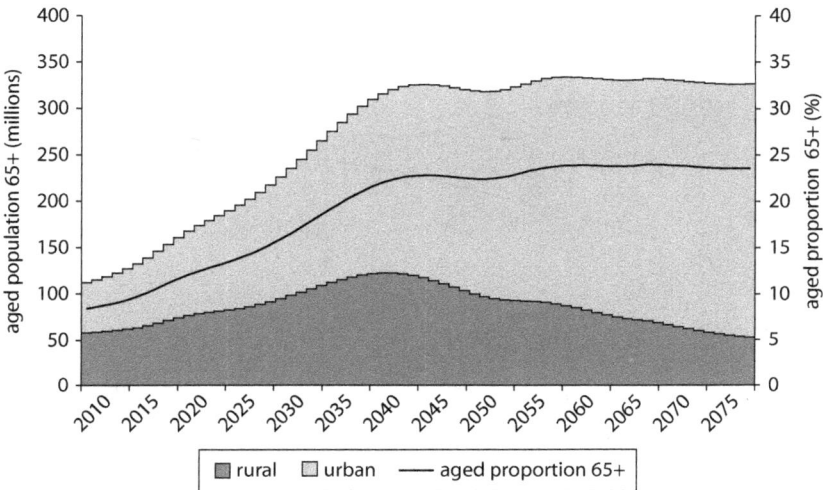

*Source:* World Bank estimates.

*Note:* A fertility rate of 1.85 is used, the same as the medium variant of the UN population projection. The migration data are from a CASS–World Bank joint study.

higher than the growth rate for the overall population. This will result in a rapid increase in the proportion of the aged population (aged 65 and above) from 8.4 percent of the total to 22.4 percent. This proportion will level off after 2040 if policy measures are taken to increase and then maintain China's fertility. The size of the rural elderly population is projected to peak by 2040 and then to decline continuously. The urban elderly population, however, will continue to increase over time.

Rapid urbanization will drive changes in the spatial distribution of the working-age population between rural and urban areas. The Chinese government has made the decision to accelerate urbanization by 2020 by deepening the *hukou* system reform to encourage rural migrants to leave medium and small cities permanently.[1] Assuming a rapid urbanization scenario,[2] the World Bank's projections suggest that the total working-age population will increase from 944 million in 2010 to 964 million by 2015, after which it will gradually decline to 929 million by 2030 and 847 million by 2050 (see figure D.2). Patterns of change in the sizes of working-age populations differ between rural and urban areas as a result of rapid urbanization and migration. Rural-to-urban migration is generally driven by demand according to age, gender, education, and the skills of migrants.

**Figure D.2    Working-Age Populations in Rural and Urban China, 2010–75**

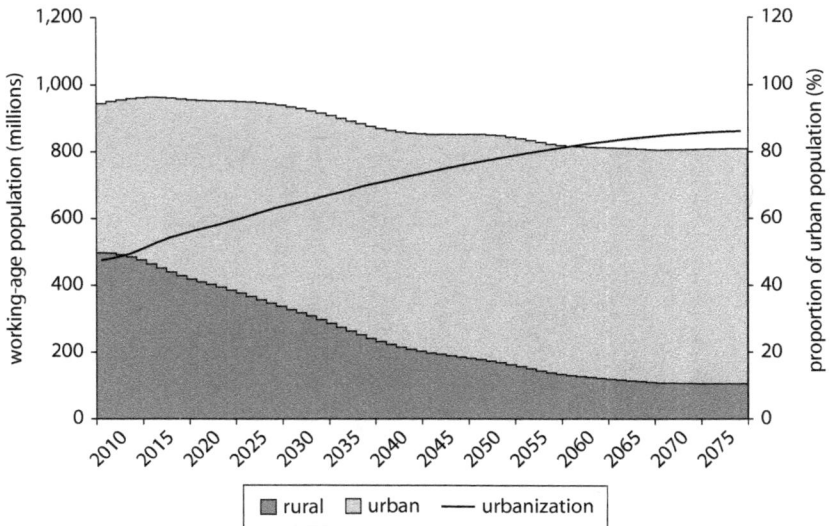

*Source:* World Bank estimates.

Migration, however, is constrained by policy and institutional factors. The majority of rural migrants are young, with an average age of 29 years (NBS 2010). With the inflow of substantial numbers of young adults into cities, the size of the working-age population in urban areas will continue to increase in the short term, while that in rural areas will continue to decline and will do so at a precipitous rate.

Migration has different implications for the burden of old-age income support in rural and urban areas. The projected flow of young adults from rural to urban areas will partially offset the effects of population aging and dampen the growth of old-age dependency ratios in urban areas. In the countryside, however, old-age dependency ratios are projected to rise dramatically. Figure D.3 demonstrates the projected pattern of old-age dependency ratios in rural and urban areas. From 2010 to 2040, the old-age dependency ratio in urban areas is projected to increase from 12.2 percent to 30.7 percent, while in rural areas it is projected to jump from 11.6 percent to 56.9 percent. From 2040 to 2065, old-age dependency ratios in rural areas are expected to remain high (but fluctuate). After 2065 old-age dependency ratios should decline as the elderly remaining in rural areas gradually pass away.

Industrialization combined with urbanization in China has indeed shifted millions in the rural labor force into nonagricultural sectors in

**Figure D.3    Old-Age Dependency Ratios in Rural and Urban China, 2010–75**

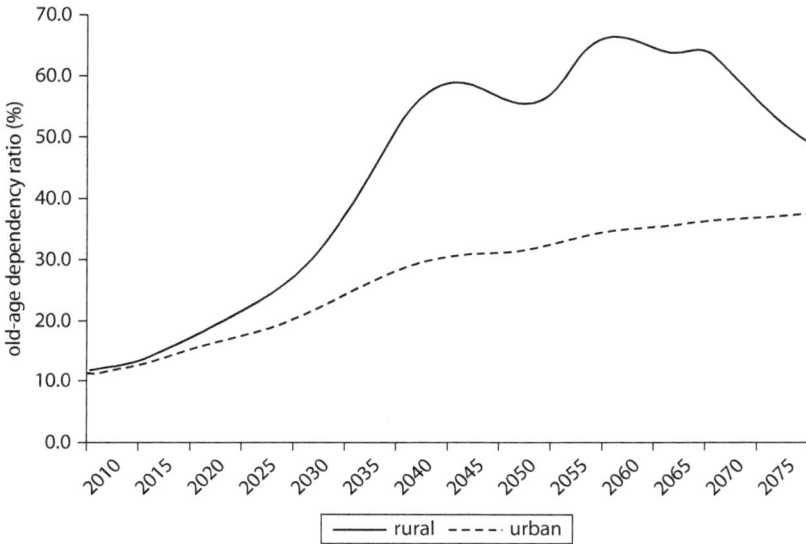

*Source:* World Bank estimates.

urban areas. At the beginning of reform and the period of opening up, agriculture was the dominant sector in the economy and absorbed a huge proportion the country's surplus labor. In 1978 agricultural employment accounted for nearly 70 percent of total employment. Rapid economic growth created millions of nonagricultural jobs and transformed the country's economic structure. By 2008 agricultural employment had dropped to just 39.6 percent of total employment and accounted for less than 12 percent of GDP. With this massive rural-to-urban migration, rural employment leveled off and then began to decline while urban employment has increased substantially. As shown in figure D.4, total employment rose from 647 million in 1990 to 775 million in 2008. Over this period, urban employment increased by more than 100 million while rural employment rose slightly and then began to decline from 491 million in 2001 to 473 million in 2008.

China's internal migration is the largest peacetime migration observed in human history. Starting in the mid-1980s, the volume of rural migration has sustained an upward trend. The number of rural migrants amounted to 78.5 million in 2000, rising to 140.4 million by 2008 (see figure D.5). Compared with total urban employment, the share of rural migrants increased from 33.9 percent in 2000 to 46.5 percent by

**Figure D.4    Employed Population, Urban and Rural Areas, 1990–2008**

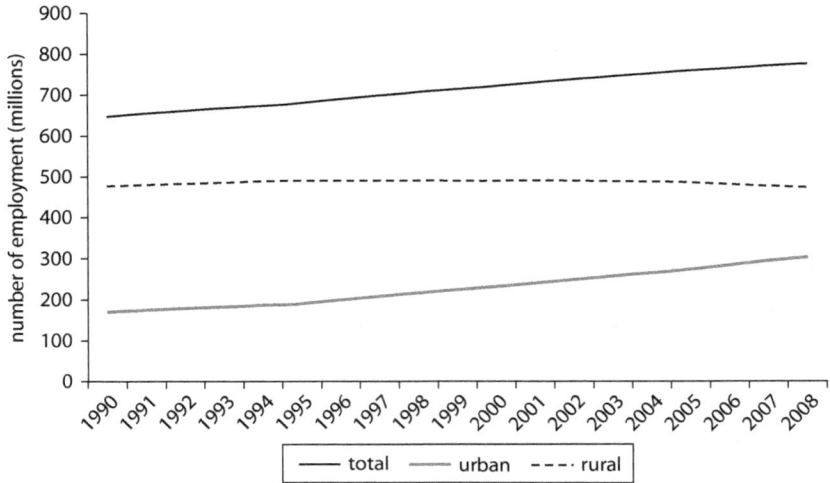

*Source:* NBS 2009.

**Figure D.5    Trends and Shares of Rural-to-Urban Migration in China, 2000–08**

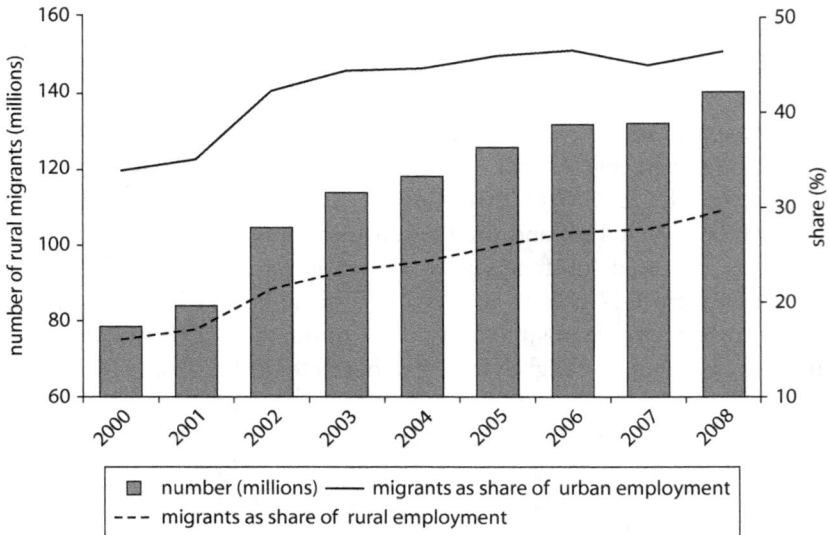

*Source:* NBS 2009.

2008—nearly half the total. The number of rural migrants accounted for 16.0 percent of the rural labor force in 2000 but rose to 29.7 percent by 2008. With the expansion of nonagricultural sectors and urban economies, the number of persons counted as surplus rural labor in China has declined as rural migrants have increasingly entered nonagricultural sectors. The strong demand for rural migrants generated by rapid growth has resulted in the emergence of labor shortages beginning in 2003. Although the global financial crisis inflicted a temporary shock to employment, the problem of labor shortages reemerged as the economy recovered, and are increasingly visible in urban labor markets. The rate of wage growth of rural migrants has remained in the double digits since 2003. Empirical evidence suggests that China's labor market has reached a Lewisian turning point: a transition from unlimited surplus labor to limited surplus labor (see Cai and Wang 2009). This will have important policy implications for China's economic growth and socioeconomic transformation.

The supply of labor is a critical ingredient for economic output and growth. As labor supply increases, so does capital accumulation until a new output equilibrium is reached. With the projected shrinking of the labor force in China, postponing retirement by raising the retirement age could be one option for increasing the labor supply and mitigating the challenges of population aging. The following two sections discuss the effects of an increase in the retirement age on labor supply and the pension system. A sound pension system, especially in rural areas, offers another mechanism for coping with demographic and socioeconomic change. This appendix does not discuss the rural pension scheme but instead focuses on understanding the effects of an increase in the retirement age on the urban labor supply and the urban pension system.

## Effects of an Increase in the Retirement Age on the Labor Market

At present, labor shortages are not confined to coastal areas. In fact, the transfer of labor-intensive industries into inland areas has caused labor shortages in those regions as well. The widespread problem of labor shortages suggests that labor has become scarce as China's economy modernizes, a pattern of development that has also been observed in Japan, the Republic of Korea, and Taiwan, China. Increasing the labor *supply* is clearly one of options for addressing the problem of labor shortages.

Increasing the labor supply by encouraging older workers to remain in the labor market and to retool their skills will have a certain and, in most cases, gradual impact. Such a process of encouraging people to work longer would coincide with when labor force growth is expected to be low or stagnant in urban areas and shrinking in rural areas as a result of declining fertility in prior decades as well as recent migration.

To illustrate the labor supply effects of an increase in the retirement age in urban areas, two scenarios have been modeled. First, we have modeled an increase in the retirement age for women from 51 to 60 years (the same as for men). According to China's labor regulation, female officials and white collar workers retire at age 55 while the rest retire at age 50; thus, it is reasonable to select age 51 as a starting point. Assuming a gradual increase in the retirement age at a rate of six months per year, the increase in the retirement age from 51 to 60 years will take 20 years, or by the end of 2029 if begun in early 2010. Second, we have modeled an increase in the retirement age for both men and women to 65 years. After the retirement age for women reaches 60 years (the same as for men) in 2029, the simulations assumed that the retirement age would be increased at the same rate of six months per year until the age for both men and women reaches 65. Figure D.6 shows the projected impact of these changes on the labor supply. An increase in the retirement age for women from 51 years to 60 years old would increase the proportion of the working-age population (defined as persons aged 15 to the retirement age) by about 10.9 percent by 2029. If the retirement age were to be further increased further from 61 to 65 for both men and women, the working-age population would increase by 18.4 percent by 2039 before leveling off.

The incremental effect of an increase in the retirement age on the labor supply will also be determined by other factors that impact the supply and demand for labor. From the perspective of labor supply, individual participation in labor market is determined by variables of wage, individual wealth, and preference for leisure. On the demand side, individual skills and productivity will be the key to meeting the job requirements of enterprises. Figure D.7 shows that labor market participation rates vary significantly by age and gender. In the urban labor market, older workers tend to have lower rates of labor market participation than do younger workers, and men have higher rates of labor market participation and withdraw from the labor market later than do women. In 2005 in the urban labor market, women aged 51–60 years have a participation rate of 33.2 percent, while both men and women aged 61–65 years old have a rate of 23.2 percent. Thus, the actual marginal impact

**Figure D.6    Labor Supply Effects from an Increase in Retirement Age**

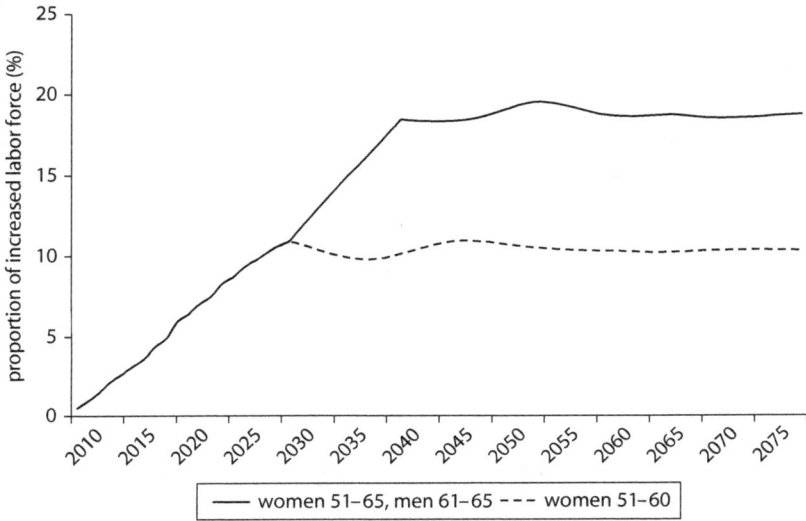

*Source:* World Bank estimates.

**Figure D.7    Labor Force Participation Rate in Urban China, 2005**

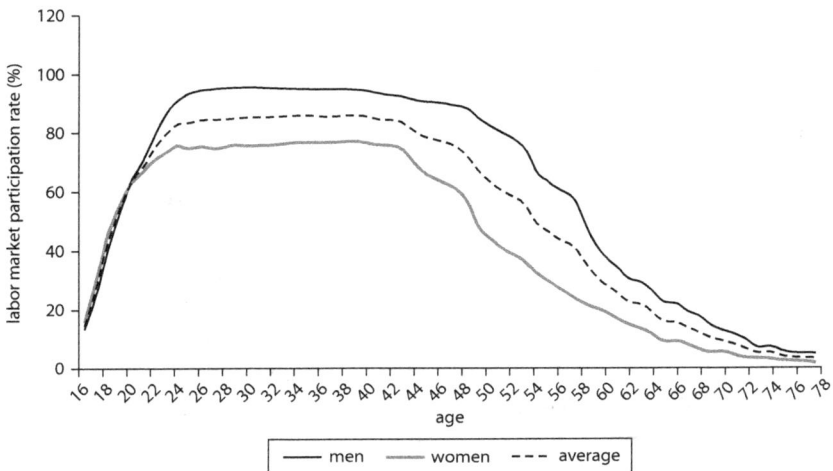

*Source:* NBS 2005.

of an increase in the retirement age would be less than one-third the supply of older workers aged 51–65 years. Certainly, changes in the legal retirement age would significantly affect labor supply decisions by these cohorts who would have been eligible for benefits sooner but now have to work longer.

The impact of an increase in the retirement age also reflects such factors as job opportunities, discrimination, and the informalization of the economy. At a given wage level, job opportunities are one of the important factors that affect individual behavior regarding labor force participation. When an economy is in recession, job opportunities are limited. Such adverse labor market conditions will discourage some older workers from working and encourage them to depart the labor market permanently. Discrimination against older workers would exacerbate this pattern. The degree of informalization in the urban labor market has been increasing during China's economic transformation, though the share of informal sector has stabilized in recent years. In the formal sector, workers generally have better working conditions, higher salaries, and better protection under the law. If an increase in retirement age is mandatory, the enforcement of the law is easily implemented. Thus, older workers can, in principle, work longer if they so choose. But workers in the informal sector will be hired and fired regardless of their age because the labor law and laws regarding pension participation are often not applied to these workers anyway.

The impact of an increase in the retirement age on youth employment has been an ongoing concern in China. Some observers argue that increasing the retirement age will reduce the number of jobs for younger workers entering the labor force. This argument—referred to by economists as the *lump of labor fallacy*—is based on an erroneous assumption of substitution between older and younger workers under a fixed level of labor demand. In the 1980s and 1990s, many OECD countries had experienced high and sustained unemployment, which was believed to reflect the existence of a fixed number of jobs in their economies. Several of these countries, therefore, enacted policies aimed at increasing the demand for the unemployed such as work-sharing arrangements, weekly limits on hours, and early-retirement programs. Empirical evidence, however, suggests that such policies were ineffective in reducing unemployment. Rather, they resulted in higher real wage rates and, consequently, *reduced* rather than increased total employment (see Kapteyn and others 2004).

Analysis of OECD countries suggests that little empirical evidence exists that older and younger workers are input substitutes. On the contrary, the evidence points toward their being complementary (see figure D.8). This conclusion is strengthened by a recent study of 21 OECD countries between 1960 and 2004, which suggests that changes in the rates of employment among older workers (aged 55–64) have small but positive effects on the employment of younger workers (aged 16–24) and on those in between (aged 25–54) (see Kalwij and others 2009). As economies grow and evolve (and as technologies change), the skills required of new workers also change. As a result, when someone retires from a particular position, it is unlikely that exactly the same skills will be required of his or her successor. Similarly, as workers spend time accumulating experience in a particular profession, job-specific knowledge, skills, and judgment make older individuals useful even when younger new workers begin their careers with new and different skills that older workers are unlikely to develop.

In China the modest and gradual increase in the labor force participation among older workers that would result from an increase in the retirement age would not decrease prospects for youth employment. From 2000 to 2005, labor market participation rates increased for most older

**Figure D.8    Change in Employment Rates in OECD Countries by Age Group, 1997–2007**
*percentage points*

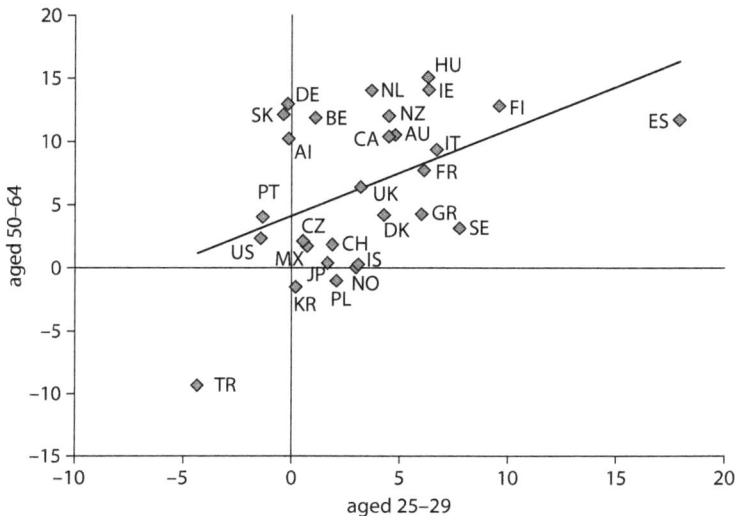

*Source:* OECD (via direct communication).
*Note:* OECD = Organisation for Economic Co-operation and Development.

workers (see figure D.9) despite there being no changes in the retirement age. In fact, nothing prohibits individuals from retiring from formal sector employment and rejoining the formal sector as a contract employee or simply moving to employment in the informal sector. The unemployment rate among youth dropped from 16.1 percent to 9.1 percent over the same period. This can be attributed largely to rapid economic growth, which generated millions of new jobs. In the late 1990s, most laid-off and unemployed urban workers were unskilled, female, or older workers laid off during the painful period when state-owned enterprises were reformed. In spite of declining unemployment, youth unemployment has gradually become a more pressing issue in China. As is the case in a number of other countries, youth unemployment is more than twice that of adults. In the context of the global financial crisis, youth workers, including migrants and college graduates, have faced challenges in the urban labor market and suffered from rising rates of unemployment. Cai and Wang (2009) show that youth unemployment is a structural issue in China and that substitution between young and old workers is weak or nonexistent. In the context of rapid growth, the excess demand for labor resulting from growing urban

**Figure D.9    Labor Market Participation Rates of Older Workers in China, 2000–05**

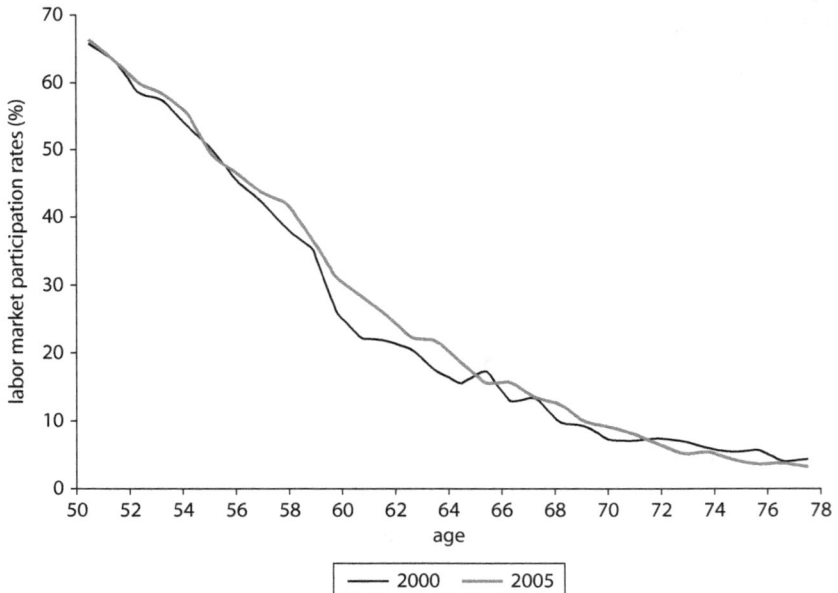

*Sources:* NBS 2000 and 2005.

economic output more than outstrips the substitution effect that would result from increasing labor participation among older workers. In the meantime, technological advances change the skills required of the workforce. Although older unproductive factories may have been able to employ many unskilled workers, newer, more technologically driven factories need workers with stronger technical skills. This means that as China's economy changes, its demand for skills also changes.

## Effects of an Increase in the Retirement Age on the Urban Elderly

### Old-Age Insurance System

Increasing the legal retirement age is one of several options to address the dramatic consequences of aging worldwide. In China this option is still under discussion. In addition to the lump of labor fallacy (discussed above), another reason for concern over increasing the retirement age might be that the average retirement age is actually lower than the minimum age at which workers become eligible for a full pension. In the late 1990s, early retirement was prevalent because of widespread enterprise restructuring and retrenchment. At that time, the discussion of increasing the legal retirement age was sensitive, particularly because many enterprises had large numbers of workers who were not employable after restructuring. As a result, justifiable concern was expressed that increasing the retirement age could contribute to rising unemployment and early retirement, particularly in some regions of the country. With enterprise restructuring largely completed and tightening urban labor markets in many cities in China, policy concerns over increasing the retirement age may not be as prevalent as they were previously. Some local authorities, such as those in Shanghai,[3] have experimented with a flexible system of retirement ages and with deferring retirement for senior managers, technicians, and skilled workers. In coastal areas, a few provinces have significantly increased local minimum wages and improved welfare to attract new workers to mitigate labor shortages.

An increase in retirement age could both materially improve the financial sustainability of the existing social pooling component in China and increase the benefits provided from the current Individual Accounts or NDC balances. Increasing the retirement age will slow the growth of the system's old-age dependency ratio, leaving more financial resources available to support China's aging society. Raising the retirement age has opposite effect on revenues and expenditures: Encouraging older workers to work longer will result in more contributors who would otherwise have retired, thus increasing revenues; meanwhile, social pooling expenditures would fall because benefits are paid for fewer years even though annual benefits at retirement are higher as a result of additional years of service credit. In the case of Individual Accounts or NDC benefits, expenditures are simply deferred; their lifetime cost is unchanged.

The effects of increasing the retirement age will also depend on any design changes adopted for the urban old-age insurance scheme. The existing scheme is financially unsustainable as a consequence of several factors, including legacy costs and aging. Simulations estimate the projected liabilities of the baseline scheme to be the equivalent to 141 percent of 2001 GDP (see Sin 2005). The system dependency ratio (that is, the number of beneficiaries supported by each worker) is projected to increase from 16 percent to over 50 percent in about seven years and to increase further to 100 percent over a 30-year period under the pension policy framework adopted in 1997. If an NDC scheme were adopted, legacy costs separately financed, and the retirement age increased, the projected medium-term cash flow imbalances driven by rising system dependency ratios would be far easier to manage.

## Public Policy Implications of Increasing the Retirement Age

As discussed above, encouraging older workers to remain in the labor market promises substantial economic benefits. For these benefits to be realized, older workers must have incentives to stay in the labor force, and structural barriers to their continued employment must be reduced. For example, individuals will make decisions about their participation in the labor force in response to tax incentives, particularly when wage taxes reduce their compensation for each additional year of work and retirement benefits do not materially increase as a result of working longer. Figure D.10 depicts the relationship in 12 study countries between unused labor capacity (that is, the share of workers retired among the elderly population) and the tax foregone to retirement (that is, a measure of income loss for continued labor force participation). Clearly, decisions regarding retirement timing reflect the incentives in place for continued employment. Burtless (2009) demonstrates further that the level of *net* replacement rates impacts departure rates from the labor force for persons between 60 and 64 years of age. Existing incentives for early retirement as well as disincentives for delayed retirement, therefore, must be considered when making changes to the statutory minimum retirement age.[4]

**Figure D.10    Retirement Incentives Matter: Implicit Tax on Remaining in Work**

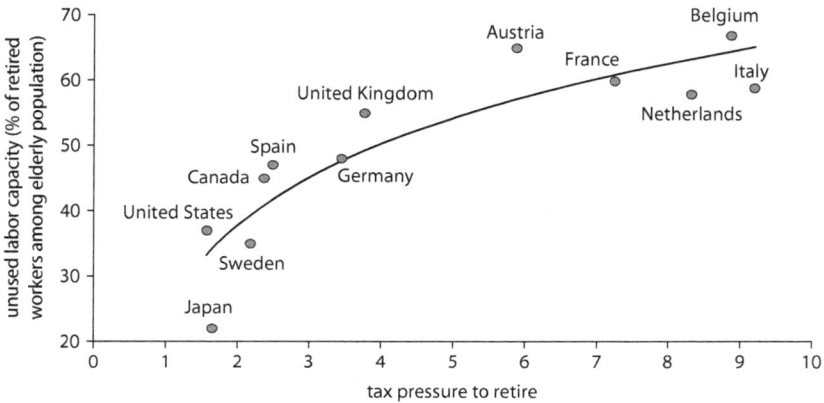

Sources: Gruber and Wise 1999; Hofer and Koman 2001.
Note: The unused labor capacity is the percent of retired workers among elderly population. The tax pressure to retire is an index 1 of 10 where 1 is the lowest level of induced pressure to retire due to the tax system and 10 is the highest level of pressure.

Pension benefit design and qualification criteria often create strong incentives for early retirement, including the following:

- Insufficient (or nonactuarially determined) adjustments for early or late retirement[5]
- Earnings tests that reduce benefits because an individual continues working (the use of such tests is often justified by the nonactuarial nature of the benefit calculation)
- Tax exemption of benefits that create high net replacement rates
- High net-benefit levels that are typical of unsustainable schemes
- Low minimum retirement ages linked with social pressures to retire to "make room" for the younger workers (as was discussed earlier) and
- Special early-retirement provision in many countries (including China) for workers in hazardous professions as well as generous benefits for disability.

Encouraging older workers to work longer will require the government to address the gaps between worker wages and productivity, institutional and policy barriers, and age and gender discrimination. In China's urban labor market, older workers are less likely to be working part-time or be self-employed and are at greater risk of becoming economically inactive beyond the age of 50. This is especially true for women. Therefore, policies are needed to provide a supportive environment and to remove existing obstacles to working longer. Keeping the elderly in the labor market, as well as creating sustained demand for elderly workers, will require a major rethinking of labor market institutions and practices, three of which are highlighted below.

### Addressing the Productivity-Wage Gap

Addressing the productivity-wage gap for elderly workers is necessary to promote efficient employment. The productivity-wage gap means that workers at all ages should be compensated in accordance with their productivity. If work rules prohibit lateral assignments or demotions when an individual's productivity falls below his or her compensation (as can be the case when productivity declines among older workers), employers will attempt to lay off elderly workers and will be reluctant to hire older workers even when they are well qualified. Cross-country empirical evidence suggests that worker productivity grows during mid-career but may begin to decline when approaching the retirement age. If seniority rules or wage restrictions prohibit less productive older workers from receiving lower compensation, employers have an incentive to let such workers go. This leaves policy makers with two options: upwardly adjust the productivity profile or downwardly adjust wages. The resistance to the latter is often reenforced by pension rules such as those that exist in China that calculate pension benefits based on wages earned in the final years before retirement.

### Strengthening Lifelong Learning

Strengthening lifelong learning is crucial in a world of changing technologies, knowledge, and increasing life expectancy, and it is especially important in China, where the profile of labor market skills requirements is changing—and will continue to change rapidly with the continued evolution and transformation of the economy. As suggested above, individuals during their lifetime have to be trained and educated in such a way as to position themselves for rapidly evolving and changing demands in the labor market. Although the importance of lifelong learning is widely recognized internationally, its actual implementation is generally lacking, and discussions of how to best finance it are ongoing. Governments and employers should contribute to the financing of lifelong learning (because both profit from an up-to-date and educated workforce), but most financing will have to come from workers themselves because they profit directly from developing sustained and higher skills.

### Policies Supporting Labor Mobility

Policies to support labor mobility are equally important for older workers in China. Policy measures that support labor mobility include the following: (1) eliminating the fragmentation of pension and other social insurance provisions, (2) supporting the portability of accrued pensionable and other rights, (3) gradually eliminating *hukou* residency requirements, and (4) processing work permits without regard to an individual's place of origin. In addition (as was discussed above), lifelong learning is essential to mobility as economies evolve. Social policies and labor laws can support mobility as individuals age and undergo changes in their family structure (such as raising children and getting divorced). As people live longer and are able to work longer, they are typically not as productive later in life. Not only enterprises but individuals and families as well will have to accept the cultural changes driven by population aging.

## Conclusions

This appendix examined the impacts of population aging on labor markets and pension systems in light of China's great rural-to-urban migration. It has provided empirical evidence to dispel the myth that delaying retirement and encouraging older workers to remain in the labor force will adversely affect employment, particularly for younger workers, and it suggested that public policies that reduce incentives for older workers to exit the labor market can still be supportive of economic growth and the sustainability of the pension scheme. The following recommendations emerge from this appendix:

- An increase in the retirement age could improve the sustainability of the pension system and increase levels of income replacement
- China's growing demand for labor will be partially met by migration and would benefit from encouraging older workers to remain in the workforce longer
- An increase in the retirement age would need to be accompanied by other reforms if anticipated gains in labor market efficiency are to be attained.

## Notes

1. See Wen Jiabao's *Report on the Work of the Government* (2010), delivered on March 5, 2010.

2. According to the World Bank's projections, the proportion of the urban population to the total population will rise from 46.6 percent in 2008 to 64.9 percent in 2030, almost 5 percentage points higher than what was projected by the United Nations Population Division (2009). In 2008, the *China Statistical Yearbook* showed that the proportion of the urban population was 45.7 percent. The 2010 census found an urban population share of fractionally under 50 percent, and in 2011 China crossed the 50 percent urban mark for the first time in its history. The World Bank's projections can, therefore, reasonably be used as an upper bound of China's population changes in the future.

3. In February 2010, a news report stated that Shanghai plans to establish a flexible system of retirement ages for three categories of workers (senior management personnel, technical personnel, and skilled personnel). These workers can postpone their retirement age if approved by their working units. See details at http://news.sina.com.cn/c/2009-02-20/124117255268.shtml.

4. An OECD publication provides a comparative view of early-retirement incentives in its member countries (see OECD 2009).

5. For a definition and discussion of actuarial fairness, see Queisser and Whitehouse (2006).

## References

Burtless, G. 2009. "Preparing the Labor Markets for an Aging Population: Designing Public Policy to Increased Labor Force Participation." In *Pension Reform in Southeastern Europe: Linking to Labor and Financial Market Reforms*, ed. Robert Holzmann, Landis MacKellar, and Jana Repansek, 127–48. Washington, DC: World Bank.

Cai, F., and M. Wang. 2009. "Employment Shock of the Financial Crisis and Its Countermeasures." *Academic Updates* 20: 16–31.

Gruber, J., and D. A. Wise, eds. 1999. *Social Security and Retirement around the World*. Chicago: University of Chicago Press.

Hofer, H., and R. Koman. 2001. *Social Security and Retirement in Austria*. Vienna: Institute for Advanced Studies.

Kalwij, A. S., A. Kapteyn, and K. De Vos. 2009. "Early Retirement and Employment of the Young." RAND Working Paper Series WR-679. March. http://ssrn.com/abstract=1371889.

Kapteyn, A., A. S. Kalwij, and A. Zaidi. 2004. "The Myth of Worksharing." *Labour Economics* 11: 293–313.

National Bureau of Statistics (NBS). 2000. "Population Census, Micro-Data." Unpublished report, NBS, Beijing.

———. 2005. "One Percent Population Sample, Micro-Data." Unpublished report, NBS, Beijing.

———. 2009. *China Statistical Yearbook*. Beijing: China Statistics Press.

———. 2010. "The 2009 Monitoring Report of Rural Migrant Workers." http://www.stats.gov.cn/tjfx/fxbg/t20100319_402628281.htm.

OECD (Organisation for Economic Co-operation and Development). 2009. *Pensions at a Glance. Retirement-Income Systems in OECD Countries*. Paris: OECD.

Queisser, M., and E. Whitehouse. 2006. "Neutral or Fair? Actuarial Concepts and Pension-System Design." OECD Social, Employment and Migration Working Papers No. 4, OECD, Paris.

Sin, Y. 2005. "China Pension Liabilities and Reform Options for Old Age Insurance." Working Paper 2005-1, World Bank, Washington, DC.

United Nations Population Division (UNPD). 2009. *World Population Prospects: The 2008 Revision*. New York: United Nations. http://esa.un.org/unpp.

# Voluntary Savings Arrangements

## The Objectives and Role of Voluntary Savings Arrangements in the Chinese Pension System

Effective multipillar pension systems in all countries undergoing population aging must rely significantly on voluntary retirement savings to supplement the benefits paid from mandatory pillars. For supplemental savings schemes to address the limitations of public systems, they require (1) group arrangements organized on the basis of employment—such as the current Enterprise Annuities (EAs)—sponsored by individual employers, (2) the extension of this concept for groups of workers within a common industry or for all the members of a trade union or worker organization, or (3) individual arrangements that provide retirement savings products on a retail basis.

Supplemental elements of the pension system should be designed to fulfill several interrelated purposes, including the following:

- *Supplementing the limited income replacement capacity of mandatory pillars.* The mandatory elements of pension systems operate most efficiently when they provide only a basic level of income replacement for

---

This chapter draws from Hinz (2007).

average participants. The replacement rates required to prevent poverty in old age and achieve effective consumption smoothing over the life cycle will vary considerably across individuals because of differences in income, patterns of earnings, and the need for income replacement (which varies with income). To operate efficiently, basic pension pillars should be relatively simple in design and modest in size. Imposing very high contribution rates serves only to distort decisions within the labor market. This suggests that basic pillars should be designed to ensure a minimum level of income for all workers (for poverty prevention) and provide only limited income replacement beyond this minimum income level for others.

The design of the urban old-age insurance scheme in China is already consistent with this principle: It replaces under half of lifetime income for a typical worker and a generally lower percentage for workers earning more than the average (this is particularly true for persons who experience rising levels of earnings over their working life). To adequately smooth consumption from work to retirement, total replacement rates from all sources of between 60 percent and 80 percent of pre-retirement earnings are often required. Achieving these levels of total income replacement will require significant supplementary retirement savings for all but the lowest-income workers. Saving 10 percent of wages and investing them in long-term financial products specifically designed to achieve returns closely correlated with the long-term growth of wages should provide the additional 20–30 percent of income replacement required to smooth income adequately for most workers. This would most efficiently be achieved by supplementary Occupational Annuities (OAs) and Individual Annuities (IAs) that can be tailored to the varying circumstances and preferences of China's rapidly evolving labor force.

- *Improving the efficiency of consumption and savings decisions.* One of the core macroeconomic challenges facing China in the coming decades is the establishment of an efficient long-term balance between consumption and savings. One of the primary motivations for retirement savings is to spread consumption over the life cycle. In the absence of a well-designed retirement savings scheme, however, individuals cannot efficiently manage the various costs and risks of saving to include longevity risk (that is, that one will outlive one's savings) as well as investment risk. In response, many individuals will engage in high levels of "precautionary saving." This results in overall levels of savings that are higher than what is collectively necessary as individuals separately seek to manage their risks. A well-designed and supervised supplemental pension system can improve the efficiency of consumption and facilitate rational savings behavior by (1) providing savers with a supply of appropriate investment instruments specifically designed for long-term pension savings, (2) achieving economies of scale in the administration of a retirement savings scheme to lower investment costs, and (3) pooling mortality risks during the payment of benefits when individuals reach retirement and begin to draw on their supplemental savings accounts.

- *Facilitating the efficient operation of labor markets and promoting enterprise development.* China continues to move toward more open and competitive labor markets. This requires employers to have the means to attract and retain workers with the attributes and skills appropriate for their respective industries. For this to happen, it will be important to establish an environment in which employers benefit from investing in the human capital of their workers through training and other skills development. Employers must have the means to create appropriate market incentives to retain the highly skilled workers they have trained. Otherwise, competitors will simply hire workers trained by other employers at marginally higher wages, thereby exploiting the value of the other employer's investment. Supplemental OAs can provide employers with the means to retain workers by offering the promise of future benefits and by giving them access to lower-cost investment vehicles, the efficiency of a collective savings regime, and the support of expertise in the management of their savings. The specific characteristics of a particular employer-based pension scheme may have different appeal to workers with different characteristics, thereby improving the efficiency of allocation of labor.

- *Promoting the depth, breadth, liquidity, and development of domestic capital markets.* Funded occupational and individual annuities can provide a large source of long-term savings and capital formation. In many countries with well-developed supplemental private pension systems, accumulated assets exceed 100 percent of GDP. These assets provide the underlying capital to facilitate the development and operation of the institutions that support capital market development, including asset managers, custodians, and brokerage and trading houses. Savings that are channeled into investment vehicles specifically designed to support retirement income production create the demand for long-term instruments and improve the quality of asset management services. This increases the depth of capital markets and facilitates the development of long-term instruments.

- *Contributing constructively to the management of population aging.* The decline in the working-age population in China, projected to begin about 2015, will impose significant challenges for the maintenance of economic growth. The most direct way of addressing this problem is to develop a means to encourage workers to remain in the labor force at older ages. Supplementary pension systems can be designed to help address this problem by creating additional incentives for continued work. Each year of additional work and contributions will provide a commensurately greater level of retirement income that can help offset incentives to retire at the earliest age of eligibility under the public system.

## Conditions Necessary to Fulfill These Objectives

To achieve the objectives discussed above, a system of supplementary pension savings must fulfill several conditions:

- *Broad access on an equitable basis to savings instruments.* Supplemental OAs and IAs should be easily accessible on equivalent terms for all economically active individuals. For those employed in the formal sector, this can be best accomplished through the promotion of employment-based schemes such as the existing EAs. These schemes, however, have reached only about 6 percent of the workers in the formal sector because many are employed by enterprises that are too small for such a scheme to be cost effective or that possess characteristics, such as very low earnings, that do not make it attractive or feasible. Moreover, more than half of the labor force is not engaged in formal sector employment and would not have access to employer-based schemes anyway. A fully effective supplemental system will need to provide all workers *access* to savings instruments designed to provide secure retirement income at a reasonable cost. This could be accomplished by designing products available at an individual retail level on terms similar to those covered by EAs.

- *Meaningful and consistent incentives to save within the scheme.* Pension savings need to be distinguished from other types of savings and treated appropriately as long-term deferred consumption. Achieving the right level of saving requires providing the proper implicit signals regarding the required level of savings needed to reach targeted levels of income replacement. Although overall savings in China remain high, savings are not uniformly distributed. Some share of individuals, especially those of moderate income, may require meaningful economic incentives (or explicit subsidies) to stimulate them to save more. In most countries this is achieved by affording supplementary retirement savings special tax treatment in which income taxes are deferred for funds contributed to designated retirement savings schemes. Low-income individuals, who do not pay much in the way of income taxes, often require additional incentives, such as matching contributions or other credits. For the system to operate successfully, incentives should be provided in a similar form and level throughout the economy.

- *Investment instruments specifically designed for retirement savings.* Pension savings schemes have specific characteristics that must be addressed during their design. First, they operate over a very long time horizon. Second, because they are designed to provide income to individuals who have left the workforce, they should be invested with low tolerance for risk. Levels of risk tolerance, however, vary across individual circumstances and across any given individual's life cycle, typically diminishing in direct proportion to the individual's proximity to retirement. Providing the necessary financial incentives and creating the capacity to effectively supervise retirement savings schemes requires that funds afforded preferential tax treatment be segregated and identifiable. International experience strongly suggests that most individuals lack the skill and knowledge required to make optimal decisions regarding their investments for retirement, and many do not wish to make such decisions. This suggests that the pension scheme should be designed to provide a relatively small number of products to fulfill the most common risk, return, and holding period characteristics. Investment choices within a scheme are then limited to these alternatives as is the eligibility for preferential tax treatment.

- *Low-cost operations to preserve savings during accumulation.* The long-term nature of pension savings and limited capacity of individuals to defer income makes supplemental funded pension schemes extremely cost sensitive. Generally, a one percentage point increase in administrative costs reduces retirement income by 15–20 percent. Thus, supplemental pension schemes must be designed to keep operating costs as low as possible. This can be achieved through the imposition of restrictions on fees and expenses and by facilitating competition within the retirement savings market.

- *Cost-effective and reliable mechanisms for converting savings into post-retirement income.* Transforming individual pension savings into retirement income requires a means of converting the balances of individual savings accounts into a secure income stream. At retirement, the design challenge for supplemental pension schemes shifts from providing access to a broad segment of the working population and managing investment risk to providing a mechanism for individuals to manage the uncertainty surrounding how long they might live. This requires the pooling of mortality risk into large pools backed by low-risk assets that enable individuals to convert the funds in their accounts into a secure income stream at retirement.

- *In addition, supplementary pension schemes must be perceived by participants as being secure and reliable.* The success of any pension system is strongly influenced by the behavior of its participants in response to their perceptions about its security and reliability. Most individuals will never be capable of making independent judgments about the quality of asset management or the security of the institutions in which their savings are invested. This requires strong market regulation and oversight. Otherwise, workers will be reluctant to participate or will engage in inefficient levels of precautionary savings to compensate for their perceptions of risk.

## A Design Framework for Supplementary Pension Schemes

The proposed supplemental OAs and IAs need to be designed in accordance with the core principles below to (1) have the capacity to provide a substantial level of income replacement for a broad segment of China's population and (2) be consistent with the objectives and attributes outlined above.

### Investment Products Should Be Tailored Specifically for the Needs of the Scheme

Saving for retirement in an efficient and secure manner requires investments to be aligned with the needs of the scheme. The vast majority of individuals lack the knowledge and capacity to formulate and implement an appropriate investment plan and to exercise prudent judgment when choosing among a complex array of investment alternatives. Participants in retirement savings plans worldwide have a well-documented propensity to avoid making choices and to exhibit considerable inertia once a decision among investment alternatives has been made. This makes the allocation of their investment assets inefficient because the risk and return characteristics appropriate to pension savings change considerably as individuals age. In theory, investors should seek higher returns by exploiting risk premiums for longer-term investments when they are younger and should accept lower potential returns in exchange for greater security as they become older. In China savings at the household level (in part because the investment markets remain at an early stage of development) have been concentrated either in very low-yielding bank deposits that produce returns well below average wage growth or in what have proven to be extremely volatile equity markets. Neither is consistent with the needs of long-term savings schemes.

Unfortunately, the kind of investment products that are needed—long-term and low-cost products that can gradually offer lower levels of risk as individuals approach retirement—are not necessarily the products that financial service providers have an incentive to develop and sell. This is especially the case when it is more profitable to sell short-term and higher-risk alternatives. Creating efficient markets for supplementary pension products, therefore, requires the establishment of a set of permissible products and the careful oversight of the markets in which those products are sold. This requires achieving a balance between (1) limiting choices and steering individuals toward options that are most appropriate for their circumstances and (2) offering a sufficient range of options to accommodate individual degrees of risk tolerance while still facilitating market competition to keep the cost of investment products low. Achieving the necessary balance while enabling the investment markets to develop and operate efficiently will require careful design and effective market oversight.

This can be achieved by dividing allowable savings products into two groups. The first would be arrangements under which sellers agree to deliver a defined level of post-retirement income in return for a stream of payments made up to retirement. Such an arrangement is generally referred to as an annuity contract and is typically sold by insurance companies that underwrite both investment and mortality risk. These arrangements are most efficient when a large pool of contracts is pooled to manage the unknown life expectancy of any one individual. The second group would be investment management contracts, under which sellers agree to manage accumulated savings within an established set of parameters in return for a fee. Under such an arrangement, the investment risk is borne entirely by the individual. On reaching retirement, he or she must then decide how to best convert accumulated savings into an income stream during his or her retirement.

Both of these types of savings products should be permitted, but their permissible characteristics should be carefully restricted. At the most basic level, this can be achieved by simply restricting the use of the term *pension savings product* to specifically designed and licensed products available to supplementary pension scheme participants. In addition, access to tax preferences or other subsidies should be restricted to licensed pension savings products to provide the necessary incentives and to distinguish them from other investment products.

Annuity products should be licensed and sold as group products for employer-sponsored schemes or directly to individuals. The pricing and terms of group contracts should be regulated by the China Insurance Regulatory Commission (CIRC) following a general set of parameters, although pricing could be reviewed on an individual contract basis. IA contracts should be specified by age groups (this is most easily done by birth year) and be required to be marketed in easily comparable units, for example, by presenting the cost in relation to a specified payout unit (such as per 1,000 RMB per year). The pricing, fees, and underlying investments for each age band should be defined and regulated by the CIRC.

### Investment Products Must Have Appropriate Risk and Return Characteristics

Pension investment products should likewise be limited to a set of defined products with risk and return characteristics appropriate to the nature of pension savings and offered at reasonable cost. International experience strongly suggests that individuals in general make poor decisions regarding the investment of their retirement savings. This underscores the importance of restricting licensed products to channel savings to a limited set of appropriate choices. The best way to achieve this objective is by using what are known as *life-cycle portfolios*. These are products that vary the composition of underlying securities to create portfolios with risk and return characteristics appropriate for savers of different ages. The central principle is that an individual's capacity (and willingness) to assume risk gradually diminishes as retirement approaches. Such products are now becoming prevalent in many international markets. By making such products the default option (to which individuals are assigned on the basis of their age if they do not affirmatively select another option), the decision process would be far easier and would channel retirement savings into reasonably constructed portfolios that would not require adjustment as individuals age. A limited number of alternatives could be phased in at a later date to allow flexibility to those who wish to opt out of the basic life-cycle framework.

The evidence from developed financial markets indicates that most variation across investment portfolios is the result of how investments are allocated across broad classes of assets. Life-cycle portfolios can, therefore, be effectively defined using relatively narrow ranges of acceptable allocation among major asset classes deemed appropriate for differing stages of the life cycle. In this way assets can be gradually shifted from more volatile but higher-earning investments to more predictable but lower yielding investments as cohorts near the retirement age. The basic parameters governing asset allocation should be supplemented by additional limits to constrain underlying portfolios within an overall risk parameter. Limits must be designed specifically for the Chinese market and should evolve in response to market development as new products are introduced and experienced is gained.

Within such a framework, individual savings would be assigned to an investment option as a function of the individual's birth year. Cohort-specific products should adjust as the cohort ages, gradually progressing through asset allocation and risk standards that decrease permissible risk as the retirement age nears. These could be defined within five-year age bands. Permissible fees and expenses for licensed products must be defined through regulation. A reference benchmark for each age grouping, derived from the asset allocation rules and permissible risk parameters, should be created and published by the regulatory authority along with a comparison of performance of individual products against the benchmark. This would provide an easily interpretable mechanism for evaluating the performance of a given investment product and would facilitate competition in the market on the basis of performance against a common standard. Such an approach has been implemented successfully in several countries.

Age-related portfolios based on long-term strategic asset allocation standards should become the default investment product for all supplementary pension schemes to include employer-sponsored arrangements (such as the proposed OAs) and those provided in the individual retail market. Both employer arrangements and retail schemes should offer annuity and managed products on equivalent terms. Investment products could be provided by any licensed financial institution (such as banks, investment companies, or insurance companies) capable of meeting the licensing criteria established by the supervisory authority. Creating a transparent and easily understood performance metric in the form of benchmarks for age-related products will encourage performance based on competition in the market. Competition on equal terms across products and type of providers will help keep costs low. Market participants will have to be rigorously supervised based on a common set of standards developed by the authorities. Coordinating supervision of financial markets is a crucially important challenge—but one that must be addressed in any event.

Making life-cycle products the default option will channel a large portion of voluntary retirement savings into long-term instruments. Initially, this will direct funds into more stable long-term equities capable of utilizing long horizons to seek growth opportunities, but it will also stimulate demand for longer-term debt instruments, thereby gradually extending the maturity of fixed-income products in China and facilitating the development of a longer yield curve for interest rates. Such an outcome has been observed in other countries and offers secondary developmental benefits for the economy. Imposing parameters to manage portfolio risk will require the development of risk management expertise by institutional investors and will facilitate their introduction of risk management instruments. This, too, will benefit the markets and, ultimately, the economy.

### Supplemental Pension Schemes Must Be Supported by Appropriate Tax Policies

At present, the tax treatment of supplementary pension savings remains uneven and insufficient to direct savings into pension-specific products. Ministry of Finance Document 34, issued in February 2008, appears to limit contributions to supplementary pensions that are excluded from the taxable income of sponsoring employers to 4 percent of total wages, a level that is unlikely to generate enough additional income to adequately supplement the reformed system of Basic Pensions. Before the issuance of this document, tax preferences were set at the provincial and municipal levels and varied widely by jurisdiction. No exclusion from income taxation is provided for contributions from workers or for individual savings outside the EA system. One municipal government has undertaken a pilot to allow the exclusion of some group pension insurance products at a cost of up to 8 percent of employer payroll. Elsewhere, no direct economic incentives are given for the purchase of annuity products for retirement.

To foster a robust supplementary savings scheme, a uniform national policy on the tax treatment of supplemental pension savings is needed. Most importantly, tax incentives need to be accessible to all, regardless of an individual's source of earnings. A permissible ceiling of income that can be excluded from taxation should be at least as large as the (roughly) 8 percent of individual earnings now allowed under the EA scheme, provided that funds are contributed to standardized and licensed pension savings products. For an average full career worker, this would generate a benefit sufficient to provide an additional 20 percent of income replacement if investments earn a rate of return slightly higher than economy-wide wage growth. The availability of tax preferences should be constrained by a ceiling to prevent very high-income individuals (who are not at risk of poverty in their old age) from unduly benefiting from the exclusion.

Investment earnings from licensed pension products should be exempt from all taxation until they are taken as income in retirement. Benefits received in retirement (and any pre-retirement withdrawals) should be taxed as regular income. This is needed to recapture some of the foregone tax value and to avoid providing an unduly large tax benefit to higher-income individuals. Such an approach to the tax treatment of pension savings would be in line with prevailing international practice and would create incentives for retirement savings by treating it as deferred consumption for tax purposes.

Favorable tax treatment should be accessible to all individuals who want to save for retirement, including those who purchase products at the retail level as well as groups of workers who earn benefits through an OA or similar employment-based arrangement. Workers covered by an employer scheme should not be permitted to make additional individual tax-deferred savings in excess of the limits imposed for individual schemes.

Preferential tax treatment should be limited to savings invested in one of the licensed pension savings products outlined above. Linking favorable tax treatment and licensed pension savings products is crucial to the development of a consistent and secure investment framework in which products are licensed and properly regulated and supervised.

Favorable tax treatment should be applied on an equivalent basis to purchases of annuity contracts and to investment management products, provided that contracts and products are properly licensed. Although withdrawals before retirement should not be strictly prohibited, tax subsidies should be recaptured by imposing a special tax or other penalty on such withdrawals. Transfers among pension providers should be permitted, of course, so that workers leaving an employer-sponsored scheme can transfer their savings to a retail or insurance product without incurring additional costs.

### Supplemental Pensions Schemes Should Be Accessible to All

Supplemental retirement savings products should accessible to all individuals and employees of small and medium enterprises (SMEs). Reaching the self-employed, persons working in the informal sector, and those employed in SMEs is essential to achieving the full potential of a supplemental retirement savings system. This challenge is made more difficult because these individuals tend to have less capacity to save as a result of lower incomes and less stable and shorter-term working arrangements. This limitation can be partially addressed through access to favorable tax treatment and to a program of matching contributions, as outlined above, but it also requires access to a retail market for pension savings products sold at reasonable costs. Because of the small size of such accounts and the fixed costs of administering them, such a market typically does not develop rapidly on its own. The process can be accelerated by making participation in this market a precondition for licensing any pension savings product, thereby forcing providers to offer the same products at the retail level that they offer to more profitable employer-based schemes. Inevitably, this will result in cross-subsidies that favor the retail market— both for investment management products and for annuity contracts—as a result of economies of scale in administration and the potential for adverse selection with respect to mortality in the individual annuity market. Such cross-subsidies should be carefully evaluated, and adjustments in the rules may be required in the future. Initially, however, they are justified to create the perception that the system is fair and equitable and to overcome the challenges inherent in reaching the informal and low-wage sector.

Reaching workers in SMEs will require adjustments in the current EA framework to create a structure for worker organizations or groups of small employers to sponsor pension schemes. This could take several potential forms, including the creation of a collective investment product that might be offered to smaller employers and the development of multiple employer arrangements based on a common industry or workers organization. The Ministry of Human Resources and Social Security (MHRSS) has been considering these alternatives for several years but has yet to put forward a proposal. The promulgation of a legal and regulatory framework to (1) extend the EA system to workers associations and groups of employers and (2) create collective investment arrangements should be a priority for both the MHRSS and the China Securities Regulatory Commission (CSRC).

### Structures Are Needed to Efficiently Convert Savings into Retirement Income

It is important to create a structure to convert pension savings into retirement income. One of the most difficult challenges that supplementary pension systems face is how to manage the conversion of accumulated retirement savings into a stream of reliable post-retirement income. Individuals have uncertain and variable life expectancies following retirement and typically lack the analytical skills and self-discipline to effectively manage the drawdown of their savings. The presence and perception of risk will decrease the efficiency of savings as individuals engage in precautionary behavior.

An optimal solution to this problem is the purchase of an annuity contract that pools mortality risk. Experience has demonstrated that this is difficult to achieve in private insurance markets because individuals are better able to assess their own life expectancy than can annuity providers. When conversion of account balances is optional, a strong tendency is seen for only those with above average longevity to make such a purchase. In addition, individual annuity sellers—who underwrite both the investment and mortality risk of these contracts—have a strong financial incentive to select lower-cost customers (that is, those with shorter life expectancies) and to avoid those with statistically greater longevity.

These challenges can be partly addressed by channeling as large a share of supplementary savings as possible into the annuity market and by collectivizing the risk. Similar to improving investment decisions by exploiting the tendency of inertia in making financial decisions, the purchase of annuities should be made the default payout from supplementary pension schemes. On reaching a specified age, coordinated with the projected transition from work to retirement on which the investment parameters are established, individual account balances should be automatically converted into an annuity contract. Individuals who have sufficient credits within the basic pension system—or have adequate savings to produce a prescribed level of retirement income—could be given the choice to take a phased withdrawal of funds or to continue to invest them in an alternative product.

This transition from savings to income is likely to be most efficient when the default standard is a phased conversion of account balances into annuity contracts over a 10-year period around the assumed retirement date. This limits exposure to short-term fluctuations in asset values and interest rates. Annuity contracts should also be required to be inflation indexed to protect the purchasing power of benefits. This is likely to require public intervention in the development of annuity markets, because China currently lacks such instruments in its private insurance market. The provision of long-term government-backed debt instruments to support the efficient underwriting of annuity contracts will likely become necessary for these instruments to develop, although they will not be required on a large scale for many years.

Several approaches to organizing an annuity market merit consideration. One would be to require all annuity conversions to be aggregated in a publicly managed pool from which private vendors would bid to underwrite a randomly selected portion of contracts, thereby benefiting from large groups and avoiding adverse selection. Another would be to simply combine supplemental savings with the mechanism used to pay benefits from the old-age insurance system. If an NDC architecture is adopted for the public system, this would provide important liquidity to the system during the early stages of benefit payouts.

### Supplemental Pension Schemes Should Promote Investment in Human Capital

An essential challenge for any market economy is to create incentives for enterprises to invest in the human capital of their workers. Concurrent with the challenge of managing population aging, China will also need to transition from an economy based on low-cost commodity labor to one where value is created from intellectual capital and higher skilled and higher value-added labor. This demands market mechanisms that (1) can effectively match skills with demands and (2) create incentives for employers to invest in the development of their employees. The former can be facilitated by standardizing retirement savings products and enabling the portability of pension assets across schemes. This will require the same products to be available in the retail market as are available in employer-sponsored schemes, as well as uniform tax treatment so that workers can transition from one plan to another on identical terms. To achieve the latter, the current limit of 4 percent of the total wage bill that may be charged against expenses and exempted from tax should be retained for employers that sponsor an OA. (This 4 percent allowance would be in addition to the 8 percent of earnings that can be excluded by individuals contributing to supplemental pension schemes.) Employers should be permitted to impose eligibility conditions on their contributions, such as vesting requirements. In doing so, employers will have the tools they need to attract and retain workers in a competitive market and the incentive they need to invest in the training and development of their workforce. The current provision that permits employers to allocate contributions among workers on the basis of objective criteria such as length of service or performance would also help achieve this objective.

## The Path to Implementation

Establishing a supplemental retirement savings system that fulfills the goals and principles outlined above will require (1) creating a new legal and institutional framework for standardized pension savings products and (2) building on the existing foundation of the EAs and current insurance market to align them with the new policy framework and enhance their security.

### Creating a New Legal and Institutional Foundation

The market for supplemental retirement savings products should not be segmented (as is currently the case) on the basis of issuers of the products (which are currently differentiated as licensed EA scheme investment managers, insurance companies, and investment funds) but on the basis of a common set of permissible characteristics. A central authority that can define the various products and develop their parameters will be required. Given the linkage with tax policy, it would seem logical that this underlying framework be established under the auspices of the Ministry of Finance. A specialized unit within the ministry should be established for this purpose to promulgate standards and provide guidance and oversight to the respective regulatory authorities. Common standards that should be established by this unit include the following:

- Permissible asset classes and asset allocation parameters by age band
- Metrics for risk measurement and risk standards by product

- A methodology for establishing benchmarks for performance measurement and standards for a common performance reporting system
- Marketing limitations and standards
- Requirements for the segregation and custody of assets
- A common framework for prudential conduct, to address such issues as conflicts of interest, that would be applied across all institutions that offer licensed pension savings products
- Accounting requirements to include a common framework for the valuation of assets
- Requirements for independent financial audits and compliance audits
- Minimum funding requirements (that is, asset/liability standards) for annuity products and minimum capital and reserve requirements for investment products.

Once the standards for products have been established, their oversight and supervision can then be delegated to the respective authorities to include CIRC (for insurance products), CSRC (for investment companies and other asset managers), and the People's Bank of China (for banks which wish to offer the products). Although in the abstract it might be theoretically attractive to consolidate supervisory responsibility for licensed pension products under a single authority, this would create major organizational and jurisdictional conflicts given the current allocation of regulatory authority by the type of financial institutions. To provide consistency and security for retirement savings products, the development of an overall coordination body, probably best located in the Ministry of Finance, will also be needed.

An open question relates to the role of the MHRSS with respect to the oversight of employer-based OAs. Under current provisions pertaining to the EA, its supervisory authority currently extends to the licensing of investment managers and the establishment of quantitative limits on portfolio composition, as is contained in MHRSS Document No. 23, promulgated in 2004. The World Bank recommends replacing current portfolio limits and the licensing process with the requirement that EA scheme assets be invested in standardized new supplemental retirement savings products. These new products would be more directly aligned with the need to align savings by age rather than the current practice of pooling all workers from a given sponsor into a common portfolio. This would free the MHRSS to focus its oversight effort on issues relating to the performance of trustees, the governance process, the integrity of record keeping, and other issues related to the agency risks inherent in employer-sponsored schemes.

Creating a uniform and appropriate tax framework would need to be handled at a national level through the Ministry of Finance. A legal framework for establishing national tax policies may be required to supersede provincial and municipal authority with respect to supplemental retirement savings. Establishing a defined set of standardized products should facilitate the differentiation of authority between local and national levels, provided that the legal basis for taxation is amended as necessary to reserve authority over the treatment of such entities for national authorities. Existing provincial tax limits that differ from national standards as well as other conflicting initiatives would need to be preempted by national standards.

Establishing a means to convert supplemental retirement savings into reliable annuity payments will require a strategic decision whether to rely on a public clearinghouse with managed competition or to integrate the provision of annuities with the basic pension scheme.

### Enhance the EA System and Insurance Products to Support Wider Participation

A well-designed and efficiently functioning employer-sponsored system provides an important foundation of supplemental savings. By virtue of possessing the capacity to facilitate savings through payroll deduction, employer-based schemes have proven to be highly effective in increasing pension savings. To be effective, they must be perceived as fair and reliable. This demands effective supervision. The current EA scheme remains in a formative stage. Defining standard investment products to replace the current MHRSS investment framework and assigning responsibility for the licensing and oversight of financial institutions to their respective specialized authorities will reduce the demands on the MHRSS and enable it to focus on a narrower range of issues more consistent with its comparative expertise. The following additional steps are recommended:

- Separate the responsibility for overseeing supplemental pension schemes from the very different job of supervising social security institutions by creating a specialized unit for this purpose with resources consistent with its scope of responsibilities
- Develop a comprehensive oversight strategy grounded in risk assessment of the programs of individual EA scheme sponsors and licensed institutions

- Raise the level of legal authority above MHRSS circulars by establishing a national law and refocus the authority and mandate of the MHRSS on such issues as the role of employers and other licensed intermediaries in managing contribution flows and ensuring the integrity of individual savings accounts
- Develop a comprehensive framework for prudential regulation that addresses potential conflicts of interest among parties (sponsors, trustees, and asset managers) involved in the administration of the system
- Distinguish clearly the roles and responsibilities of the MHRSS in relation to the provincial labor authorities to ensure that oversight of the system is undertaken in a consistent manner
- Develop a system of reporting that provides participants in EA schemes with reliable information on their savings and the performance of their investments in relation to benchmarks.

### Create an Institutional Framework for SMEs

Two possible approaches are seen to extend the occupational pension system to smaller entities. The first is to allow the marketing of pension products to multiple employers within a common administrative structure organized by a licensed service provider. The second is to allow multiple employers and groups of worker associations to sponsor an EA scheme. Together, these would provide the legal basis for smaller enterprises to cost effectively offer workers the opportunity to participate in supplemental pension schemes.

The first approach merely requires allowing the basic EA scheme framework to be extended to establish a means for licensed trustees to market a bundled product of custody, record keeping, and asset management to smaller entities rather than requiring them to formally sponsor an EA scheme and engage service providers separately. This would result in what is known as a *master trust* type of arrangement.

The second approach would require the establishment of a carefully constructed governance structure—although this challenge would be considerably diminished if investment management was strictly controlled through licensing and the oversight of pension products by financial services authorities. The required governance structure would perform the same functions of the *Pension Councils* created under existing EA scheme regulations. A stronger set of rules that impose "fit and proper" standards and an overall set of prudential standards should be established to fill a critical gap in the current regulatory structure.

## References

Hinz, R. 2007. "The New Enterprise Annuities: The Need to Strengthen a Key Element of the Chinese Pension System." Mimeo, World Bank, Washington, DC.

Holzmann, R., and R. Hinz. 2005. *Old Age Income Support in the 21st Century*. Washington, DC: World Bank.

Jackson, R., and N. Howe. 2004. *The Graying of the Middle Kingdom*. Washington, DC: Center for Strategic and International Studies.

Organisation for Economic Co-operation and Development (OECD). 2002. *Supervisory Structures for Private Pension Funds: Survey Analysis*. Paris: OECD.

Sin, Y. 2005. "China: Pension Liabilities and Reform Options for Old Age Insurance." World Bank Research Working Paper 2005–1, World Bank, Washington, DC.

Trinh, T. 2006. *China's Pension System: Caught between Mounting Legacies and Unfavourable Demographics*. Frankfurt: Deutsche Bank Research.

Whitehouse, E. 2007. *Pensions at a Glance*. Paris: Organisation for Economic Co-operation and Development.

———. 2009. *Pensions at a Glance*. Paris: Organisation for Economic Co-operation and Development.

World Bank. 2005. "Evaluation of the Liaoning Pension Reform Pilot." Working Paper 38183, World Bank, Washington, DC.

# Glossary

*Accrual rate.* The rate at which pension entitlement is built up relative to earnings per year of service in a defined-benefit scheme, for example, 1.0 percent of the salary basis per year of applicable service.

*Accrued pension (benefit).* The value of the pension to a member at any point before retirement, which can be calculated on the basis of current earnings or also include projections of future increases in earnings.

*Actuarial fairness.* A method of setting insurance premiums according to the true risks involved.

*Additional voluntary contributions.* Contributions to a pension scheme over and above the employee's mandatory contribution rate.

*Administration.* The operation and oversight of a pension fund.

*Adverse selection.* A problem stemming from an insurer's inability to distinguish between high- and low-risk individuals. The price for insurance then reflects the average risk level, which leads low-risk individuals to opt out and drives the price of insurance higher until insurance markets break down.

---

This glossary is drawn from Robert Holzmann and Richard Hinz, *Old Age Income Support in the 21st Century* (Washington, DC: World Bank, 2006), and OECD, *Private Pensions: OECD Classification and Glossary* (Paris: OECD, 2005), used with permission. Terms indicated in parentheses are synonymous with the terms listed.

*Aging from above.* Growth in the elderly population resulting from increases in life expectancy.

*Aging from below.* Process by which decreasing fertility rates gradually lead to an increase in the proportion of the aged relative to the working age population as the working age population grows more slowly than the elderly population.

*Annuity.* A stream of payments at a specified rate, which may have some provision for inflation proofing, payable until some contingency occurs, usually the death of the beneficiary or a surviving dependent.

*Annuity factor.* The net present value of a stream of pension or annuity benefits.

*Average effective retirement age.* The actual average retirement age, taking into account early retirement and special regimes.

*Balancing mechanism.* Adjustment to a notional interest rate that accommodates deviations between assets and liabilities created by long-term demographic and other changes to preserve long-term financial sustainability of the pension fund.

*Beneficiary.* An individual who is entitled to a benefit (including plan members and dependents).

*Benefit.* Payment made to a pension fund member (or dependents) after retirement.

*Buffer fund.* Fund established to provide liquidity to accommodate sudden exogenous shocks and temporary demographic shifts affecting pension system finances.

*Contribution base.* The reference salary used to calculate the contribution.

*Contribution ceiling.* A limit on the amount of earnings subject to contributions.

*Contributory pension scheme.* A pension scheme where both the employers and the members have to pay into the scheme.

*Custodian.* The entity responsible, as a minimum, for holding the pension fund assets and for ensuring their safekeeping.

*Defined benefit.* A pension plan with a guarantee by the insurer or pension agency that a benefit based on a prescribed formula will be paid.

*Defined contribution.* A pension plan in which the periodic contribution is prescribed and the benefit depends on the contribution plus the investment return.

*Demographic transition.* The historical process of changing demographic structure that takes place as fertility and mortality rates decline, resulting in an increasing ratio of older to younger persons.

*Dependent.* An individual who is financially dependent on a (passive or active) member of a pension scheme.

*Disclosure.* Statutory regulations requiring the communication of information regarding pension schemes, funds, and benefits to pensioners and employees.

*Discretionary increase.* An increase in a pension payment not specified by the pension scheme rules.

*Early leaver.* A person who leaves an occupational pension scheme without receiving an immediate benefit.

*Early retirement.* In a state-sponsored scheme, retirement before reaching the state's pensionable age for receipt of full benefits.

*Earnings cap (ceiling).* A limit on the amount of earnings subject to contributions.

*EET system.* A form of taxation of pension plans, whereby contributions are exempt, investment income and capital gains of the pension fund are also exempt, and benefits are taxed from personal income taxation.

*ETE system.* A form of taxation whereby contributions are exempt, investment income and capital gains of the pension fund are taxed, and benefits are also exempt from personal income taxation.

*Final average earnings (final reference wage).* The fund member's earnings that are used to calculate the pension benefit in a defined-benefit plan; it is typically the earnings of the last few years before retirement.

*Financial asset.* The market value of any investments held by a pension fund.

*Full funding.* The accumulation of pension reserves that total 100 percent of the present value of all pension liabilities owed to current members.

*Funding.* Accumulation of assets in advance to meet future pension liabilities.

*Funding plan.* The timing of payments of contributions with the aim of meeting the cost of a given set of benefits under a defined-benefit scheme.

*Implicit pension debt (net).* The value of outstanding pension claims on the public sector minus accumulated pension reserves.

*Indexation.* Increases in benefits by reference to an index, usually of consumer prices, although in some cases of average covered wage growth.

*Individual account.* An accounting entry that specifies accumulated contributions and other accumulations in the case of defined-contribution schemes and contribution histories in the case of defined-benefit schemes. Individual accounts can also be individual asset accumulations in the case of funded schemes.

*Individual pension plans (personal pension plans, voluntary personal pension plans).* Access to these plans does not have to be linked to an employment relationship. The plans are established and administered directly by a pension fund or a financial institution acting as pension provider without any intervention of employers. Individuals independently purchase and select material aspects of the arrangements. The employer may nonetheless make contributions to individual pension plans. Some individual plans may have restricted membership.

*Intergenerational distribution.* Income transfers between different age cohorts of persons.

*Intragenerational distribution.* Income transfers within a certain age cohort of persons.

*Legacy costs.* Cost of financing the implicit debt (that is, the present value of benefit promises to current beneficiaries and current workers before the implementation of the reform) over and above (a) the value of the pay-as-you-go asset (under a new contribution rate) and (b) the financial assets set aside to prefinance accrued rights.

*Legal retirement age (normal retirement age).* The normal retirement age written into pension statutes at which employees become eligible for pension benefits, excluding early-retirement provisions.

*Mandatory contribution.* The level of contribution the member (or an entity on behalf of the member) is required to pay according to scheme rules.

*Marginal pension.* The change in the accrued pension between two periods.

*Matching defined-contribution (MDC) approach.* An approach whereby worker pension contributions are matched by contributions made by an employer or by a state subsidy.

*Means-tested benefit.* A benefit that is paid only if the recipient meets qualifying conditions, such as income falling below a certain level.

*Minimum pension (guarantee).* The minimum level of pension benefits the plan pays out in all circumstances. A guarantee can also be provided by the government to bring pensions to some minimum level, possibly by "topping up" the capital accumulation needed to fund the pensions.

*Moral hazard.* A situation in which insured people do not protect themselves from risk as much as they would have if they were not insured. For example, in the case of old-age risk, people might not save sufficiently for themselves if they expect the public system to come to their aid.

*Noncontributory pension scheme.* A pension scheme where the members do not have to pay into the scheme.

*Nonfinancial (or notional) defined-contribution (plan).* A defined-benefit pension plan that mimics the structure of (funded) defined-contribution plans but remains unfunded (except for a potential reserve fund).

*Normal retirement age.* See *legal retirement age.*

*Notional (or nonfinancial) accounts.* Individual accounts where the notional contributions plus notional interest rates accrued are credited and determine the notional capital.

*Notional (or nonfinancial) capital.* The value of an individual account at a given moment that determines the value of annuity at retirement or the transfer value in case of the transfer of accrued pension rights from another scheme.

*Notional (or nonfinancial) interest rate.* The rate at which the notional accounts of notional defined-contribution plans are annually credited. It should be consistent with the financial sustainability of the unfunded scheme (potentially the growth rate of the contribution base).

*Occupational pension scheme.* An arrangement by which an employer provides retirement benefits to employees.

*Old-age dependency ratio.* The ratio of older persons to working-age individuals. The old-age dependency ratio may refer to the number of persons over age 60 divided by, for example, the number of persons aged 15–59, the number of persons over 60 divided by the number of persons aged 20–59, and so forth.

*Pay-as-you-go.* In its strictest sense, a method of financing whereby current outlays on pension benefits are paid out of current revenues from an earmarked tax, often a payroll tax.

*Pay-as-you-go assets.* The present value of future contributions minus pension rights accruing to these contributions.

*Pension coverage rate.* The number of workers actively contributing to a publicly mandated contributory or retirement scheme, divided by the estimated labor force or by the working-age population.

*Pension liabilities.* Balance of the obligations to current workers and retirees at a point in time.

*Pension lump sum.* A cash withdrawal from a pension plan.

*Pension spending.* Usually defined as old-age retirement, survivor, death, and invalidity-disability payments based on past contribution records plus noncontributory, flat universal, or means-tested programs specifically targeting the old.

*Pensionable earnings.* The portion of remuneration on which pension benefits and contributions are calculated.

*Portability.* The ability to transfer accrued pension rights between plans.

*Price indexation.* The method with which pension benefits are adjusted taking into account changes in prices.

*Replacement rate.* The value of a pension as a proportion of a worker's wage during a base period, such as the last year or two before retirement or the entire lifetime average wage. Also denotes the average pension of a group of pensioners as a proportion of the average wage of the group.

*Retirement age.* See *legal retirement age.*

*Supplementary pensions.* Pension provision beyond the basic state pension on a voluntary basis.

*Support ratio.* The opposite of the system dependency ratio: the number of workers required to support each pensioner.

*Swiss indexation (mixed indexation).* A method with which pension benefits are adjusted taking into account changes in both wages and prices.

*System dependency ratio.* The ratio of persons receiving pensions from a certain pension scheme divided by the number of workers contributing to the same scheme in the same period.

*System maturation.* The process by which a pension system moves from being immature, with young workers contributing to the system, but with few benefits being paid out because the initial elderly have not contributed and thus are not eligible for benefits, to being mature, with the proportion of elderly receiving pensions relatively equivalent to their proportion of the population.

*Target replacement rate.* The targeted level of wage replacement at retirement for an average wage worker.

*TEE system.* A form of taxation of pension plans whereby contributions are taxed, investment income and capital gains of the pension fund are exempt, and benefits are also exempt from personal income taxation.

*Transition costs.* Costs of financing finance both the benefits paid to current retirees and to prefund the accounts of workers who have yet to retire.

*Trust.* A legal scheme, whereby named people (termed trustees) hold property on behalf of other people (termed beneficiaries).

*Trustee.* A person or a company appointed to carry out the tasks of the trust.

*Universal flat benefit.* Pensions paid solely on the basis of age and citizenship, without regard to work or contribution records.

*Valorization of earnings.* A method of revaluing earnings by predetermined factors such as total or average wage growth to adjust for changes in prices, wage levels, or economic growth. In pay-as-you-go systems, pensions are usually based on some percentage of average wages. This average wage is calculated over some period of time, ranging from full-career average to last salary. If the period for which earnings history enters into the benefit formula is longer than the last salary, the actual wages earned are usually revalued to adjust for these types of changes.

*Vesting period.* The minimum amount of time required to qualify for full and irrevocable ownership of pension benefits.

*Voluntary contributions.* An extra contribution paid in addition to the mandatory contribution a member can pay to the pension fund to increase the future pension benefits.

*Voluntary occupational pension plans.* The establishment of these plans is voluntary for employers (including those in which there is automatic enrolment as part of an employment contract or where the law requires employees to join plans set up on a voluntary basis by their employers).

*Voluntary personal pension plans.* See *individual pension plans.*

*Wage indexation.* The method with which pension benefits are adjusted taking into account changes in wages.

www.ingramcontent.com/pod-product-compliance
Lightning Source LLC
Chambersburg PA
CBHW070356270326
41926CB00014B/2582